C0-ARR-969

LUX ET VERITAS FLOREANT

THE
UNIVERSITY OF WINNIPEG
PORTAGE & BALMORAL
WINNIPEG, MAN. R3B 2E9
CANADA

EXILED BY THE CZAR

Mennonite Historical Series

No. 1

From the Steppes to the Prairies (1949)

By Cornelius Krahn and Others

No. 2

Plockhoy from Zurik-zee. The Study of a Dutch Reformer in Puritan England and Colonial America (1952)

By Leland Harder and Marvin Harder

No. 3

Exiled by the Czar.
Cornelius Jansen and the Great Mennonite Migration, 1874

By Gustav E. Reimer and G. R. Gaeddert

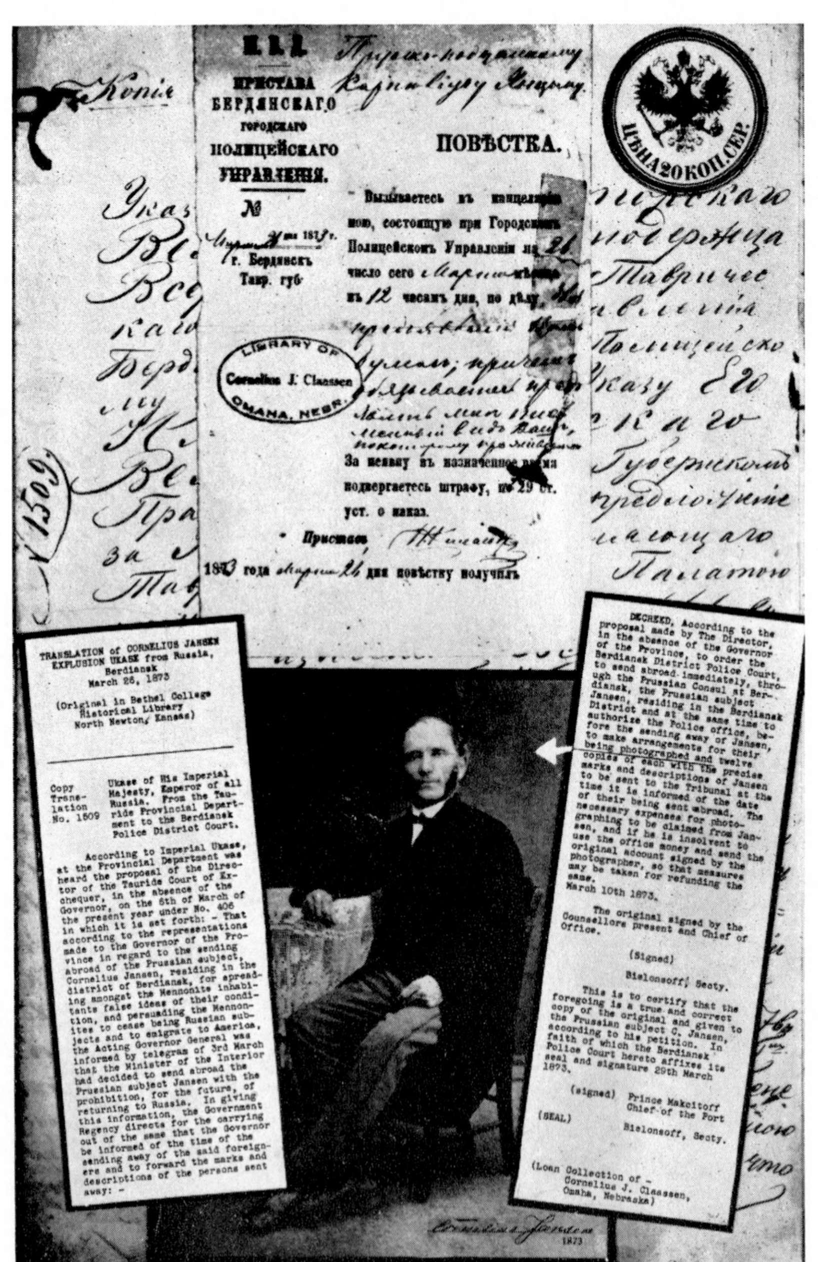

М. В. Д.
ПРИСТАВА БЕРДЯНСКАГО ГОРОДСКАГО ПОЛИЦЕЙСКАГО УПРАВЛЕНІЯ.
№
г. Бердянскъ Тавр. губ.

ПОВѢСТКА.

Вызываетесь въ канцелярію, состоящую при Городскомъ Полицейскомъ Управленіи на 21 число сего мѣсяца въ 12 часамъ дня, по дѣлу

За неявку въ назначенное время подвергаетесь штрафу, по 29 ст. уст. о наказ.

Приставъ

187 года дня повѣстку получилъ

ЦѢНА 20 КОП. СЕР.

TRANSLATION of CORNELIUS JANSEN EXPLUSION UKASE from Russia,
Berdiansk
March 26, 1873

(Original in Bethel College Historical Library North Newton, Kansas)

Copy Trans-lation No. 1509 — Ukase of His Imperial Majesty, Emperor of all Russia. From the Tauride Provincial Department to the Berdiansk Police District Court.

According to Imperial Ukase, at the Provincial Department was heard the proposal of the Director of the Tauride Court of Exchequer, in the absence of the Governor, on the 6th of March of the present year under No. 406 in which it is set forth: - That according to the representations made to the Governor of the Province in regard to the sending abroad of the Prussian subject, Cornelius Jansen, residing in the district of Berdiansk, for spreading amongst the Mennonite inhabitants false ideas of their condition, and persuading the Mennonites to cease being Russian subjects and to emigrate to America, the Acting Governor General was informed by telegram of 3rd March that the Minister of the Interior had decided to send abroad the Prussian subject Jansen with the prohibition, for the future, of returning to Russia. In giving this information, the Government Regency directs for the carrying out of the same that the Governor be informed of the time of the sending away of the said foreigners and to forward the marks and descriptions of the persons sent away: -

DECREED, According to the proposal made by The Director, in the absence of the Governor of the Province, to order the Berdiansk District Police Court, to send abroad immediately, through the Prussian Consul at Berdiansk, the Prussian subject Jansen, residing in the Berdiansk District and at the same time to authorize the Police office, before the sending away of Jansen, to make arrangements for their being photographed and twelve copies of each with the precise marks and descriptions of Jansen to be sent to the Tribunal at the time it is informed of the date of their being sent abroad. The necessary expenses for photographing to be claimed from Jansen, and if he is insolvent to use the office money and send the original account signed by the photographer, so that measures may be taken for refunding the same.
March 10th 1873.

The original signed by the Counsellors present and Chief of Office.

(Signed)

Bielonsoff, Secty.

This is to certify that the foregoing is a true and correct copy of the original and given to the Prussian subject C. Jansen, according to his petition. In faith of which the Berdiansk Police Court hereto affixes its seal and signature 29th March 1873.

(signed) Prince Makcitoff
Chief of the Port

(SEAL)

Bielonsoff, Secty.

(Loan Collection of -
Cornelius J. Claassen,
Omaha, Nebraska)

1873

I. Cornelius Jansen was expelled from Russia because of his migration activities. The Russian Expulsion Ukase, top, and on left and right, an English translation. (See also p. 201).

EXILED BY THE CZAR

Cornelius Jansen and the Great Mennonite Migration, 1874

By

GUSTAV E. REIMER

and

G. R. GAEDDERT

1956
Mennonite Publication Office
Newton, Kansas

Printed by The Mennonite Press
North Newton, Kansas

Foreword

The great migration of Mennonites from Russia, Poland and Prussia to the prairie states and provinces in the 1870's has been investigated and presented repeatedly. Some significant pioneer work was done by C. Henry Smith in *The Coming of the Russian Mennonites* (Berne, 1927). Numerous local commemorations resulted in the publication of some material. Valuable source material was presented by Georg Leibbrandt and Ernst Correll (*Mennonite Quarterly Review*). *From the Steppes to the Prairies* (Mennonite Historical Series, Vol. I) contained some original contributions. Meanwhile, additional sources have come to light which have made it possible to present one significant aspect of this event with more accuracy and greater detail.

The question particularly treated in this book is, how did the Mennonite migration of the 1870's come into being, and what were the factors that gave it such magnitude? However, in addition to this, no other research has presented in such minute detail the spiritual and cultural atmosphere of the Danzig and Russian Mennonites during the time prior to the migration. Above all, this study makes it overwhelmingly clear that Cornelius Jansen was to a large extent responsible for the initiation and scope of the migration. That he played an important role has been previously recognized but the extent to which this was the case and how this movement originated and developed from step to step are fully revealed by these new sources. This study remains within this framework. It does not give an answer to questions such as, how many Mennonites were involved in this movement, where did they settle and what were the pioneer conditions? The primary concern is to portray, on the basis of the available sources, the background, origin and development of the migration centering around Cornelius Jansen, the Moses of the movement. In addition to this, the relationship of the English Society of Friends to Cornelius Jansen and the Mennonites of Russia as well as their aid during the great migration are here presented for the first time in great detail. This contact continued in America among the Jansen children.

The title *Exiled by the Czar,* expresses the climax of the activities of Cornelius Jansen for the sake of religious liberty and the maintenance of the peace witness among the Mennonites, for which he was exiled.

The new sources were made available through the Cornelius Jansen Collection by the late Cornelius Jansen Claassen, Omaha, Nebraska, a grandson of Cornelius Jansen, who collected and preserved all available diaries, letters, books and other sources pertaining to Cornelius Jansen and turned them over to the Bethel College Historical Library. Meanwhile, the other relatives made available additional sources.

Cornelius J. Claassen also inaugurated the research project which resulted in this book. Gustav E. Reimer, formerly Germany now Uruguay, who was an exchange student at Bethel College, 1948-50, wrote the first chapters of the book, "Preparation for a Task" and "Great Issues." G. R. Gaeddert, who formerly taught at Bethel College, was active in the Kansas State Historical Society and wrote a number of books, continued the work. He wrote the major parts of the chapters "The Promised Land" and "Settlement in Retrospect." D. Paul Miller, professor of sociology at Nebraska State Teachers College, Wayne, Nebraska, who wrote his doctor's dissertation on "An Analysis of Community Adjustment: A Case Study of Jansen, Nebraska" (University of Nebraska, 1953) contributed the sections in the last chapter "The Ranch," "The Early Jansen Community," "The Town of Jansen," and "Peter Jansen in Public Life." The undersigned wove this material, heavily footnoted, into a whole, including some of the most important writings by Cornelius Jansen and other documents found in the appendixes.

Meanwhile, the initiator of this project, Cornelius J. Claassen, had passed away in 1952. His brother, Aaron J. Claassen, Beatrice, Nebraska, who from the beginning cooperated in this project, continued as sponsor. He not only made the completion of this project financially possible but contributed also for its publication. The Historical Committee of the General Conference Mennonite Church accepted the manuscript for its Mennonite Historical Series.

John F. Schmidt of the Bethel College Historical Library assisted in the preparation of the manuscript and proof-reading. Delbert L. Gratz, Aaron J. Claassen and others made helpful suggestions in reading the proofs. The Mennonite Historical Library, Goshen College, Goshen, Indiana, made available some sources of the Ernst Correll Collection. Mrs. J. E. Claassen Linscheid made some pictures available.

January, 1956
North Newton, Kansas

Cornelius Krahn, Secretary
Mennonite Historical Committee

STATEMENT BY SPONSOR

I wish to express our appreciation to Cornelius Krahn and John F. Schmidt of the Bethel College Historical Library for directing and helping with the research, examination and verification of records, preparing the manuscript and helping with the publication of this book. I regret that my brother, Cornelius Jansen Claassen, who initiated this project in 1949, did not live to see it completed. He passed away in 1952.

May the unwavering stand of Grandfather Cornelius Jansen in upholding our Mennonite peace principle, based on the teachings of Jesus Christ, be an inspiration to all who read this book.

Beatrice, Nebraska — Aaron Jansen Claassen

Contents

The chapters "Preparation for a Task" and "Great Issues" were written by Gustav E. Reimer. The major parts of "The Promised Land" and "Settlement in Retrospect" were written by G. R. Gaeddert. The sections "The Ranch," "The Early Jansen Community," "Town of Jansen," and "Peter Jansen in Public Life," of the chapter "Settlement in Retrospect," were written by D. Paul Miller (see Foreword).

I. Preparation for a Task

Background and Youth

Cornelius Jansen was born in Prussia, and lived in Prussia, Russia and America. His ancestors very likely came from the Netherlands like those of most of the Mennonites of the Vistula Delta area.

The father of Cornelius Jansen, Daniel Janzen,[1] was baptized at the Tiegenhagen Mennonite Church on June 4, 1815. His wife, Anna Buhler, daughter of Wilhelm and Anna (nee Warkentin) Buhler, was born at Petershagen in 1797 and was baptized at the same time and place with her future husband. It is unknown when they died.

Besides their son Cornelius, they had one daughter, Johanna, born November 10, 1823, at Tiegenhof; who was married to Peter Penner (1816-1895) of Petershagen. (See Appendix I).

Cornelius Jansen lost his mother when he was about ten years old. At one occasion, he later related, his mother once appeared to him after her death. Because of the loss of his mother, his boyhood days may not have been very happy. In later years his youth appeared to him as rather "worldly." Peter Jansen, in his *Memoirs,* related of his father that "in his younger days he was fond of dancing and a great favorite with the ladies. Once in a great while he would refer to this episode of his life in a humorous and rather depreciating manner."[2]

His father, Daniel Janzen, was a textile maker and merchant at Tiegenhof. In his store young Cornelius had to fill and light the long tobacco pipes of the customers. He probably attended only the village school at Tiegenhof.[3]

Johann Heinrich Zimmermann mentions in the obituary he wrote for Cornelius Jansen[4] that for some time Cornelius stayed with Gerhard Penner, later elder of the Heubuden congregation, who originally came from Marienburg. It can be assumed that he was employed in different occupations in order to complete his professional training as a merchant.

Cornelius was baptized in his home church at Tiegenhagen by Elder Peter Regier, probably at the customary age of twenty or twenty-one.

As a young man he visited the Mennonite colonies in South Russia with some friends, making the entire trip on horseback. He also went to Berdyansk where there were a few Mennonite families at that time, some of whom, like the Sudermanns, being recent immigrants from West Prussia. There he observed the advantages of the seaport of Berdyansk as a future exporting place for grain. When later, after his marriage, he and his wife decided to go to Russia, he chose to make Berdyansk his home.

Marriage

A very important event in the life of Cornelius Jansen was his marriage. Even though he married an orphan, the traditions of this family were so strong that they were to affect his life very definitely. The father of his wife came from a farming family, while her mother, as the Jansens and the Buhlers, belonged—at least for many generations—to urban Mennonite families.

On May 4, 1848, Cornelius Jansen married Helena von Riesen, age twenty-five, at Schidlitz, a suburb of Danzig. Her father, Peter von Riesen, who had died the year before (born November 11, 1779, died September 24, 1847), had been a miller but occasionally dealt with other articles on the sideline.

Peter von Riesen[4] was married three times. Being the oldest child of a large farming family at Kalteherberge, near Danzig, he married for the first time on August 19, 1800, when only twenty years old. His first wife was a 43-year old widow with children.

Not long after that, in 1804, his parents with all his younger brothers and sisters went to South Russia where they settled in the Molotschna colony, most of them (see Appendix I), later joining the Kleine Gemeinde. All these brothers (and their descendants) contracted their names to Friesen, a custom which we find frequently among the von Riesens in the 18th and the beginning of the 19th century. Their father, Abraham, used both spellings. The close relationship to the Kleine Gemeinde left its definite impact on the Cornelius Jansen family, as we shall see later.

When his first wife died on March 19, 1818, Peter von Riesen wasted little time, even for those days, before choosing a new mate. On June 21, he married Margaretha Harder, who was born on August 23, 1796, at Marienburg. Her parents were Claas Harder, a leather merchant at Marienburg, and Helena Sudermann, the daughter of a vinegar manufacturer at Caldowe near Marienburg.[5] Through her mother, Margaretha Harder was a first cousin to Elder Leonhard Sudermann, Berdyansk, whom Cornelius Jansen always called *Onkel* though they were about the same age.

Margaretha was an orphan—her father had died in 1810, her mother in 1814—and perhaps she was living with relatives at Danzig. At least the wedding took place at Danzig. Nine children were born to Peter and Margaretha, of which several died in infancy. Peter von Riesen's first marriage had been childless. When Margaretha died of tuberculosis at the age of forty, on February 3, 1837, seven children were still living.[6]

Peter von Riesen married a third time, again as in the case of his second marriage, a young girl. Her name is not known. There were no children and the marriage was not a happy one.[7]

Peter von Riesen belonged to the Mennonite congregation at Danzig[8] but in some ways differed from his brethren. At that time many of the Mennonite merchants in the city of Danzig grew prosperous with the result that more and more broke away from original restriction of nonconformity to the world. Though Peter von Riesen had become a well-to-do citizen[9] he tried to observe simplicity and nonconformity as much as possible. These same principles were stressed by the Kleine Gemeinde in Russia, and considering the close ties which linked him to this conservative congregation, one might ask why he was the only member of his family to remain in

West Prussia, especially since he wanted his children to emigrate to South Russia. Whatever his reasons were, he tried to promote the same spirit in Prussia and also tried to help his brethren in Russia.

Menno's Books Banned

In the Kleine Gemeinde, where primarily books by Mennonite authors were read, a need was felt for a new edition of Menno Simons' *Fundamentbuch* of which only some old Dutch editions or the selections by Deknatel were available. Peter von Riesen undertook to have this main work of Menno revised, and printed several thousand copies in a three-volume edition. He intended, after having delivered the number ordered by his friends in Russia, to sell the rest among the Mennonites in West Prussia. He was, however, prevented from doing so by the Mennonite elders.

This strange story is told in a small booklet *Eine seltsame Begebenheit* by P. Toews,[10] who published a correspondence exchanged in 1835 and 1836 between Peter von Riesen and his brother Abraham Friesen, who was a minister at that time, and later elder of the Kleine Gemeinde in the Molotschna settlement, South Russia. Peter von Riesen did not fail to obtain the permission of the local censor, the censorship being very severe in Prussia at that time for all printed literature.

The printing was not yet finished when a volume came into the hands of a Lutheran farmer who was displeased at some passages in which Menno defends himself against the Reformed and Lutheran clergy. As soon as Mennonite ministerial leaders learned of this they were afraid that others of their neighbors would be stirred up. It was at the time when the Mennonites began to be concerned for the loss of their privileges. While the progressive wing, especially the urban groups, were moving toward complete emancipation and were striving for full rights as citizens, the conservative wing—especially the congregational leaders—tried to avoid any publicity whatever, for fear that it might remind the public and the authorities of their somewhat unstable legal position. The Mennonite elders and ministers of the West Prussian congregations immediately held a conference, followed by three others, where they decided to confiscate the writings of the founder of their own church. Peter von Riesen was summoned twice before the conference, and finally was ordered to deliver the whole edition and threatened with excommunication for failure to do so.

Out of consideration for his family and after an intense inner struggle, he agreed. Excepting the books destined for Russia and a few copies for some friends, a list of which he submitted, and copies for his own family,[11] he delivered the rest to Elder Peter Regier. The books were stored in the attic of the Tiegenhagen Mennonite Church where they were to remain for about twenty years, exposed to great damage from moisture, mould, and mice.

A letter from Elder Abraham Regier of Heubuden to the congregations in South Russia terminated the sale of these books there. That meant more than a financial loss for von Riesen. This undertaking certainly had been something extraordinary and he perhaps felt bitter about the failures of one of his life's ambitions. Six months later he wrote a letter to all the elders and ministers who had signed the decisions of the conference, asking each one to make a copy of the deposited books and to read it for his own benefit. He was persuaded that once they really read the book they would change their minds and also that they would try to improve their work for the salvation of their congregations. Finally, he hoped that his children would be able in the future to free the books and return them to their proper destination. Later the elders graciously permitted the exportation of the confiscated copies of the Menno Simon's *Fundamentbuch* to Russia whence some have found their way to America, where they can even now be found in some homes of former members of the Kleine Gemeinde and in historical libraries.

It was Peter Regier, elder of the Tiegenhagen congregation and the person who confiscated Peter von Riesen's books, who officiated at the marriage of Helena von Riesen to Cornelius Jansen. This seems to indicate that their marriage was not performed in the home of the bride as was customary. In that case the Danzig elder would have been in charge. Later on, however, the young couple lived at Schidlitz with Helena's younger brothers and sister.

The only sources of information we have for these first years, are a few account books.[12] Cornelius Jansen kept an accurate record of all expenses they had. Anna von Riesen, the sister of Mrs. Jansen, who lived with the Jansens during her lifetime, remained financially independent. While their expenses were at first divided into three parts, later on they apparently had an arrangement by which her help in the house made up for board and room. But she paid all extra expenses, which consisted mostly of gifts for others.

In these account books even items of a few pennies or kopecks are listed. Cornelius Jansen always advanced the necessary amounts of money to Anna von Riesen or paid the expenses directly, as for instance even a birthday gift for himself, until from time to time they settled the account. Though the books show an extreme exactitude they also reveal the generosity of the family. No doubt the preciseness in financial matters was an important factor for the successful living together of Anna von Riesen with the Cornelius Jansens for nearly fifty years.

Though the account books, preserved especially for the time from 1848-1856, do not give exact figures on the financial situation of Cornelius Jansen or the von Riesens, they sometimes reveal some interesting facts from which we can draw some conclusions as to their standards and their way of living, and, to a small extent also concerning some events. We learn from the entries that Anna von Riesen did some horseback riding and even owned riding equipment. Shortly after the Jansen's wedding, in July 1848, Abraham von Riesen must have married, for there is an item: "For Abraham's wedding gift, 13 taler."

Migration to Russia

On February 12, 1849, the first child was born to Cornelius and Helena Jansen, a daughter, who—according to the custom in Mennonite families—got the name of her grandmother, Margaretha. As in every middle-class home, the young infant was taken care of by a "Frau Annchen," as the nurses were called.

They made a trip to Kozelitzke, apparently to visit Gerhard Penner, brewer and farmer, who later became the elder of the Heubuden congregation. They visited the "Dominik," the famous Danzig fair which was always held in August, at that time already better known for its entertainments rather than for its economic importance.

Beginning in 1850 there appear entries regarding the migration to Russia. A traveling carriage was bought. More shopping was done and passports were obtained. The exact date of the departure is uncertain, but from June 21 the expenses were made out in Russian money. The last entries in Prussian currency were made on June 14. Therefore, we can conclude that they left Danzig during the week after June 14, 1850, and passed the Russian border before June 21. On this trip Cornelius and Helena Jansen and their small daughter were accompanied by Helena's sister Anna and by her youngest brother, Johannes. As for Mrs. Jansen's two other brothers, Heinrich, the elder, probably had left before, while Abraham evidently stayed on at Schidlitz.

What were the reasons for this migration to Russia? Helena Jansen (daughter) says[13] that when her father and mother were married, her mother "made it a condition that sooner or later they would go to South Russia and make their home there as all her father's brothers and sisters had gone there previously." Even after a separation of more than forty years, the family ties between the relatives in West Prussia and in Russia were indeed very strong. Relatives who are mentioned before and during the first time are "Onkel Klaas Friesen" and "Onkel [Heinrich] Neufeld," brother and brother-in-law of Peter von Riesen,[14] Jacob Friesen, Blumstein, apparently a cousin, (Hermann) Harder, Gnadenfeld, and Rudolph Riesen, Berdyansk, cousins of Mrs. Jansen from her mother's side. The Sudermanns, cousins of Mrs. Jansen's mother, are also mentioned.

There were probably no economic reasons for this move, although we do not definitely know the occupation and financial situation of Cornelius Jansen. It seems to be a part of the exodus of the whole von Riesen family.

The daughters of Peter von Riesen were more loyal than his son in adhering to the principles of their father, and it is not impossible that, as daughter Helena expresses it, Mrs. Jansen was the motivating agent for a migration to Russia. Yet, Cornelius Jansen, in a letter written in 1870, said that he disliked the many restrictions to which the Mennonites were subjected in Prussia.[15]

The trip made by carriage took several weeks. This traveling was usually done by several families in a group. Between the settlements in South Russia and Prussia there was always a coming and going of visitors in both directions. Those who went for the first time would usually go with someone who already had made the trip. For the Jansen group the leader was an Epp, apparently from

South Russian settlements and well acquainted with problems involved in such a trip.

Berdyansk

At the end of July the Jansens were in Berdyansk, a city situated on the Sea of Azov, at the mouth of the Berdyanka River which formed a natural port. Founded in 1735, Berdyansk was not incorporated until one hundred years later. At this time it began growing more rapidly, being the nearest exporting place for large wheat-producing German settlements, and in 1897 it had twenty-seven thousand inhabitants. Among the first Mennonites to move into this city was Abraham Sudermann who came there from Caldowe, West Prussia, in 1841 and built and operated a treadmill. Being a minister, he started to gather a congregation which, however, was independent only a short time, from 1865 to 1876, when it was under the eldership of Leonhard Sudermann. Before and after that time it was affiliated with one of the Molotschna congregations, first Gnadenfeld, later Rudnerweide.[16]

Here at Berdyansk they apparently first visited with their friends—the Sudermanns. Rudolph Riesen, Mrs. Jansen's oldest brother, was already established at Berdyansk. But as yet the Jansens did not stay. We also find them visiting and making contacts in the Molotschna settlement.

Finally, they chose Berdyansk as their future home and bought a *Wirtschaft* there, as it is referred to. This term usually means a farm, or an estate, but it is rather vague. Sources do not disclose whether Cornelius Jansen immediately engaged in the business of grain buying and exporting.[17] The *Wirtschaft* was bought in equal parts together with the sister and the two brothers of Mrs. Jansen, so that each one of the following owned one fifth: Cornelius Jansen, Helena Jansen, Anna von Riesen, Johannes von Riesen, and Abraham von Riesen. The latter was still in Prussia but intended to follow later.

In the fall they moved to Berdyansk, where they were established at Heinrich von Riesen's home from November 23, 1850 to July 22, 1851. Apparently they were living with them, but the accounts only reveal that the Jansens were paying for the food. For two weeks following, from July 22 to August 6, 1851, they only paid for the noon meals. At this time, apparently, the new home was established.

One of the outstanding events was that of March 21, 1852, when the first son was born to Cornelius and Helena Jansen. The traditions were again observed, the boy being given the name of his grandfather, Peter.

The account of the expenses for the household at Berdyansk from the time of their arrival in 1850 to the time of their departure in 1852 are preserved. This account does not show anything of agricultural or mercantile undertakings and activities, but it gives an idea of the food they bought, the kind of furniture purchased, and other household expenses. Cornelius Jansen himself specified their total expenses during their first sojourn in South Russia (except the expenses for the *Wirtschaft* as purchase, inventory, repairs, new buildings, etc., which were recorded separately and divided into five parts). Following is the account as he computed it, in three currencies:

HOUSEHOLD EXPENSES IN BERDYANSK, 1850-1852[18]

	Banco Rubles	Silver Rubles	Taler	Groschen	Pf.
1. Housekeeping	2961.86	846.24½	940	8	2
2. Miscellaneous Expenses	581.06	105.02	184	14	0
3. Alms and gifts	250.52	71.57½	79	15	10
4. Trips to Tashtshenak and the Mennonite colonies	311.86½	89.10½	99	9	2
5. Furniture and household articles	1785.32½	510.09½	566	23	2
6. Board to Heinrich von Riesen	625.25	187.50	210	20	0
TOTAL	6525.88	1864.54	2071	21	4

Back to Prussia

The strange fact that the Jansens left Berdyansk after such a short stay, in all references, has been explained by the outbreak of the Crimean War. This, however, has to be questioned. They left Berdyansk in the fall of 1852, while war was declared by the Turkish Sultan Abdul Medschid about one year later on October 4, 1853. It is doubtful too, whether the war could be predicted so early, because it was not until July 2, 1853, that Russian armies moved into the Danubian principalities, thus creating the cause for war. It was two and a half years after the Jansens left that Berdyansk was threatened by military events, and the other Mennonite residents fled to the Molotschna settlement.[19]

It seems, therefore, that we have to look for other reasons. There is a possibility that they were of a financial nature. When the Jansens and the von Riesens left Danzig in 1850, they did not dissolve all financial connections. They had a considerable amount of their money invested in West Prussia, mostly in mortgages on farms, and in bonds (*Pfandbriefe*).[20] While at this time and in the years to come their financial interests in West Prussia were taken care of by C(arl) H(einrich) Zimmermann, it could be possible that because of certain regulations their personal presence became necessary or desirable.

There are two other factors to support this assumption. The legacy of Peter von Riesen was not yet settled. When Peter von Riesen died, three of his children, Abraham, Anna, and Johannes, were still minors. The inheritance was administered by guardians who were responsible to the probate court. As late as June 14, 1855, the Stadt-und Kreisgericht at Danzig, referring to a rendering of accounts by the guardians, mentioned the fact that the inheritance of Anna von Riesen had not yet been completely probated.

Secondly, during the time shortly before the Jansens left Berdyansk an event occurred which certainly was not without repercussions for the family. Heinrich von Riesen of Berdyansk, Mrs. Jansen's oldest brother, died. From the account book we learn that this must have happened between July 10 and September 30, 1852.

Already in September, 1852, the grain warehouse was rented to Jacob Buhler,[21] a young Mennonite, who was a friend of the Lutheran pastor from Neuhoffnung, Eduard Wüst. Neuhoffnung was a village, settled by immigrants from Württemberg, Germany, and was situated half way between Berdyansk and the Molotschna settlement. This settlement was founded by Lutherans who had separated from the Lutheran church and established separatist *Brüdergemeinden*. Wüst, a representative of the so-called new Pietism, was instrumental in introducing the pietistic movement also to the Mennonites. The first contact of this new Pietism with the Mennonites was made at Berdyansk.[22] Sermons preached by Wüst in Berdyansk in 1851 and 1852 were later printed. We can assume that during this time Cornelius Jansen became acquainted with this movement which was to have an important influence on his later life. Since the property was already rented out in September, 1852, it is possible that for some weeks they visited in the Molotschna settlement before returning to Prussia. The account book of Anna von Riesen also refers to a trip through the Crimea which must have been made in August of the same year.

The journey back to Danzig, as Peter Jansen relates, "was made by private conveyances drawn by post horses, the usual way of quick travel in those days." Peter also relates that after entering Prussia, they saw for the first time in their life a railway train. His father, he writes, "tried to induce mother and aunt to abandon the carriages and finish the journey by rail in a few hours. However, the ladies were afraid, and my mother decided to continue by horse power, which took them several days instead of so many hours." [23]

On November 18, 1852, they arrived at Danzig. The following days they apparently looked up all of their friends. Louis Eduard Zimmermann, one of their friends at Danzig, reports in his diary that he met them several times. He remarked that Cornelius Jansen as well as his wife talked very interestingly about Russia. Another time he reported about a party at his home where also "Herr und Madame Jansen" were present. Other guests were the Abraham von Riesens, Pastor Jacob Mannhardt and his wife, the ministerial candidate Johannes van der Smissen and the Gerhard Penners from Kozelitzke. This entry again speaks of Cornelius Jansen's conversational gifts and powers.[24]

This gives a little glimpse of their acquaintance at that time, and of their friends. In the years following, J. Mannhardt and G. Penner were to become determined opponents in the conflict which developed in West Prussia over the question of nonresistance, as the leaders of the liberal and the conservative wings respectively. At this time, however, there were no differences, and the relations between Mannhardt and Cornelius Jansen also seem to have been good. In 1854 J. Mannhardt founded the *Mennonitische Blätter,* the first Mennonite periodical in Germany. At one time he asked Cornelius Jansen for comments or explanatory notes on an article on the Mennonite settlements in South Russia. Later, when Cornelius Jansen was back at Berdyansk, there appeared a report in the *Mennonitische Blätter* (1858. p. 18) on a mission festival held in a grain warehouse at Berdyansk at which Nicolai Schmidt, Steinbach, and Eduard Wüst spoke. Though the author is not named, the style of the article gives the impression of being from Cornelius Jansen's pen. Possibly the meeting place was his also.

For the first part of this stay in West Prussia the Jansen family again lived at Schidlitz, together with Mrs. Jansen's brother, Abraham. Though they lived in a separate apartment they shared the household expenses with the Abraham von Riesens, to whom they also paid a small rent for the apartment.[25]

The account books give no evidence of Cornelius Jansen's business activities. They report, instead, an occasional visit to friends in the country, as to Kozelitzke (Gerhard Penner), to Renkau (Andreas Penner), to Marienburg and other places. The family also made excursions enjoying the beautiful scenery surrounding Danzig. In June 1854, they spent some time at Zoppot which at that time had become an established beach resort. In 1855 they visited Kahlberg, another resort north of Elbing on the narrow tongue separating the Haff from the Baltic Sea. In 1855 they must also have traveled through some other parts of Germany, an event referred to in the account books, without giving additional information.

Among the people named in the account books, there frequently appear, besides those already mentioned, an uncle and an aunt von Roy, and also a person always called "Herr Calculator." The latter apparently had something to do with the financial affairs of the von Riesen family, and probably as an expression of gratitude he received as a gift quite an expensive fur coat to which all members of the family contributed.

Occasionally South Russia is mentioned, for example when Jacob Buhler was sending the rent, or when uncle Claas Friesen was given his brother Peter's fur coat (*Stadtpelz*) by the von Riesen children. Unfortunately, our sources do not cover the time very well, otherwise they would reveal some of Cornelius Jansen's concern and activities in connection with Berdyansk.

Since neither the obituaries nor other general sources give any information on the purpose or major business activities of Cornelius

Jansen during this four-year stay in West Prussia, except for the latter years, we must assume that he had intended to stay only as long as necessary and to go back immediately after all financial matters were settled, and that his returning to Berdyansk finally was delayed by the Crimean War.

Persuaded by the opportunities of Berdyansk he may have tried to induce others to go there. While the Jansens were living at Danzig, a certain cooper, Fick, departed in 1854 taking along a small loan and also Jansen's great traveling carriage (*grosse Journaliere*). Later this same cooper, Fick, was living at Berdyansk.

While the Jansens were still at Berdyansk among the Mennonite residents who held their gatherings in a schoolhouse, the need had been felt for an adequate church building. However, Berdyansk Mennonites as a whole were not very prosperous at that time, and not in a position to realize their goal by their own means. Now while sojourning in West Prussia, Cornelius Jansen began raising a fund for this purpose by collecting money among the brethren of the West Prussian congregations.[26] Apparently in collecting money he began with his own family, each member giving forty *taler.*

Later on this campaign was also supported by the *Mennonitische Blätter.* Set back by the Crimean War, it took several years and more money had to be raised among the brethren in Germany and South Russia, before the church could be erected.

Charity, as it seems, did not take the last place in the Jansen family budget. They contributed, for instance, to the Bible Society, and repeatedly to the aid for victims of the Vistula River floods which caused great damage in the spring of 1855. Frequently money was sent to Pastor Fliedner, the founder of the deaconess work, and director of the institutions of charity at Kaiserswerth, Rhineland. He also supported Pastor Schneller and his work among the orphans at Jerusalem. A New Year's greeting was received from *Waisenvater* Schneller, in 1868.

Peter Jansen relates that his parents brought back to Berdyansk a Lutheran governess, Sister Sophie, who had been trained as a nurse at Kaiserswerth. In the account book of Anna von Riesen we find repeated mention that money was sent "für Sophie nach Kaiserswerth." At one place we find noted that Anna von Riesen paid a total of 500 taler for "Sophiechen" at Kaiserswerth. This would mean that Sister Sophie's training was paid for by Anna von Riesen, possibly together with the Jansens.[27]

It must have been during this time that Cornelius Jansen asked for the Menno Simons books of his father-in-law in order to take them to Russia when he would leave. However, the Mennonite elders still had scruples, and before complying they sent to the consistory of the Lutheran church at Königsberg, East Prussia, to which institution they had no relation or obligation whatsoever. They asked for the opinion of the Lutheran church leaders who did not object.[28]

In 1855 the front of the Crimean War approached Berdyansk. All the Mennonite residents fled to the Molotschna settlement and did not dare return for nearly one year. Only once during the whole war did English ships appear at the port of Berdyansk.[29]

Though no letters are available from that time, we can assume that Cornelius Jansen was kept well informed on the events in South Russia. Seeing no possibility of returning to Berdyansk as long as the war continued, he probably decided in the fall of 1855 not to lose any more time by waiting, and bought a farm at Wickerau, near Elbing, West Prussia. This, however, turned out to be only temporary.

On February 25, 1856, the peace congress opened at Paris, and on March 30 the peace treaty was signed. On March 23, Cornelius Jansen's third child was born, named Anna after the second grandmother and perhaps also after her aunt. If Cornelius Jansen intended to go back to Berdyansk as soon as possible, he was now delayed by this family event, which for some time excluded a long and strenuous journey. About three months later he hurried back. One reason probably was that Jacob Buhler, to whom he had rented his place, had died suddenly of typhoid fever in 1855 while being away from Berdyansk.[30]

Before leaving, Jansen sold his recently acquired farm at Wickerau to Mrs. Jansen's youngest brother, Johannes, who had become engaged in April, 1856, to a sister of Mrs. Louis Eduard Zimmerman of Danzig, she being also a niece of Elder Gerhard Penner.

Russia Again

The Jansens left West Prussia in the summer of 1856, probably not before the wedding of Johannes von Riesen, which took place on

July 8. Peter Jansen described this journey briefly. "A lot of cooked and preserved provisions were taken along to help out the rather meager and dirty fare of the roadside inns,"[31] but probably also because it was a lot cheaper this way. They traveled in covered carriages, one of them driven by a coachman whom Cornelius Jansen had engaged for this service. This time they apparently did not stop for a longer time at the Mennonite settlements but drove directly to Berdyansk.

At Berdyansk, Cornelius Jansen "set about repairing the damage done to his buildings by the ravages of war and neglect and re-establishing his grain business."[32] The accounts for the Berdyansk *Wirtschaft,* especially for the first years from 1856 to 1859, show many signs of construction activity, partly reconstruction. An account from December 1859 indicated that about 1,500 silver rubles had been spent for repairing and two thousand silver rubles for new buildings, mainly for the new large house which was constructed during this period. [33]

Peter Jansen relates, furthermore, that Cornelius Jansen formed a partnership with Abraham Matthies, who had a large store in the village of Rudnerweide, which was the one nearest Berdyansk in the Molotschna settlement.[34] From the account books we discover that he had another partner in another village of the settlement, Jacob Enns at Halbstadt. These partners bought the grain from the farmers and shipped it to Berdyansk where it was stored in the granaries of Cornelius Jansen until it could be sold at a suitable price. The role of the partners was not only to serve as agents for Cornelius Jansen, but it was also important that they disburse a certain amount of money because they had to pay the farmers who were usually short of cash. Cornelius Jansen would bring the amount for the grain that was sold or send it with friends or members of the family whenever they went to the villages, or when the partners came to Berdyansk. However, he never sent more than two thousand silver rubles at once. The gain or loss which Cornelius Jansen made by selling the grain was divided equally between the partners. Besides that, the books mention a 2 per cent commission which, however, went largely to the broker.[35]

The grain, exported primarily to England,[36] consisted largely of wheat, most of which was designated as "red wheat." Cornelius

Jansen also handled smaller quantities of oats, barley, linseed, and a kind of rapeseed (colza).

Since not all farmers sold their grain through Jansen's agents, some selling directly to him, especially those who did not need the money immediately; it is impossible, from the account left, to estimate the extent of his grain business. In 1871 the total amount exchanged with Abraham Matthies was 17,909 silver rubles, in the ten years before, in 1861, about half this amount. This shows that his grain business had been growing considerably during these ten years, in spite of the fact that Cornelius Jansen was not without competition.

Peter Jansen describes how the grain was shipped to Berdyansk. It was done mostly by ox teams traveling very slowly.[37] The drivers were usually not too reliable so they were not given money before they had delivered their shipments, in order to keep them from getting drunk. Often they brought along a letter from the farmer or agent, indicating the expected price of the grain. The farmers also often asked Cornelius Jansen to buy this or that for them and to send it back with the drivers. This was an additional service. It seems, however, that Cornelius Jansen bought at wholesale and stored certain goods which the farmers often needed and asked for.

The place where the Jansens had erected their buildings was landscaped in the first years after their return to Berdyansk. The large lot contained several acres back of the houses and sloping up a gradual elevation. "This," relates Peter, "my father parked, and the slope he planted to grapevines. From the crest of the hill a beautiful view was obtained, with the harbor and shipping only about a mile away. Here Father built a summer house, and often on Sundays and other festive occasions, coffee was taken there."[38]

Cornelius Jansen must have done some farming as a side line. Peter only relates that when he was fourteen years old, which would have been in 1866, his father leased a large tract of land about thirty miles from Berdyansk, where a ranch, (in Russian called a *Khutor*) was started.[39] This ranch was managed by a Russian overseer. How many other Russian hired people were employed by Cornelius Jansen, is not known. It is mentioned by Peter Jansen that the coachman usually was a Russian. The grain business certainly required some laborers, too, since the grain was carried in sacks from the wagons to the granaries and from the granaries to the ships. In the account books we find accounts only for the year 1863, and only for a night watchman and for four other servants, one male and three female, the latter four all Mennonites.

Unlike the other Mennonite immigrants to South Russia Cornelius Jansen never became a Russian citizen. In his first letter to America mentioned above he gave an explanation for his attitude. He preferred Russia to Prussia because here he could, even as a foreigner, live without the many restrictions in the economic and social areas. But "for many reasons" he distrusted and disliked the government and the living conditions not wanting to get into any irrevocable obligations toward Russia. While living in Russia he came to recognize that personal freedom is more important than earthly wealth.[40]

Public Service

In a time of growing nationalism Cornelius Jansen seems to have been more of an internationalist, maintaining certain reservations against both governments under which he lived.[41] But on the other hand he no doubt tried to be loyal to both. Only thus can we understand that he accepted an appointment for consular service.

This service was to give Cornelius Jansen his distinctive designation, the name under which he became known, especially among his Mennonite fellow-brethren: "Consul Jansen."

It is generally assumed that Cornelius Jansen for some time was a Prussian consul at Berdyansk. His daughter Helena maintained that he "served in this capacity for nine years, and later, as consul for Mecklenburg, for three years."[42] In the previously mentioned article in *Der Herold,*[43] it is said that he was appointed a Prussian consul in 1856, which office he held for nine years, and that, when he resigned, he received a personal letter of acknowledgement by Bismarck for his unselfish services.[44]

Neither the obituaries nor other family papers give the length of time of this consular service. Peter Jansen only says: "In the meantime, father had been appointed Prussian Consul, which gave him quite a standing in town and insured more respect from the natives. It was great fun for us boys to hoist the flag with the great black eagle on special occasions."[45] Cornelius, the youngest son, did not recall anything about his father's service.[46]

It is technically inaccurate that George Hume, an English engineer who came to Berdyansk in 1861, in his memoirs calls Cornelius Jansen "The German Consul,"[47] for the German Reich was not founded until 1871.

The Quakers, Robson and Harvey, who came to Berdyansk in 1867 and became very well acquainted with Cornelius Jansen, did not in their report mention anything of a public position he kept. They call him " a Mennonite merchant and farmer."[48] Very likely Jansen was not in consular service at this time any more. It thus seems inaccurate to assert, as Leibbrandt does, that Cornelius Jansen was Prussian Consul at Berdyansk as late as 1871.[49]

C. B. Schmidt, the land agent of the Santa Fe, who met Jansen while the latter was prospecting land in the western states, expresses a somewhat similar opinion when he asserts that Cornelius Jansen owed his information on the draft question during the years 1870 and 1871, "to his official position."[50]

The Berlin State Archives should have reliable information. Ernst Correll inquired via the German Embassy at Washington in 1933. The answer he obtained was very brief. It specified that Cornelius Jansen was appointed consular agent at Berdyansk by the Prussian consul at Odessa in 1859, and that his functions as such ended in 1862, when a Prussian consulate was established at Berdyansk with someone else in charge.[51]

If Cornelius Jansen's consular service ended in 1862, a personal letter of acknowledgement by Bismarck would seem plausible, because from September 5, 1859, to May 24, 1862, Bismarck was the Prussian ambassador at St. Petersburg. It would be unlikely that Bismarck would have written this letter after he had become prime minister of Prussia, to which post he advanced later in the same year.

This suggests the possibility that the periods of three and nine years, mentioned by Helena Jansen (Junior), have to be exchanged, and that Cornelius Jansen was in Prussian service three years and in the service of Mecklenburg-Schwerin for nine years. However, Peter, born in 1852, remembered distinctly having hoisted the flag "with the great black eagle" which was the Prussian service flag, while the Mecklenburg-Schwerin service flag carried the crown and anchor in the center and a bull head in the upper, inner corner.

As a souvenir of Cornelius Jansen's consular service for Mecklenburg-Schwerin, the family has preserved the waxprint of a seal reading: *"Vive Consulate Grossherzogth. Mecklenburg Schwerin zu Berdyansk."*

Cornelius Jansen apparently did not relate much concerning his consular service. There are only two records of his comments about this work. Once in his talk on the Mennonite exodus from Russia, given at Mount Pleasant, Iowa, in 1875, he said, in connection with his exile, that he sent a telegram "to the philanthropic Prince Henry von Reuss, at that time German ambassador at St. Petersburg, to whom I was known as the founder of the German consulate at Berdyansk where I had held this official position many years."[52] He was slightly more explicit in a letter written at the time when he received the order to leave the country, saying that he was "the founder and for many years the representative of the Prussian and Mecklenburg Consulate here."[53] Unfortunately both passages are not very specific. No definite conclusion regarding Cornelius Jansen's consular service can be made until more information is obtained. More information could probably be found in the official correspondence of the contemporary British consuls at Berdyansk, since at least two of them, Cumberbatch and Zohrab, were intimate friends of Cornelius Jansen.

English Contacts

With the growing importance of Berdyansk, Great Britain, at about the same time as Prussia, established a consulate in this city. We know the names of two of those British consuls, Cumberbatch and Zohrab. They probably were the only ones during the time of Cornelius Jansen. Cumberbatch was a neigbbor of the Jansens, living in one of Jansen's houses.

According to accounts preserved in the family, Mrs. Jansen was not willing to move into the new house built by Jansen after the return to Berdyansk, thinking that this would be imcompatible with the principle of the simple life. So Cornelius Jansen rented it to Cumberbatch, the new British consul who was looking for a house. Since he was a pious and simple man, Mrs. Jansen was now persuaded that one could live in a large house and not become arrogant. When Cumberbatch left town again, she was willing to move in.[54]

This friendship was to become of great importance to the future of the Jansen family. While playing with the Cumberbatch children, the older Jansen children learned their first English words. Peter Jansen relates that he sometimes accompanied Cumberbatch on his hunting trips.[55] But it seems also that between the families as a whole cordial relations developed so that Cornelius Jansen and the ladies also started learning English. English businessmen coming to Berdyansk became acquainted with the Jansens. One of them was William Melville, "a very remarkable Scot, tall and gaunt in his appearance, and truly British in thought and feeling. He was the agent of the British and Foreign Bible Society, and had remained in Odessa throughout the Crimean War, devoting himself entirely to the work of distributing Scriptures among the Russian soldiers."[56] On his distribution trips he often came to Berdyansk where he became acquainted with the Jansens. Peter writes that he was a "bachelor . . . a Presbyterian of the old school, who still believed in predestination and eternal damnation, a typical Scotchman, tall spare and seemingly austere, but withal a most lovable character."[57] Peter also described how Melville procured for the grown members of the family copies of the New Testament, with both the German and English texts, and started reading classes which helped them much in the English language.

According to an oral tradition, Melville, who had subagents working under him, stored some of his Bibles in the house of Consul Cumberbatch. When Cumberbatch left, he asked Cornelius Jansen to store the books for him.[58] Cornelius Jansen, however, not only stored the books but later became engaged in the distribution of Bibles and Christian literature, as we will see.

Since Melville was located at Odessa, his business contacts there were useful to Cornelius Jansen. Later, when the question of emigration came up, it was through Melville that Cornelius Jansen first contacted the American consul at Odessa.[59]

The more Cornelius Jansen advanced in the English, the more his help and service was asked. The ability to use English was not very common in Russia at that time. The official language, of course, was the Russian, besides which there existed the Ukrainian and other languages. The language of society was French. Among the educated the German was also widely known. The knowledge of at least one of these three languages was necessary for the foreigner to avoid complete dependence on interpreters. Cornelius Jansen sometimes served in this capacity, as for instance, at the visit of the Quakers, which event we will have to treat later.

He was also in demand because of his relationship to the Mennonite settlement. One case especially is known to us, that of George Hume, through the memoirs he wrote.[60] It illustrates Jansens role in the introduction of labor saving agricultural machines among the Mennonites in South Russia. Hume was an English naval engineer who happened to come to South Russia and at Odessa became acquainted with William Melville, who introduced Hume to his wealthy friend, William Wagner.[61] Hume relates "that the two friends were very deeply interested in the Mennonite section of the German colonies. It was at Melville's instigation that I became filled with enthusiasm at the idea of going into the interior to investigate the situation, which fruition was destined to effect a complete economic transformation in the whole of the farming industry in South Russia."

Being financially backed by Wagner, Hume associated with a friend, William Graham, also an English engineer, and in 1861 went to Berdyansk, provided by Melville with letters of introduction to Cumberbatch and Jansen. Graham and Hume established their headquarters at Berdyansk, and from here they went to work after the arrival of the machinery from England. "Introduced by Mr. Jansen," as Hume writes, he "started out on a journey through the Mennonite colonies with a view to introducing the reaping and threshing machinery, which had not hitherto been seen there."

In order to expand their business, Graham and Hume dissolved their partnership in 1863, Graham staying on in Berdyansk, while Hume moved to Poltava and later on to Kharkov. Before he departed, he again visited the German colonies "armed with an introduction from Mr. Jansen," and made the acquaintance of the leading men.[62] The Jansens soon cultivated cordial relationships with W. Graham and his family. Even after they had migrated to America they kept in touch with the Graham and Hume families by correspondence.[63]

Other English friends of the Jansens named in the diary of Margarete (Margaretha) Jansen, 1866, are "the Wagstaffs,"[64] and especially the successor of Consul Cumberbatch, Consul Zohrab and his wife. The Zohrabs were even invited to the birthday parties which were usually reserved for closest relatives and most intimate friends. Zohrab often called at the Jansen home, once cleaning Mrs. Jansen's sewing machine, at other times giving medical advice, playing piano, or telling interesting stories. Often Margarete went over to the Zohrabs, either to do some needle work together with Mrs. Zohrab, or to take drawing lessons.[65]

Besides these English friends the Jansens came into contact with many other foreigners, especially since Berdyansk was a port, meeting also captains, businessmen, etc.[66] All these contacts beyond the Mennonite group gave to the Jansen home a cosmopolitan atmosphere.

Mennonite Friends

The fact that mere business acquaintances of Cornelius Jansen became his lifelong friends prompts us to take a look at the friends he chose from his own group, the Mennonites. While as a merchant he was in contact with many people, the number of those who could rightly be called friends of the family was rather small. Significantly enough, they all belonged to a certain group having several characteristics in common. They were on the progressive side, supporting the efforts made for better education, but at the same time they were also influenced by one or several of the pietistic movements which spread among the Russian Mennonites in the middle of the century encouraging warmer religious life, a more active church life, and stressing missionary zeal. Yet they kept away from excesses, and, remaining loyal to the traditional institutions, none of them joined the Mennonite Brethren or other movements which developed during this time. They were more or less neutral in the many controversies and quarrels which swept the Molotschna settlement almost without interruption from the time of Johann Cornies to the migration to America.

We have already heard of Abraham Matthies, the business partner of Cornelius Jansen. Abraham Matthies, Rudnerweide, was elected to the ministry in the Rudnerweide congregation at the Molotschna in 1840.[67] He belonged to those who early got in touch with the Pietists at Hoffnungsfeld, having as early as 1845 heard the initial sermon of Eduard Wüst with whom he became favorably impressed. He was also one of the founders of the so-called *Bruderschule* at Gnadenfeld,[68] but otherwise he remained in the background. When he died suddenly in 1866 the Jansen family was deeply grieved.

Another friend was Jacob Reimer, Felsenthal,[69] who belonged to a small and distinctive group called *Einsame* or, erroneously sometimes "Quakers" though they had no connections with the Society of Friends.[70] They tried to live a quiet and contemplative life, favoring but not insisting on celibacy and community of goods. Since Reimer was the owner of a large estate it was profitable for Jansen to do business with him. Even though Cornelius Jansen did not share the specific views of the *Einsame,* Jacob Reimer meant more to him than a customer only.[71]

Besides these two, there were, of course, others with whom Cornelius Jansen maintained lasting friendships. We mentioned before the relatives of Mrs. Jansen, mostly belonging to the Kleine Gemeinde. The one who seems to have been in closest contact with the Jansens was Jacob Friesen, Blumenort, a deacon of the Kleine Gemeinde.[72] There certainly were others of whom we do not know. There were also good friends in the Vistula region, for instance Mrs. Jansen's youngest brother, Johannes, who with his family came to Berdyansk later in order to stay with the Jansens for some time. Of the other friends Elder Gerhard Penner, with whom Cornelius Jansen always maintained a correspondence, ought to be mentioned.

Contact was maintained mostly by correspondence or occasional visits. There were others in the immediate neighborhood, in the city of Berdyansk, with whom Jansen associated regularly. Of these, too, we have already spoken in other chapters, and we only review them here.

The most intimate friend of Cornelius Jansen for many years, perhaps for all his life, in spite of diversities of opinion in later periods, was Leonhard Sudermann. We shall have to deal with him repeatedly; therefore, at this time, only a short characterization is given. Leonhard Sudermann, born in 1821 as a farmer's son in West Prussia, came to South Russia in 1840 after his father's death, with his mother, nearly all his brothers and sisters who had emigrated in previous years. In 1841 he married Maria, the daughter of Abraham

Sudermann, miller and Mennonite minister at Berdyansk. Leonhard Sudermann also settled at Berdyansk, but his occupation there is unknown.

Like many others at that time he was influenced by Wüst, became his friend and remained so even when the more ardent followers of Wüst—the later founders of the Mennonite Brethren Church—deserted him at the end of his life.[73] The year Wüst died (1859), Leonhard Sudermann was elected to the ministry in the Berdyansk congregation, which was affiliated with the Gnadenfeld congregation. When the Mennonite congregation at Berdyansk became independent, Sudermann became the elder in 1865. One of his first acts as elder was to introduce a Sunday school for the children of his congregation on Sunday afternoons.[74] Though he had only an elementary training,[75] he was considered an educated man. His preaching was appreciated for its warmth, its simplicity and modesty, and also for the many quotations of hymns that were interwoven in it.[76] Since Berdyansk was locally separated from the Molotschna settlement, he did not participate in the religious controversies which took place there. Apparently he was a man without enemies, for whenever we find his name mentioned, it is done with attachment and high regard. The Jansen children adored him. He and his wife were the most frequent and the most welcome guests of the Jansen home.

Since Cornelius Jansen was more familiar with public and business affairs, his advice was often sought by Leonhard Sudermann. On the other hand, the grace and the moderation of Leonhard Sudermann certainly were beneficial in balancing and softening an occasional abruptness in Cornelius Jansen's nature. Leonhard Sudermann was also to become a valuable ally in Cornelius Jansen's big campaign for emigration to America.

In some aspects we can say that they both grew together, adjusting one to the other to some extent, and as we shall see, they had many views and ideas in common. It might be mentioned here that the Sudermann home probably was the only other Mennonite home in Berdyansk where many English friends of Jansen also visited, in spite of the fact that Leonhard Sudermann did not speak the English language.

In the description of the coming events we shall find many instances where the views of the two friends were in harmony, also some where they disagreed. We shall also have to deal with some of the important tasks to which Leonhard Sudermann was elected by his people.

Other Mennonite inhabitants of Berdyansk frequently visiting in the Jansen home were the old minister, Abraham Sudermann, with his family. Abraham Sudermann died in 1865, survived by his widow. Of his children we should mention Hermann, also a grain merchant,[77] and his wife. Mrs. Jansen's aunt, Mrs. Isbrand Riesen, who for some time occupied a part of the Jansen home was, until her death, a frequent guest. Perhaps her son, the cabinet maker Rudolf Riesen, should also be included. He had, like Cornelius Jansen, also retained his Prussian citizenship, the only other case we know of.[78] There were, of course, many other families in the city of Berdyansk with whom the Jansens were on friendly terms and where they were invited for weddings, engagements, funerals, and *Brautfeten,* a party usually given by relatives for an engaged couple, to which usually many relatives and friends were invited.

It seems that the Jansens had connections with only one non-Mennonite German family, the Haymanns, with whom they still exchanged letters from America, but of whom we have no other information.

According to a well-known proverb a man can be judged by his friends. That seems to apply to Cornelius Jansen, especially since he appears to have been rather selective.

A Visible and Active Church

We have previously indicated that his thoughts and religious feelings, from the time of his boyhood days until his ripe age, underwent a change. This certainly did not occur without certain influences by his friends. One of the characteristics of Cornelius Jansen was his readiness to accept something new, if he could recognize it as justified. Together with this he possessed a readiness to adjust himself to other persons and to adapt himself to new situations, a quality which, especially later in America, proved to be of great value to him.

Though Pietism was not unknown among the West Prussian Mennonites, it was not so common as yet, and not so strongly emphasized as was the case in South Russia through the activities of Eduard Wüst. Cornelius Jansen was affected by the revivalistic wave, but he always maintained reservations to the excesses of the movement, and to the theatrical manners of Wüst, who abused, as Jansen thought, the reverence of his followers, especially when he permitted women to kiss his hands.[79]

The necessity of missionary activity, of spreading the Gospel, which was stressed by the Pietists, became of greatest importance to Cornelius Jansen. Though he was in complete harmony with traditional Mennonite beliefs, he felt that the Mennonites were not active enough. To some extent he was always an outsider, maintaining a critical attitude.

The "invisible church," he claimed, has no biblical foundation. The true Christian church has to be a visible and an active one. Thus it has been from the times of the early Fathers up to Thomas á Kempis, John Hus, Menno Simons, Johannes Arndt, N. L. Zinzendorf, M. F. Roos, Paul Gerhardt, J. E. Gossner, and finally Ludwig Hofacker.[80] The Mennonite church, through its own fault, has not been "visible" (noticeable, active) enough. As a matter of fact, Cornelius Jansen somewhat reluctantly accepted the name "Mennonite." He would say: "We so-called Mennonites," or "We nonresistant Christians called Mennonites."[81]

To him the Mennonite church did not orginate with the Reformation. "It is a mistake to say, that we were founded by Menno Simons, ... We claim to be only reformed and gathered by him, and trace our history back to the Waldenses, getting near, through them, to the earliest Christian congregations of the first centuries."[82]

Crusader for Temperance

Another change he made during these years was the giving up of the use of tobacco and alcoholic beverages. He had always been moderate in their use. In the account books we find occasional mention that a bottle of wine was bought or some beer. But now he dropped these completely, and gradually also "became a great crusader against the use of the weed, although never fanatical."[83]

A quite likely way in which this happened, in harmony with the nature of Cornelius Jansen, is told by his son, Cornelius Jansen, Junior: "An incident showing Cornelius Jansen's constant desire to lead a consistent Christian life was when Jacob Reimer put his arm around Cornelius Jansen and said: 'I think that one who loves the Lord Jesus cannot smoke,' needless to say, Cornelius Jansen gave up the use of tobacco. . . . We had, as was the custom at that time when a guest was present, wine on the table. This time it was Mr. John Melville . . . I, a child at that time, came to my mother at the table, and asked to have what was in the bottom of her glass. As she started to give it to me, Mr. Melville put his hand on her arm and said: 'don't,' and then he apologized and told father, also at the table, of the danger and evils of drink; both parents, open to conviction, from that day on banished intoxicants from the table, and eventually, when they came to the United States, became convinced and consistent abstainers."[84]

The use of tobacco was, at that time, still generally accepted among the Mennonites, except for the Kleine Gemeinde, and so was the moderate use of beer and strong drinks, while wine, being more expensive, was in general reserved for the more well-to-do.

The aversion against alcohol in the Jansen family can, however, be partly explained by some shocking events which involved closest relatives. Peter Jansen related this in a talk he gave in a temperance society at Berlin (Kitchener), Ontario, in 1873. Some of the closest relatives indulged in the abuse of alcohol, and two of them died accidentally while under the influence of alcohol.[85]

We shall see, in following chapters, that Cornelius Jansen, strongly supported in this matter by his wife, whose relatives were members of the Kleine Gemeinde, became a fighter for the cause of temperance.

Spreading Christian Literature

Being true to what he believed, Cornelius Jansen acted accordingly. He not only criticized the lack of activity within his church, but started to work on his own. That was not necessarily preaching, for he was never elected to the ministry. There were other ways, and the one he chose was the distribution of Bibles and Christian literature. We have seen that he was first engaged in his work by Melville. But he did not stop there. When he had to leave Russia, he could proudly record that from the fall of 1864 until spring, 1873, he had been distributing Christian literature in the value of 1880.00 silver rubles.[86]

In this work of spreading Bibles and other Christian literature

Cornelius Jansen did not confine himself to his own group. We find listed in his account book Bibles or New Testaments in many languages besides German and Russian, often in Hebrew, for the many Jews living in South Russia; Bulgarian, for Bulgarian colonists settling not far from Berdyansk; and also French, being read preferably by the educated intelligentsia; and Italian, for many merchants and others in the city of Berdyansk which as a seaport was very cosmopolitan in its population. Even Testaments with double text are mentioned.

We have a list of books he received in 1867 from Oncken, Hamburg.[87] Among the many devotional books, tracts, sermon books, Christian stories and primers, we note especially several books by Spurgeon and Bunyan, while only one book by Beyschlag on Renan was occupied with actual theological questions.

Under January 28, 1869, we note that he, together with his friends Cornelius Friesen, Berhnard Buhler, Penner, and Leonhard Sudermann, decided to buy for 25 silver rubles from the Oncken's Tract Society at Hamburg, tracts for distribution. He also received Christian literature in the Russian language from the firm of J. G. G. Blissmer at St. Petersburg, of which we have accounts for the years 1869-1871.

Cornelius Jansen was aided in the distribution of Bibles for the "British and Foreign Bible Society" by Leonhard Sudermann, Hermann Harder, Gnadenfeld, a Friesen from Marienthal, a certain Thomsen, and especially by Abraham Matthies.[88] A Lutheran pastor by the name of Rheinbach is also mentioned frequently.

In recognition of his services for the Society he received in 1872 a large fifteen pound Bible, printed in 1871, "in grateful acknowledgement of kind and friendly services rendered for many years, in promoting the object of the Society in South Russia," as the dedication reads, signed in London, May, 1872, by Jackson and Bergue, secretaries of the Society.[89]

As he had for Melville, Cornelius Jansen also acted as an agent for James Watt, who maintained a Bible storehouse at Odessa, handling mostly German Bibles, Russian New Testaments and primers.[90]

He also interceded for the native Russians who, having broken with the Greek Orthodox Church, were severely persecuted by the priests. Daughter Helena relates the following incidents in a paper given years later in Mount Pleasant, Iowa:

> Two Russian farmers (brothers) living in quite good circumstances had come to the conclusion that the pictures of their holy saints which every Russian family must have according to the number of children in it, were of no account. They consequently removed them from their houses all together. Of this notice was given to the priest, who, with the authority he possessed, had both of these men torn away from their wives, children and occupation and thrown into prison. My father visited them frequently, taking refreshments to them and speaking words of encouragement. These indeed they needed, for it is not an easy thing, to have in prospect the standing in the pillory, which punishment many had suffered already before them; or to be imprisoned at the time of harvest, when they were so much needed at their homes.
>
> The wife of one of these men asked the officer on her knees with many tears to let her husband out, only for that time, that he might reap what he had sown before he was imprisoned, but she was refused. My father interceded for her, but even his exertions were in vain. The judge said to him, 'Had this man been a robber or a murderer, he might, because of your warranty, have been liberated for this time, but one who has turned away from the *Pravoslavnaya church* which means 'right believing Church,' has done a crime in offense to spiritual things and cannot be helped.' Consequently these poor men remained imprisoned until they were released by death about a year after.
>
> Of instances like these, I could mention many, but I will only speak of one more.
>
> There is in Russia a sect called 'Besspopovitz' which means without pope or priest. They go very seldom or not at all to the public worship of the Greek Catholic Church nor fast before Easter like the other Russians must do, but they eat vegetables, butter, milk or things with the exception of meat. Smoking or any use of tobacco is looked upon by them as a vice and is not allowed because they believe it against the Bible. . . .
>
> Now there are two girls, also belonging to this sect; they often worked for us, and we found them to be honest and diligent persons. Once however, when my mother sent for them, their house was empty and we were told that they, with their parents had been imprisoned for not attending any of the services connected with the Russian Church.
>
> My parents asked the judge with whom they were acquainted whether he could do anything for them, but he assured them he could not.

> This took place previous to our leaving Russia. After coming to this country, my mother inquired in letters about these poor girls and was informed that they had been 'sent to Siberia.'

It was events like these that greatly perturbed Cornelius Jansen and caused him to advocate and work unceasingly for immigration to America. By reason of his many contacts, official and otherwise, he was aware of the fact that, as we shall see later, the special religious and economic privileges of the German colonists In Russia, including the Mennonites, were about to be withdrawn.

The Jansen Home and Library

It seems appropriate at this time to take a look at the literature to be found in the Jansen home at Berdyansk. The Bethel College Historical Library has reconstructed the collection of books originally in the possession of Cornelius Jansen. Besides the *Fundament-Buch* of Menno Simons in the edition of Peter von Riesen, and the *Geschichte der Martyrer* by Isaac von Dühren, we find *Beitrage zur Kenntniss der Mennoniten-Gemeinden in Europe und Amerika* by Reiswitz and Wadzeck, (Berlin, 1821). Mennonite hymnaries are also represented.

Some of the books still preserved, which must of course, be only a few from the library Cornelius Jansen possessed, are also listed in the above mentioned list of books ordered from Oncken, as were several story books and the history of the Christian church.[91] Not missing in this collection is a book of sermons by Ludwig Hofacker, whom Wüst had declared his ideal, and whose sermons at that time were much read among the Mennonites of South Russia.[92] We also find in the library John Milton's *Das Verlorene Paradies* (Altona, 1762). Several times in his *Letter Book,* writings of Sören Kierkegaard (1814-1855), the Danish philosopher, are mentioned. We are not surprised to find that Cornelius Jansen was interested in this great critic through his book, *Christentum und Kirche.*

According to an entry in his account book (*Journal,* 1860) in February, 1864, he kept the German newspapers edited in St. Petersburg and Odessa, which he ordered not only for himself but also for other Mennonite friends at Berdyansk. Of other periodicals he received we mention here the *Mennonitische Blätter.* We have only a list of these periodicals for the years 1871 and 1872. At that time Cornelius Jansen's interests had partly shifted and we find on his order list Christian magazines in both German and English languages, some of them especially for children.[93] An obvious shift of interests was brought about for Cornelius Jansen by the visit of a Quaker delegation to South Russia in 1867. Before we, however, turn to this important event, let us take a look at the Jansen home as it was at this time.

Having dealt with the varied contacts the Jansens had, we can easily imagine that the atmosphere of the Jansen home was, especially for a Mennonite home, rather unique. The composing elements expressed themselves in family relationships, in customs and habits, in thinking and behavior, in friends and books.

In some respects the Jansen home was that of the German *Bürger* in the middle of the nineteenth century. The city of Danzig at this time had already lost its patriciate, but the patrician heritage had been partly taken over by the new classes of wealthy townsmen and to some extent also by the well-to-do Mennonite merchants. Out of this environment came some basic elements of the way of life as followed by the Jansens. While among the rural Mennonite groups the Low German was still prevailing, a pure High German was spoken in the Jansen home.[94] The children very likely attended the elementary Mennonite school at Berdyansk, which was taught by David Goerz from 1869 to 1873, and received training by governesses.[95] The Christmas tree was a symbol of great joy in the Jansen home,[96] which must have been an exception among Mennonites in South Russia. It was different for the Mennonites in the Palatinate, who became acquainted with this custom earlier. It was brought to America by them and used at Summerfield, Illinois.

Another home element was given with the Mennonite traditions, strongly stressed by relationship to the Kleine Gemeinde. It had been a rule for the wealthy Danzig Mennonites that the clothing had to be simple in appearance, but made from finest materials. This principle was valid for the Jansen family, Mrs. Jansen especially, was very strict in this respect. While Anna von Riesen would sometimes buy a hat or have a dress made, Mrs. Jansen tailored all clothes for herself and her daughters. Clothing, in her view, was used primarily to cover the body rather than to beautify.[97] No jewels or fashion attire was worn, but the watches and watch chains, the eyeglass frames and cases were of the best quality and always of gold or silver.[98]

The close relationship to the Kleine Gemeinde revealed itself also in a certain seriousness, in the avoidance of loud gaiety. The diaries of Margarete Jansen which serve as a main source here, reflect also the spirit of the home.[99] Though Margarete always tried to maintain a cheerful disposition, she sometimes, especially when together with other young people, reproached herself for what she thought was excessive joy.[100]

Though there were several servants in the home, the children were habituated to work, and it is therefore, only natural that the girls, for instance, learned to milk the cows.

To the three children already mentioned, we have to add three more, born after the return to Berdyansk. They are: Johannes (John), born October 16, 1854, Helena (Helen), born November 14, 1859, and Heinrich, later named Cornelius, April 30, 1863. We observe the custom of giving names which are traditional in the family. The name of the youngest son was changed to Cornelius about at the time when they came to Canada.[101]

Besides these six children, the two children of Mrs. Jansen's brother, Abraham von Riesen, whose parents both had died early, were educated largely in the Jansen home. They are Heinrich and Anna von Riesen,[102] about the same age as the two oldest Jansen children. From 1871 to 1873 we find Heinrich at Danzig, staying with the Louis Eduard Zimmermanns, and apparently getting a professional training as a merchant, during this time aiding Cornelius Jansen with the printing of his pamphlets.

What we said about the different influences certainly pertained to every aspect of the daily life. The daily meals were as follows: Breakfast (*Frühstück*), noon dinner (*Mittag*), a light meal at four in the afternoon, called *Kaffee,* and the evening meal, called *Tee,* the latter receiving its name from the fact that in the evenings tea was usually served, prepared in the Russian *Samovar.* Here an adjustment to the Russian environment becomes obvious. In the rural Mennonite tradition the afternoon snack was called *Vesper.* At the evening meal, called *Abendbrot,* usually some soup was served.

Names of the dishes and the baking were mentioned, as for instance, *Apfelmus, saure Klopse, Eierbier, Pfeffernüsse, Raderkuchen, Pfannkuchen,* and others, show Mennonite traditions as well as standard items of the Danzig citizen's kitchen.

The family life can be called peaceful and harmonious. When the family gathered for the meals, thanks was rendered, and after the evening meal a devotional service was held, called *Abendsegen.* In the twilight hour they liked to sit together and sing songs.[103] Cornelius Jansen was very musical and a music-lover. He played the piano and the flute and had a good voice. He also saw to it that his children learned to play an instrument.

Although the facilities for education were, as we saw, not too good in South Russia, the Jansens offered their children that which was available, but without forcing them strongly when they were old enough to use their own judgment.

Margarete, who in 1866 knew enough English to make occasional English remarks in her diaries, also took French lessons. Peter at this time was taking Russian, of which language Cornelius Jansen, of course, had a fair knowledge too, since he had to use it in dealing with Russian customers of wholesalers.[104]

As we have already seen, good reading material was richly provided in the Jansen home, even special books and periodicals for the children. The Sunday morning was devoted to the church service, and when, for some reason, the family did not go, they gathered at home and one of the parents would read a sermon.

To this home, characterized by solidity, simplicity and cordiality as its outstanding features, the visit of representatives of the British Society of Friends was to add a new note.

Guiding the Quakers

In June, 1867, an English Quaker minister, Isaac Robson, from Huddersfield, had been "liberated" by a Yearly Meeting of the Society of Friends "for religious service" in South Russia, chiefly amongst Molokans, and also in northern Italy.[105] In the beginning of August another minister of the Friends, Thomas Harvey, of Headingly Hill, Leeds, who felt it his duty to accompany Robson, got the approval of the Society.

These two, both already widely traveled, started on their trip the same month. To some extent they patterned their travel route after that of some other Quakers, Stephen Grellet, an American of French origin, and William Allen, a Britisher, who paid a visit to South Russia in 1819.[106]

Robson and Harvey first went to South Germany where they got into contact with the Mennonites, in order to get information about them, and especially also about the Mennonites in South Russia. In September, 1867, we find them at Odessa, where they submitted a petition to the czar "in support of nonconforming Russians now imprisoned," which afterwards proved to have results.

Of their arrival at Berdyansk the report says:

> Tenth month 9th . . . about 4 A.M. we landed at Berdyansk and with difficulty got admission into the hotel where dirt and discomfort prevailed. To our relief, however, in a very short time Cornelius Jansen, a Mennonite merchant and farmer, who had been advised of our coming, called with a conveyance and most kindly took us to his own house. During our stay here of several days we received the most affectionate attention from this interesting family, consisting of parents, six children, and aunt, all of whom speak English, and who, in their principles and habits, have much in common with Friends. There are about seventy Mennonite families at Berdyansk. We had two appointed meetings with them, attended by about seventy and a hundred, respectively. Both of them we thought to be seasons of Divine favour. We also attended their own meeting on First-day morning, which was conducted with much simplicity and seriousness. The arrangements of the house resemble those of Friends, except that the ministers' gallery has a reading desk in the centre; men and women sit separately. We had a good deal of social intercourse with the ministers and other members of the congregation, when much inquiry was made respecting the principles and practices of Friends—especially on Baptism and the Supper. We were impressed with the agreeable and candid spirit in which our explanations were received, and felt these occasions to be profitable and refreshing. Cornelius Jansen interpreted efficiently for us, both in public and in private.
>
> Knowing that we wished to visit the Mennonite colonies, Cornelius Jansen informed us that he was ready to accompany us, having finished his harvest the day before our arrival. He also remarked that had we come at the time originally proposed, he would have been placed in considerable difficulty. Thus our undesired detention at Sevastopol was made the means of bringing us to the field of labour at a time when our truly kind friend was able to leave home comfortably, and also when the Mennonite farmers generally were at liberty to receive our visit.
>
> Cornelius Jansen, having provided bedding, and a supply of food for men and beasts, which was stored in his own carriage, drawn by

> three horses, after a touching parting opportunity with the family we left early on the 15th of Tenth Month for the interior, entering at once upon the steppe, an apparently boundless and treeless, though not barren, expanse. We passed through several villages, and not numerous trains of wagons laden with wheat for Berdyansk. Many of these trains consisted of rude Russian bullock-wagons, with drivers to match, contrasting very strongly with the neatly-made horse-waggons, with well-dressed drivers, from the Mennonite and other German colonies.
>
> Our first day's travel of sixty versts brought us to Rudnerweide, the nearest Mennonite village, where we were hospitably received by the widow, Barbara Matthias. The 'eldest' principal minister soon called upon us, and proposed our having a meeting in the next morning, to which we gladly acceded. He said his wife had received her first impression under the ministry of S. Grellet when he visited their colonies in 1819.[107]

For several days they visited the Mennonite villages, speaking at gatherings in churches which were, in spite of the shortness of the announcement, always crowded, and sometimes in schoolhouses and homes. At these gatherings they addressed the people, and also answered the questions about their particular beliefs. Of the meeting at the Rudnerweide church they report: "At the close the four or five ministers who were present showed their love by the accustomed kiss, and expressed cordial satisfaction with what had been said."

Other churches they visited were Gnadenfeld, Neukirch, Ohrloff, and Halbstadt. It is interesting to note that Cornelius Jansen, who, without doubt, directed the tour, took the Quakers only to those churches which at that time were known as the more progressive, but not to the Petershagen and Pordenau groups. Cornelius Jansen also brought them to Felsenthal one afternoon. The report says: "Our kind companion took us a long drive to call on a family who, with a few others among the Mennonites, are erroneously termed, Quakers. It was a disappointing visit, and we failed to obtain an opportunity for serious conference on their peculiar views."[108] For two days they visited, together with Nikolai Schmidt, Steinbach, the Molokans, whose villages were not far from those of the Mennonite settlement. In the meetings they held with them, Cornelius Jansen translated from English to German, and Nikolai Schmidt from German to Russian. The Molokans had been visited previously by another Quaker, John Yeardley, for whom Nikolai Schmidt had also served as an interpreter.

On October 23, they left the Mennonite settlement for Nikopol, 90 verst away, still accompanied by Cornelius Jansen. Because of the danger of missing the road during the darkest hours of the night they were obliged to stop at an inn. When they arrived at Nikopol the next morning, the steamer they wanted to take to Kherson had left two hours before. Forced to wait three days for the next steamer, they discovered in this town seventeen Mennonite families, with whom they held a meeting, admonishing them to organize themselves and to establish regular church services.

After having provided for their comfort as well as possible, Cornelius Jansen returned home the following day. The report reads: "We parted this morning from our true friend, guide, and interpreter, Cornelius Jansen, who left us to return home. His valuable services, rendered with a ready mind, and true brotherly kindness to two perfect strangers, in the name of disciples, will, we trust, not lose an abundant reward."[109]

Isaac Robson, one of the Quaker ministers who had been visiting the Mennonites in South Russia, felt compelled to summarize the essentials of his message to them. In the beginning of 1868 he sent a letter, addressed "To the Mennonites in South Russia," to Cornelius Jansen.[110]

After reviewing the many privileges the Mennonites enjoy in Russia, he came to his main point: "Is it not His purpose that you should not only be blessed yourselves but also that you should be a blessing to others—that 'your light should so shine before men that others seeing your good works should also be brought to glorify your Father who is in heaven?' Is it not His purpose that you should be instrumental in spreading the knowledge of the truth of the Gospel of Christ to those who are now sitting in darkness—sunk in ignorance and superstition? Are you prepared, dear friends! to give a good account of this your stewardship? I do not forget the difficulties of your position nor the danger which might result from attempts to enlighten your more ignorant neighbors. But I feel it right to endeavor a little to stir you up by putting you in remembrance of these things."

To this Cornelius Jansen agreed fully. He immediately translated this letter and sent it to Odessa to have it printed. It was soon sent back, some sentences being entirely crossed and blotted, with the notice that it could not be printed in Russia.

One of the passages not permitted for publication was the one above quoted without which the letter lost most of its worth. About his reaction Cornelius Jansen says: "This refusal to reprint such a brotherly letter awakened in me and several others real suspicion, and gave the first serious thought concerning our real position under the Russian government, as to how little our so-called religious liberty was worth."[11,1]

This passage, in Cornelius Jansen's own words, expresses what we may call one of the turning points of his life. Thus far, when refusing the Russian citizenship, it had been perhaps due more to an uncertain feeling of antipathy. Now his situation became clear to himself. Becoming conscious of his position he felt the limitations so much more; these were not economic restrictions as in Prussia, but restrictions involving religious liberty—freedom in thought and expression. Perhaps he had always considered Berdyansk as a more or less temporary place of abode. But now, getting more uneasy than before after this experience, he felt prompted to look around for another place of refuge. Shortly after the visit of the Quakers in South Russia, another event occurred which was to affect the situation of Cornelius Jansen and his family greatly.

II. Great Issues

War and Peace

On November 9, 1867, the parliament of the North-Germanic Confederation had passed a new conscription law (*Reichswehrgesetz*), revoking the privileges of the Mennonites. This did not come unexpectedly. In fact, since the main part of West Prussia had been incorporated into the Prussian Kingdom in the first division of Poland, in 1772, they could no longer be without a certain anxiety. Frederick II, after many appeals, had granted them their old privileges but not unconditionally. Every year they had had to pay 5,000 talers for a military school (*Kadettenhaus*), at Culm, West Prussia, an obligation which Cornelius Jansen called " a continual offence to our feelings." [1]

It is not our purpose here to give a complete review of the development and the problems in connection with the Mennonite principle of nonresistance in Prussia.[2] However, since this question will be of increasing importance in the life of Cornelius Jansen, we must take the main points of this development into consideration.

The rise of nationalism in Germany, of which the Napoleonic wars brought the first general manifestations, did not leave the Mennonite congregations unaffected. The process of emancipation, however, did not advance at the same pace everywhere. The urban Mennonite groups showed a more liberal attitude, and earlier so than the rural ones. The same difference existed largely between the western Mennonites including those in the Palatinate, and the ones in the East, who as a whole, were more conservative.

This difference became evident when in 1848, the Frankfurt Parliament, at the instance of a Mennonite from Krefeld, Hermann von Beckerath, rejected an amendment to the Constitution, introduced in favor of the West Prussian Mennonites, exempting them from military service.[3] Though the rulings of the Frankfurt Parliament did not have legal force, they were highly symptomatic.

The emigrations from West Prussia to Russia, especially those after 1848, had, in part, been motivated by the threatening loss of the privilege of military exemption. A continuous emigration to Russia from 1852 to about 1870 and a gradual weakening of the principle in Prussia are the reasons why the final emigration from West Prussia to America, was in general, not very strong.[4] Since many had friends and relatives in Russia, an emigration to that country was not unusual. It can be said that up to 1868, the main body of the West Prussian Mennonites was not willing to give up the privilege without making strong efforts for its retention. Prussia's successful wars in 1864 and 1866 did much to integrate the Mennonites, especially their young people, into the German nation, which gradually resulted in the giving up of the principle of nonresistance.[5]

Many urban Mennonites, especially, gave up their principle of nonresistance. Others wanted to retain it in the form of noncombatant service. Among those who were persuaded that a change of the Mennonite position was necessary, and eminently worked for it, was Jacob Mannhardt, pastor of the Danzig Mennonite congregation and editor of the *Mennonitische Blätter,* founded in 1854. This monthly magazine, of which Cornelius Jansen was a subscriber, favored under Mannhardt the abandonment of the principle of nonresistance and the introduction of mixed marriages.[6] In considering the question, we have to bear in mind that those who were ready to give up nonresistance were eager to obtain something else instead: the full recognition of their church, and a higher social standing for themselves. Unsatisfied with the limited corporate rights they wanted the full corporate rights which would transform their church from a sect (*Sekte*) to a free religious association (*freie Religionsgemeinschaft*).[7]

Jacob Mannhardt, knowing that time was in his favor, was careful enough to avoid a split between the Danzig church and the rural congregations. Yet in January, 1868, after a long period of silence as to this delicate problem, he opposed, in an editorial, the proposed noncombatant service.[8] But when in March, 1868, the king issued an order-in-council which left to his Mennonite subjects only the alternative of either accepting the noncombatant service or leaving the country, Jacob Mannhardt and the majority of the West Prussian Mennonites considered this question settled.

Of those who still were opposed, some emigrated to Russia as did Elder Johann Toews of the Ladekopp congregation who had been a member of the delegations to Berlin in October, 1867, and February, 1868.[9] The rest gathered around Elder Gerhard Penner, of the Heubuden congregation, who, advised by his friend and mediator, the Baron von Brauchitsch, Klein Katz, did not yet give up, but hoped for an act of grace on the part of the king.

Finally, the nonconforming groups had to recognize that they too had no other choice than to emigrate. On April 25, 1870, the elders and ministers assembled for a conference on this question, but no agreement was reached. Shortly afterwards, on May 3, 1870, the more determined gathered again and elected a deputation which was assigned to look for adequate location in Russia.[10]

When the two delegates, Elder Wilhelm Ewert of Nessau near Thorn, and Peter Dyck, minister of the Rosenort congregation, came to Berdyansk in 1870, on their extensive tour, they got the same advice which they apparently had received during their visit the year before. While they conferred with Leonhard Sudermann and Cornelius Jansen the latter insisted that they should consider an emigration to America, and advised them to send a delegation there.[11]

America on the Horizon

Cornelius Jansen's recommendation was not given accidentally. He had been reading of the great number of Mennonites in North America[12] and had received more information about this country from one of the Quakers, with both of whom he had maintained correspondence after their visit. He later said: "Now it appears to us a clear and wonderful guidance in the hands of our Lord, that the next year our beloved friend Isaac Robson paid a visit also to America, whence he brought us all the information we needed."[13]

The more information Cornelius Jansen received, the more he became persuaded that America was the country where the Mennonites could live in full freedom. In the beginning, however, this was a rather personal affair, concerning himself and his family, and perhaps a few friends from Prussia, but not any larger group and not yet his fellow Mennonites in South Russia.

To the Mennonites of South Russia, the idea of going to America was something new because none had ever done it, and there were no contacts between the Mennonites in South Russia and those in America.

That was a little different in West Prussia. First of all, the Prussian Mennnonites were in contact with the other Mennonite groups of Germany, of which some had gone to America recently. Mennonites in South Germany, for instance, had connections with the group at Summerfield, Illinois, which had emigrated only about twenty years previously. In 1868, the Mennonite pastor at Friedrichstadt, Carl Justus van der Smissen, had received a call to serve as professor at the Mennonite school at Wadsworth, Ohio. Jacob Mannhardt was in contact with John Oberholtzer, the co-founder of the General Conference. They probably exchanged their papers.

A few families of the West Prussian Mennonites had also emigrated to the United States, among them being two with whom Cornelius Jansen entered in correspondence later: Peter Wiebe, Rolla, Missouri, and Gerhard Wiebe, Newbourgh, Ohio, a half brother to Elder Johann Wiebe of Fürstenwerder, West Prussia.[14] Johannes D. Dyck spent the years from 1848 to 1858 in America before going to the Trakt, Samara. But those who had gone there, had gone as individuals and for personal reasons.

America, at that time, was considered a country "interesting for adventurers, an asylum for criminals," as Leonhard Sudermann expressed himself.[15] Perhaps also the poor and the have-nots would take the chance to go there as did many of them from Germany up to 1870, but not the prosperous Mennonite farming families in West Prussia who were left as a last group of objectors to military service.

Strangely enough, another man started promoting America as a country for a possible emigration—Jacob Mannhardt. Though he did not approve of emigration in general, he maintained that in case some wanted to do so, America was by far preferable to Russia. As early as September, 1869, Mannhardt published the first letter by an immigration agent of the State of Virginia who had heard of emigration plans among the West Prussian Mennonites. More letters followed, by agents and private persons, in nearly every following issue, some warning, but most of them favorable and encouraging.[16]

The publicity which was given to these letters by Mannhardt, was not without result. In February, 1870, Mannhardt, could report that a group under the initiative of Elder Abraham Esau, Tiegenhagen, which thus far had planned to go to Russia, now had cast their eyes on America. The Danzig Mennonites, though they did not consider emigration at all, were even willing to share expenses of a deputation to America.[17]

These America-plans, however, proved to be without solid foundations, as the ensuing conferences revealed which we already mentioned. At the first larger meeting no conclusions were arrived at. Those seriously considering to emigrate were in the minority, and later they chose their delegates, not for America but for Russia.[18] However, shortly after those delegates, Peter Dyck and Wilhelm Ewert, had returned from their inspection tour, the situation changed completely, for Russia also was about to introduce a general military service.

Conscription Rumors

For the Mennonites in Russia, contrary to their brethren in Prussia, the revocation of their privileges came suddenly and unexpectedly. To Cornelius Jansen as well, though he always had maintained reservations against Russia, the news came like "lightning from a clear sky."

Cornelius Jansen reported that he first heard of the new law in preparation "when the Governor-General von Kotzeboo [von Kotzebue] told a friend of mine in 1870, that the law of universal military service already confirmed by the Emperor, would also destroy our privileges. A few weeks afterwards, being personally acquainted with this governor-general, I called upon him at Odessa, where in circumstantial conversation he convinced me for certain about our dark future."[19] An illuminating detail is given by Cornelius Jansen, Jr., Pasadena, Calif., "When father Jansen asked him [the governor-general] point-blank, he hedged about and would not come out straight, till father said: I ask you as a father, is it true? Whereupon he answered: If you ask me so I have to say the report is true" (Answer to Questionnaire).

The friend here mentioned by Cornelius Jansen was Isbrand Friesen, also a resident of Berdyansk, orginally a Mennonite, but who had now left the Mennonite church and who held some administrative position owing to which he was in contact with the Governor-General von Kotzebue. Dietrich Gaeddert stated that he knew of the contemplated change of the *Privilegium* long before this time.[20]

We do not know the exact time of Cornelius Jansen's trip to Odessa, only that it was, as he says, "a few weeks" after Friesen had told of the news. For a description of the coming development we have to rely in part on the report of Dietrich Gaeddert, written twenty years later but, in the data given, based on his diary entries, and undoubtedly correct.

According to this report the Mennonites did not believe Isbrand Friesen but thought that he, who apparently had left the Mennonite church for ambitious reasons, now wanted to show off against his former coreligionists. That also was the result of a first conference of the elders on this matter on December 18, 1870 (o.s.), to which Friesen was invited. However, shortly afterwards another meeting was held. An explanation is given by Ab. Görz,[21] who writes that Isbrand Friesen in a letter of November 19, 1870 (o.s.), informed Peter Schmidt, Steinbach, of his conversation with the governor-general. In order to make sure, Elder Johann Harder sent a telegram to Senator Eduard von Hahn at St. Petersburg. Senator von Hahn, who had been the supervisor of the Mennonite colonies for many years, and therefore, was fully acquainted with their situation, in his answer suggested that the Mennonites should send a deputation to St. Petersburg. This was what was decided on at the second conference, held on January 8, 1871 (o.s.). (o.s. = old style calendar).

We can assume that Cornelius Jansen was not idle during this time. Strangely enough, Dietrich Gaeddert in his report does not mention Cornelius Jansen and his activities until January, 1872.

Although the papers of Cornelius Jansen do not refer to his activity in the cause of emigration previous to 1870, we are well informed on his correspondence from February, 1870, up to his expulsion in 1873. One of the sources for this information is his letter-book, entitled *Correspondenz,* in which he kept track of all letters he wrote during this time, entering date, address, and, in a few words, the contents. Brief as these notes are, they are of greatest value to us, because this very period seems to be the most important in the life of Cornelius Jansen, and the initiation of the emigration movement his major achievement. His work was a threefold one, and consisted of gathering information on the conditions in America, influencing his brethren in Russia and West Prussia in their decision, and of contacting government officials of Canada and the United States.

This work began as a one-man campaign by Cornelius Jansen and finally led to one of the greatest Mennonite voluntary mass migrations in recent history.

Contacting American Mennonites

Though Cornelius Jansen received his first information on North America through Mannhardt's book and from Isaac Robson in 1867, it seems that he did not come into contact with American Mennonites before 1870. His first letter for this purpose he wrote on February 15, 1870 (o.s.), which he mentioned in the preface of his *Sammlung von Notizen über Amerika,* and which was partly reproduced in *Mennonitische Blätter,* (No. 7, Sept., 1870). It was addressed to Daniel Hege, an immigrant from the Palatinate, and the first secretary of the General Conference Mennonite Church, who had, unknown to Jansen, died in 1862.

Christian Krehbiel, another immigrant from South Germany, writes about this letter in his autobiography: "The letter came into the hands of John Oberholtzer, who, at that time, was the publisher of a Mennonite periodical and president of the General Conference. Conditions among the European Mennonites were then less well known to those in the East than to us in the West. Accordingly, Oberholtzer sent Jansen's letter to me in Summerfield. . . . Obviously, so important an inquiry must have an answer and I undertook to reply." Christian Krehbiel states that he wrote Jansen at length depicting American conditions as fully and as truthfully as he could closing his letter with a paragraph "that in this country every farmer and every businessman in ordinary circumstances must be his own best workman."[22]

Cornelius Jansen answered soon. Used to the European labor system, he did not understand Krehbiel's final remark. "He could see that if a hired hand was sick one's own son would feed the horses; or if a maid was ill or away one's daughter would do the milking; but that every owner must be his own best worker, that he could not understand."

In a second letter, written on December 24, 1870, Christian Krehbiel explained himself in more detail on the labor situation in the United States. This explanation was so important that Jansen not only included it later in his collection of letters from America, but also prepared himself and his family for this situation.[23]

On April 8, 1870, John F. Funk,[24] Elkhart, Indiana, wrote to Cornelius Jansen stating that he had received his letter "a few days ago" in which Jansen had related that some Mennonites of the Ukraine were contemplating leaving the country and asked for information about settlement possibilities in America. Judging by the content of Funk's letter this must have been the first letter which he received from Jansen and was probably written at the time that Jansen wrote the letter to Daniel Hege.[25] Funk's letter contains information about settlement possibilities, exemption from military service, and the promise to send more information, and to help the Mennonites from Russia establish new homes in America.

In his next letter Funk acknowledged the receipt of some postcards and a letter dated January 22, 1871 (o.s.), which he received from Cornelius Jansen. Funk wrote that he was sending him the requested copies of *Der Herold der Wahrheit* and some books, that Isaac Robson had been his guest, that he would help the delegates when they would come and that a Mennonite can be freed from military duties in America by paying three hundred dollars. This correspondence continued from some time.[26]

In a letter which Peter Jansen wrote to John F. Funk at the occasion of the death of his father, Cornelius Jansen, he stated that "the correspondence of Father's with yourself was really the first step taken toward the Mennonite immigrations to the United States." This claim was repeated by Funk in his article on "Cornelius Jansen"

(*Family Almanac,* 1896) and more recently in the *Mennonite Quarterly Review.*[27]

To this we must say that Cornelius Jansen's contact with the American Mennonites cannot be considered "the first step" in this event. Contacts with English Quakers and the consulates preceded this step. In addition to this we have a clear record from the pen of Cornelius Jansen himself in the preface to *Sammlung von Notizen über Amerika* (see Appendix IV) in which he states that through the book by Mannhardt on *Die Wehrfreiheit* . . . his attention was first called to the fact that there were numerous Mennonites in America and that this compelled him to gather information about their religious life. It is further implied in this preface that he wrote his first letter to the American Mennonites on February 15, 1870 addressed to Daniel Hege which was answered by Christian Krehbiel, as we have seen. Weighing the statement of the father with that of the son it must be remembered that the father wrote about these events while they were taking place while his son wrote according to hearsay a generation later.

The most concrete, if not the most important information which Cornelius Jansen obtained about conditions in America evidently came neither from Christian Krehbiel nor John F. Funk but from a number of Prussian Mennonites who had recently gone to America and secured farms there. Peter Wiebe, who had purchased a farm at Rolla, Missouri, and later settled at Halstead, Kansas, received a letter from J. v. Riesen of Berdyansk dated February 28, 1871 (o.s.), which contained a long list of questions. It is evident that this inquiry was written because of Cornelius Jansen's activities. On May 20 Peter Wiebe replied in a very detailed letter answering his twenty-four questions.[28] He not only wrote him his own impressions but also gathered information from others, reporting how much a farm costs, how much the crops yielded, what the wages for hired help were, the cost of the trip, etc. etc.

A similar letter was written by Gerhard Wiebe of Newbourgh, Ohio, on September 22, 1872, to his brother, Elder J. Wiebe near Danzig in which he not only related his own impressions but also included a letter from John Oberholtzer, Milford Square, Pennsylvania, dated September 9, 1871 which contains some detailed information regarding the status of the nonresistant Mennonites during the time of the war.[29]

These were busy years for Cornelius Jansen obtaining and conveying information regarding the pending conscription law and about a possible emigration to America. Information was obtained from Mennonites, land and immigration agents, consuls, delegates in St. Petersburg, etc., and it was dispersed among friends in Russia and Prussia.[30]

Delegation to St. Petersburg

For the Russian Mennonites the main event of the year 1871, was the sending of the first deputation to St. Petersburg, which was followed by many others. Though this delegation was intended first as a regional affair, it soon after was considered advisable to start an united action by all Mennonite settlements. At a conference on January 22 (o.s.), at Alexanderwohl, Molotschna, representatives from the Chortitza and Bergthal settlements also attended. Four delegates form the Molotschna and two from the Chortitza settlements were chosen, Elder Leonhard Sudermann being the leader of the delegation from the Molotschna.

They started on February 1, 1871 (o.s.), for Odessa, where they wanted to inform their immediate superiors, the president of the *Fürsorge-Komitee* for the German colonies and the governor-general of their steps; however, both were already in St. Petersburg, where our delegates arrived on February 20. They saw many high officials and it was suggested that they had come too early, for it would take about two years before the law now in preparation would be finished.[31]

They received some assurance of understanding and the promise of support. They did not get to see the czar, which had been one of their objectives, but left the capital rather satisfied with their accomplishments, after handing in a "Memorial on the question of nonresistance of the Mennonites." While at St. Petersburg, the delegates got acquainted with Theodor Hans, pastor of a Moravian congregation in the capital, who was willing to look after Mennonite interests and to inform them of any events in their case. Pastor Hans had an interest in reconciling the Mennonites with the government, but as a Moravian, he certainly was not interested in the primary problem of the Mennonites: the maintenance of nonresistance.

Later he became one of the opponents to emigration. He challenged the Mennonites, calling their attention to the responsibility they had in Russia.[32]

While Leonhard Sudermann was away at St. Petersburg, Cornelius Jansen maintained contact with him by correspondence. On February 14 he sent him the "last lengthy missive" of the Quakers; on February 25 he sent a comment on a remark of the Queen of England, who had declared the Prussian military system was worthy of imitation for its recent success in the Franco-Prussian War.[33] On his way back from St. Petersburg, Leonhard Sudermann went to Prussia to see his brother Abraham who was living there. Cornelius Jansen tried to take advantage of Sudermann's presence in West Prussia, and asked him in a letter of March 20 to plead for a deputation to America, and also to have the missive printed.[34]

Cornelius Jansen was also in continual contact with leaders of the West Prussian Mennonites, mainly with the elders Gerhard Penner and Wilhelm Ewert. He sent them copies of letters he received from his Quaker friends in England, and also from America.

Contacting the U. S. Consul

In the latter part of June, Jansen went to Odessa.[35] Here he undoubtedly made the first personal contact with the consul of the United States, Dr. Smith, from whom he had received information about America through James Watt. It was at this time that Jansen planned a trip to America either alone or with family. To the consul at Odessa, Dr. Smith, he wrote on July 20 (o.s.) 1871: "With regard of my proposed voyage thither [America] at the end of this, or at the beginning of the next year, I will take the liberty of troubling you at a future period, either personally or by letter."[36] That is probably also an explanation for some financial transactions undertaken during this time by Cornelius Jansen. On his orders 2800.00 rubles (silver) were sent to Heinrich Schütt at Hamburg, a Mennonite merchant who later rendered great services to the immigrants. For some unknown reason Jansen's trip did not materialize.

At this early phase Jansen was perhaps the only one not to hope for any acceptable results from the Russian government, and consequently proceeded unswervingly in his plans. At the American consulate he not only inquired about the United States, but was also concerned about acquainting Dr. Smith with the Mennonite people, their situation and their problems. On July 20 (o.s.), he sent him statistics and a map of the Molotschna Mennonite settlement, and also a report on Berdyansk for the year 1870.[37]

James Watt wrote on May 4, 1871, that he had seen the consul of the U. S. twice regarding immigration to America[38] and in a dispatch to U. S. Department of State, on April 1, 1871, Dr. Smith mentioned that the Mennonites "will re-emigrate if unsuccessful in their appeal."[39]

Now, after the visit of Cornelius Jansen, he was able to report more extensively.

> I have lately received a visit from Mr. Jansen, of Berdyansk by the Sea of Azoff, one of the foremost of them as to property and intelligence, who represents that the Russian Government hesitates, evades a direct answer to their petition and, in his opinion, does not intend to exempt them from military service. He informs me that there are thirty thousand families of them, numbering an hundred and fifty thousand souls.
>
> They occupy over two hundred thousand acres of land and have ninety villages; fifty of which are in the valley of Molotschna or Milk River, which flows into the sea not far from Berdyansk, and forty in that of the Dnieper between Kherson and Ekaterinoslaff. He assures me [and our consular agent at Rostoff, Mr. Martin, who knows him and many of them, confirms his declaration] that they are an industrious, quiet, law-abiding people, frugal, simple in their habits and are like the Quakers opposed to war and strife from religious principle and, therefore, cannot conscientiously enter the military or naval service.
>
> 
>
> Mr. Jansen thinks that one tenth of their number would soon emigrate to the United States if assured beforehand of respect on the part of the Government for their religious belief on the military service question. He thinks that a much larger number would afterwards emigrate when they should receive favorable reports from the pioneers.
>
> Few among them have any knowledge of America except that it is a great country beyond the seas, and he would be glad to obtain pamphlets, books or papers, in the German language, descriptive of the soil, climate, and general attractiveness of American life, for free distribution among them.
>
> There are, already, many of their religious faith in Lancaster, Bucks and Montgomery counties, Penn.; near Hagerstown, Md.; in the Shenandoah Valley, in Virginia; in Wayne, Holmes, Logan and other counties of Ohio; in Indiana, Illinois, Michigan, Iowa, and Missouri.
>
> I have no doubt but that circular letters from some of them, in the German language addressed to their religious brethren everywhere in Europe would bring in an abundant harvest of hard working faithful

> emigrants. Mr. Jansen would be glad to know whether they could obtain large tracts of land in one or several places by themselves, and whether as free homesteads or by purchases, at the established government rate, and in general what encouragement could be offered them were they to emigrate.[40]

After this letter reached Washington, some correspondence resulted between the Department of State and the Department of Interior, but only concerning the land question. Finally, a condensed report of the General Land Office for 1869 was published in English and German, and copies of this "Brief Description of the Public Lands" were sent to Odessa. Copies of this report were probably contained in the parcel of books Cornelius Jansen received from the U. S. consul in the beginning of January, 1872.[41]

Although the histories of P. M. Friesen, Franz Isaac, D. H. Epp and others, do not record events for the time between the first deputation to St. Petersburg and the beginning of the year 1872, this period was not barren of actions. Again we have to turn to the above-mentioned *Aufzeichnungen* ... of Dietrich Gaeddert for supplementary information.

The reports of the delegates at a conference on April 23 did much to calm the minds. But four months later, on August 13, another conference was held on this same matter, the deliberations of which were continued on September 15 (o.s.). It was decided to take advantage of the czar's sojourn at his summer resort in the Crimea in order to try again for a personal audience. A delegation was sent which did not succeed in seeing either the czar or the czarina, and returned after leaving petitions with both majesties. Their rereports at a conference on November 12 were less satisfactory than before.

Spreading Information

It was during this time that Cornelius Jansen began to give wider publicity to his efforts. This was achieved through the spreading of printed material obtained from America and by spreading information by correspondence far and near.[42] But even with his family helping to make handwritten copies of important items, it remained impossible to reach a larger number of people. Jansen therefore, had recourse to printing. Because of the strict censorship this could not be done in Russia. Since his nephew, Heinrich von Riesen, happened to be at Danzig, he was charged with the practical execution of this publication. On November 20 (o.s.) Cornelius Jansen ordered the printing of selected letters from America and a preface written by himself. It appeared in 1872 in Danzig under the title: *Sammlung von Notizen über Amerika.* This booklet was distributed among the Mennonites of Prussia and Russia (Appendix IV presents the preface).

Meanwhile, on January 11, 1872, a conference was again held at Alexanderwohl at which more than before a separation of opinions and interests became evident. Jansen, present at this conference, put in a word for a deputation to America and apparently he got so much support that the original purpose of the meeting, the sending of a second delegation to St. Petersburg, was not reached.

Cornelius Jansen was primarily concerned about the principles of faith. Dietrich Gaeddert gives a report on what Jansen said at this conference.[43] For his feeling and for that of many others Jansen went too far, when he condemned the transportation service rendered by the Mennonite farmers upon requirement during the Crimean War. This transportation was to be required only for food for the troops; but later on, in fact occasionally at this time, ammunition had been transported by the Mennonites. Jansen called this a violation of the principle of nonresistance. He said that instead of asking for the maintenance of their privileges the Mennonites should first ask for forgiveness for their transgressions, and then for freedom of faith and conscience.[44]

Conscription Law and Conferences

Most influential in changing the attitudes as expressed at this conference was the fact that the new conscription law, which had been introduced on June 4, 1871, had been published in the fall of the same year and had meanwhile become known to the Mennonites. It meant a disappointment insofar as the Mennonites had previously been assured that the law would not be applied to those born before its introduction. This had been changed later, and the Mennonites had to recognize that they could not count on any delay.

The large majority still hoped for a special exemption, the much more so because the military levy just decreed provided that a money substitute of 800 rubles could be paid instead.[45] However, Jansen was now backed by Leonhard Sudermann and other friends from

Berdyansk; in the colonies also groups formed who seriously considered emigration.

The following night Leonhard Sudermann and Cornelius Jansen stayed at the home of Dietrich Gaeddert where they had a long discussion on the Mennonite situation and finally agreed on emigration as the only solution.[46] Jansen had been gaining the support of Leonhard Sudermann and other friends at Berdyansk for an important step forward just a few days previous to the conference. Together with a number of brethren he had directed a letter to his friend, the British Consul, J. Zohrab, at Berdyansk, on January 3, 1872, containing several requests. They asked, whether, in case of an immigration to Canada, they could count on a special concession as to exemption from military service, and on a grant or cheap purchase of land. In addition, they inquired about the advisability of a deputation to London and Canada, and finally solicited the consul's recommendation.[47]

It was a result of Jansen's activity at the conference, that a group from the colonies also undertook to make a request similar to the one made by their brethren at Berdyansk, signed by P. Lohrenz and others.[48] They expressed the thought that they were "encouraged by the step taken by our brethren of Berdyansk," and that though they were as yet only a few, a favorable reply would induce many others to join them.

Those opposed to emigration were not willing to take the defeat and a second conference was called only two weeks later, on January 25, 1872 (o.s.), also at Alexanderwohl. Here a delegation to St. Petersburg was finally elected and authorized to find a way through which they could fulfill their obligations toward the state, without accepting military service.[49] Cornelius Jansen as well as others of the Berdyansk group are not mentioned as having participated at this meeting.[50]

The deputation did not have any success. Senator Gerngross, who was instrumental in preparing the conscription law, told them that the committee he worked with had decided unanimously that the Mennonites should serve in hospitals and sanitation service if possible, without the use of weapons. The only thing left to do would be to make an appeal to the Imperial Council, presided over by Grand Duke Constantin; this could not be done before the Council began its sessions in fall.

On the other hand, Senator Gerngross was very well informed on happenings among the Mennonites. Gerngross surprised the delegates by telling them frankly that at their first January meeting at Alexanderwohl a foreigner, [Cornelius Jansen], had made propaganda for emigration. A distorted denunciation had come into the hands of the senator, apparently sent in by an opponent of Cornelius Jansen.[52] The delegates hurridly wrote a memorandum, in which they defended themselves, refuting all charges and stressing their loyalty toward the czar and government.[52]

Contacting the British

By this time the request of the emigration party, submitted to the British consul, was well on its way. On February 3, 1872, he sent both petitions he had received to the British Foreign Secretary, Earl Granville. In an accompanying letter he briefly described the Mennonites in South Russia and explaned their situation. The consul stressed especially the importance of this Mennonite quest, which, if successful, would induce a large number of their fellow brethren and also other German colonists to emigrate during the next ten years, during which emigration was allowed to them. He wrote: "The departure of the Germans will, undoubtedly, be a serious loss to the country for they are not only much more proficient in agriculture than the native population, and consequently produce heavier crops and finer qualities but they are very hard working and therefore, in proportion to each man, they bring a much larger quantity of land under cultivation and thus increase the produce of the country."

On March 5, Consul Zohrab could reply to Cornelius Jansen, that according to information received from Earl Granville, the matter was "under the consideration of H. B. M. Government."[53] The requests were sent to Canada for consideration and report.

In their letter to the British consul the Berdyansk Mennonites had stated that for those considering emigration "the inclination may be partly for Canada and partly for the United States."[54] Therefore, on January 22 they directed a similar letter to the consul of the United States at Odessa. A reply, coming from the U. S. Embassy at St. Petersburg was delivered through Consul Smith on April 10.[55]

It was only provisory, very short and not satisfactory, especially for the first point, to which it was simply stated that "compulsory Military Service does not exist in the U.S."

Letters of Consul Zohrab to Earl Granville give a good picture of the situation during these months. While on March 15 he reported on the unsuccessful Mennonite delegation to St. Petersburg and the disappointment about the actual draft regulations, ten days later he wrote about a conversation with Cornelius Jansen:

> Mr. Jansen, one of their leading men, was with me this morning.... He thanked me for the attention H. M. government was giving to their wishes, and added that while the desire to quit a country in which their position had been so changed, was general among the Germans, still the people generally could not be persuaded that the Emperor would put in force the new laws against them, and they believed that at the last the government would give way and release them.
>
> The chiefs are fully persuaded that such a course will not and cannot be pursued by the government, and that no changes in their favor will be made. Meetings are constantly held to discuss the matter, when the leaders expose the dangers of hesitation, but as they have as yet no substantial proofs that the government will not give way, and no offers or basis on which to rest their arguments of the advantages of emigrating to Canada, they are unable to bring their assurances to conviction, but they are persuaded that when they are fully informed as to the terms on which they will be admitted to colonize in Canada, and when the Russian government will give, as they must eventually do, a refusal to their prayers for a continuation of their privileges, the determination to leave will be unanimous, and will be acted on.
>
> It is remarkable that though there is much hesitation at present, and the leaders feel even discouraged, yet whenever they cease to canvass the matter, they are immediately begged by the different villages not to cease their labours.
>
> It is natural that those interested should tremble at the prospect before them, and hesitate to come to a final decision, and try to remain where they are, and hope that their wishes will be granted. To leave long established homes, to give up positions of prosperity; to sacrifice their properties for conscience sake, are sore trials, and must demand great moral determination.
>
> That the Germans will exhibit this force of character when the hour for deciding arrives I do not doubt.

We notice here, that the British consul at Berdyansk always exchanged notes directly with the foreign secretary. The latter, however, informed also his ambassador at St. Petersburg, Lord Loftus, who was cautious enough to contact the Russian government on this proposed emigration. He stated to Prince Gortshakoff, that two points had to be cleared before an answer could be given to the Mennonite applicants, the consent of the Canadian government to receive them, and the assent of the Russian government to dismiss their Mennonite colonists.

As Lord Loftus reported to Earl Granville in his dispatch of April 3, 1872, on this conversation, Prince Gortshakoff said "that no objection would be raised by the Imperial Government to the emigration of these colonists. They were free to go in accordance with the agreements entered into on their first arrival, subject to their fulfilling all obligations in accordance with the laws."[56]

During these months, the Mennonite groups, determined to emigrate, were anxiously looking forward to the answers from Canada and the United States. Their Russian neighbors always had been envious of their prosperity and, of course, also of the privileges of the Mennonites. Not only their immediate neighbors, but the whole Russian nation, directed by the press, began to show hostile reactions to the Mennonite endeavors of either maintaining their privileges or leaving the country. One of these papers, *Russkii Mir,* wrote on March 4, 1872, that it was "a great pity that tens of thousands of Mennonites cannot reconcile themselves to the new order of things which now exists throughout the whole of Europe." It stated that, in spite of the value of the Mennonites as farmers, the principle of equality had to be maintained. "It is better to lose the Mennonites than to introduce into the State the inequality of rights and that too in favor of the foreigners and not of the native population."[57]

For the Mennonites this was a time of insecurity and uncertainty. "Impatient of waiting for combined action, some of the richer families have already sent persons to America to collect information." Thus reported Consul Zohrab on May 11, 1872. These persons, referred to by the consul, were young men belonging to well-known and wealthy families: Philipp Wiebe, Vorwerk; Peter Dück, Brodski; and Bernhard Warkentin, Altonau. They were joined on their trip to America by Jacob Baer, a German Mennonite from Bavaria. Before leaving the country two of them, Wiebe and Warkentin, went to see Cornelius Jansen at Berdyansk, in the latter part of April, 1872. For both of them Jansen wrote recommendations to J. Braun at Hamburg, probably a Mennonite, with whom Cornelius Jansen was in correspondence, and also to John F. Funk at Elkhart and to Gerhard Wiebe at Newbourgh, Ohio. Though this was strictly a private undertaking, one of the young men, Bernhard Warkentin, came to play an important role in the Mennonite immigration to America.

Although some of the notes exchanged between the British officials came into the hands of Cornelius Jansen, due to the obligingness of his friend, the Consul Zohrab, we do not have a complete record of all the correspondence exchanged on the matter of the Mennonite emigration. Some of these documents, which are a part of the Cornelius Jansen collection, were copied by Jansen, translated, and, apparently multiplied by handwriting for distribution among his brethren, as, for instance the previously mentioned letter of Lord Loftus to Earl Granville of April 3, 1872, and several letters of the Secretary of the Canadian Department of Agriculture, John Lowe. However, we do not know when and in what form he received the answer of the Canadian government. According to reports submitted by the Canadian Privy Council, the attitude of the Canadian officials was favorable to the Mennonite request. The minister of Militia and Defense observed that by law the Mennonites were "exempt from military service when balloted in time of peace or war, upon such conditions and such regulations as the Governor-in-Council may, from time to time prescribe."[58]

The minister of agriculture was able to offer "a free grant of 160 acres of best land . . . in the Province of Manitoba, or in other parts of the Northwest Territory during the years 1872 and 1873" for any person over the age of twenty-one years, and also settling possibilities in other provinces.

These answers were welcomed and considered satisfactory by Cornelius Jansen and his friends, except in one point. If the governor had the right to prescribe the conditions and regulations of the exemption to military service, could that not, under the pretext of necessity, lead eventually to a practical abolishment of this exemption? To make sure, Jansen decided to write to the governor-general directly, which he did on July 22. Jansen handed this letter to Consul Zohrab who submitted it to Earl Granville, accompanied by a letter of July 26, 1872.[59] The request was forwarded to Canada where it was answered in a positive way. The essential passage reads:

> That the intention of the Act in conferring upon the Governor General in Council the power of making conditions and regulations was to enable the Government to provide, if necessary, for the registration of the exempted persons in such a manner as to prevent persons belonging to any other denominations than those specified in the section of the Act above quoted from avoiding military duty under false pretences. That the constitution does not confer upon the Governor General in Council any power to override or set aside, under any circumstances, the plain meaning of the statute law. . . .[60]

Before, however, this answer was returned, in fact even before it was made, the Mennonites had already received an unofficial guarantee, through an agent of the Canadian government, whose sudden appearance assured the prospective emigrants that the Canadian government was more concerned about them than they could assume at that time.

Thus far the attitude of the Canadian government was more encouraging to the Mennonites than that of the U.S. authorities. Though the U.S. representative at St. Petersburg, Schuyler, did not hesitate to make a temporary reply, he reported the matter to the Secretary of State and also contacted the Russian government. The official whom he saw was more cautious in his answers than Prince Gortshakoff had been toward the British ambassador. To his question about the Russian government's intention he received the answer "that the Government could not say what they would do until they had received a petition from the Mennonites themselves asking for permission to emigrate."[61]

From his superior, the Secretary of State, Hamilton Fish, Schuyler received the advice to maintain reservations, though Fish recognized the value of the Mennonites for his country. "As Russian law, however, forbids emigration or its encouragement it would not be advisable for this government to interfere in the matter until the disposition of that government, which you proposed to ascertain, shall be known." He added, that it was improbable that Congress, in the case of the Mennonites, would make an exception and grant them money or lands "towards inducing them to emigrate or compensating them therefor."[62]

Consequently neither the representative at St. Petersburg nor any other U.S. official should do anything to encourage the Mennonites, until the Mennonite delegates came to the United States. Even the correspondence between Cornelius Jansen and the U.S. consul at Odessa ceased completely.[63]

All this could not discourage Cornelius Jansen. Meanwhile he had acquired sufficient knowledge of the situation in the states, and of the Mennonites living there, that he still considered an emigration to the United States. It was quite natural that for some time Canada was to move into the foreground in the consideration of the future emigrants.

Hespeler and Jansen

In her attempts to get immigrants from Europe, Canada had always, because of her more unfavorable geographical situation, to fear the competition of the United States. Consequently, the Canadian officials were more attentive to occasions which seemed to promise a benefit for the country. Unlike the state and railroad agencies they did not confine themselves to the battle over the immigrants when these arrived on American soil, but also sent agents to the different European countries to induce people to come to America. One of these was William Hespeler who, while working in South Germany as a special agent of the Canadian government, learned from a Russian noble, Count Menshikoff, about the Mennonite tendencies for emigration. Having communicated his news to the authorities at Ottawa, he received the order from the minister of agriculture "to proceed immediately . . . to Berdyansk," where he was to contact the British consul.[64]

Having lived among the Mennonites of Ontario, he knew about their qualities as settlers, and willingly set out to win the Russian Mennonites for Canada. The Canadian efforts at that time were also handicapped by the fact that Canada did not have her own diplomatic and consular representatives in foreign countries, and had to rely on the British officials whose interests were not always identical with those of Canada. Hespeler, who had difficulty in getting his papers for Russia, did not hide his disgust with this situation. But he was to meet even more obstacles.

When he arrived at Berdyansk on July 25, 1873, and called upon the British Consul, Zohrab, who not having received instructions from the Foreign secretary, was afraid to compromise himself, the more so since Hespeler, in an open telegram had hinted at his purpose to the Russian authorities. The consul declined any support and advised Hespeler to leave Russia without delay.

In the report Hespeler sent to the minister of agriculture on August 28, he stated:[65] "Not being pleased with the Consul's conduct, especially as I had reason to fear that he had also some other object in keeping me away,[66] I begged him to direct me to one of the leading Mennonites in the town, to which he complied . . . My first acquaintance was with a Mr. Jansen who is residing in Berdyansk where there are only a very limited number, and by him I was received in a most welcome manner. Mr. Jansen took me to all the other members of the congregation, and by every one I was treated with the greatest attention."

During a few days he also visited the Mennonite colonies, where he received an excellent impression on the character of the Mennonite people. "They are a hardy, industrious, orderly and intelligent race, and they would prove a valuable acquisition to Canada; their villages are patterns of order and industry, large orchards and gardens spring up where originally could not be found a tree."[67] He regretted not having pamphlets for distribution for the ones he had sent to Berdyansk did not arrive. "My offers and information were most favourably received, and I received assurance from all sides, that the selection of Canada for their future home is the most favourable one in view." In case the deputation which was again to be sent to St. Petersburg, would come back without result, they would take advantage of the offer of the Canadian government and send a deputation to America at government expense.

Cornelius Jansen, "one of the most zealous," asked for information on the exemption from military service about which he had written to the Canadian governor-general. "This to them a very important question, was put to me for explanation from all sides."[68] Hespeler tried to explain this, but also wrote for authentic information.

To this point John Lowe answered on September 16, 1872: "The Governor can prescribe no conditions or regulations under which or under any circumstances these persons can be compelled to serve." This finally was satisfactory, and Cornelius Jansen, to whom Hespeler forwarded a copy of this reply, translated it and speedily distributed it among his friends.[69]

Before leaving, Hespeler paid another visit to Consul Zohrab, relating his impressions. He felt "that no move will be made [by the Mennonites] till the people are made to face the change in the law and then the exodus will be general and hurried."[70] During the conversation Hespeler suggested that the consul, who was well acquainted with the Mennonites, should have "the management and direction of the movement" which was to be expected. Zohrab was quite willing to do this and expressed himself accordingly in his dispatch to the foreign secretary. The British ambassador at St. Petersburg, however, who forwarded this report with an accompanying note, strongly advised against "any further action taken in the matter by Mr. Zohrab." The ambassador, perhaps reflecting the general opinion in the capitol, was not persuaded that the Mennonites would emigrate at all. He felt that the Mennonites played a double game, "on the one hand endeavoring to exercise a pressure on the Imperial Government by a threat of emigration in order to obtain the fulfillment of their wishes whilst, on the other hand . . . simultaneously in communication with the Governments of Canada and of the United States with a view in case of failure with the Imperial Government to secure the best conditions for their future emigration.[71]

Following Hespeler's visit an extensive correspondence developed between Cornelius Jansen and William Hespeler, who now returned to Alsace to take up his work there again. The Canadian Department of Agriculture, stirred up by the news that a Mennonite delegation already was visiting Nebraska,[72] wanted Hespeler to keep in close contact with the Mennonites. The department showed its eagerness by new offers through which it tried to induce the wanted immigrants. Hespeler was asked to find an agent among the Mennonites who would get $2 per capita for all Mennonite immigrants to Canada. Hespeler however, with his better knowledge of the Mennonite character, dissuaded the department in this point, for he knew that such a proposal could only be detrimental to their efforts, for he had found them "more conscientious than their confessionalists in Canada or the United States—it would in their eyes look too much like dealing in human beings."[73]

Another constructive offer was "that the Government of Canada would bring 1,000 or more persons at one time from Berdyansk during the year 1873 at the same rate of fare as is now paid by passengers sailing from the port of Liverpool to Quebec."[74]

Jansen had been very much concerned during this time about the practical execution of the emigration. He especially felt a responsibility for the poor among those who wanted to leave. The cheapest means of transportation, of course, would have been a steamer, directly from Berdyansk to America. Jansen asked his English Quaker friends, Isaac Robson and Thomas Harvey, to secure a ship for this purpose. He also ventured to suggest to them a money loan for the needy Mennonite emigrants.[75]

> Through the English Consul at Berdyansk and other friends acquainted with shipping, an estimate has been made in showing that a steamer could be chartered to carry a hundred families from Berdyansk to New York for about 18,000 or 20,000 rubles [in round figures $3,000]. It is our opinion that as soon as one party has left many more now in indecision seeing the practicability of the undertaking will also leave, and emigration would become general, not only among the Mennonites but also among the Lutherans[76] and others anxious to escape military service. If a hundred families could go for 20,000 Rbl. that would be 200 Rbl. per family. We have, therefore, determined to require of each family intending to go a deposit of 200 Rbl. either of one's own money or paid by a friend, to be placed in the Berdyansk Commercial Bank. Thus the payment of the steamer would be insured before it would be chartered. But many of our people would perhaps reach America penniless (and what I would like to draw your attention to today is—could not an equivalent sum of 13,000 be collected by Christian friends in England to be held by them partly as a security that the steamboat owners would be paid, partly to return the 200 Rbl. to those who having given away all their money in Berdyansk in payment of the 200 Rbl., arrive in America quite in want—this money returned to them would be as a loan for five or ten years and, if necessary, a small rate of interest could be taken.
>
> My impression is—very few, if any, would require such assistance, and when once the success of the emigration was seen our own people would be willing to bear the burden of our poorer friends. By requiring a deposit of 200 Rbl. from each family we insure that only proper persons will go. The relations among our people one toward another are such that anyone who has neither 200 Rbl. nor credit for it among his neighbors is certainly not a person whose character is good—and therefore, not a person suitable to be taken.

These plans were not later realized, and we probably are not wrong if we connect this with Jansen's expulsion from Russia. The Alexanderwohl congregation and other groups, however, adopted a similar plan.[77] Also the idea of a direct boat passage to America was abandoned. All passengers went via Hamburg, Bremen or Antwerp. Only one boat, laden with effects of the emigrants was sent the planned direct way.

Hespeler, when leaving Russia had arranged with the Mennonites to meet, at a later date, with their delegates who were intending to visit their brethren in West Prussia. This was to be done when the delegation making its last appeal at that time, would return without success. So this meeting was postponed. But Hespeler, whose work in Alsace and Lorraine was interrupted by the legal transposition due to the taking possession of these areas by Germany, followed a call to Russia to meet with the Russian Mennonites again. Since he did not dare to enter the Mennonite regions, he met with a delegate from Berdyansk and two from the settlements.[78] At this time Hespeler also visited Lutheran colonies in the Crimea, in Bessarabia and Kherson, but soon, harrassed by the Russian police, had to leave. Toward the end of the year, however, the British government felt that Hespeler should apply utmost reservation until the Mennonites would receive the permission to emigrate.[79]

Still the Mennonites were not ready to ask for their passports, always hoping for an act of grace. Delegation after delegation desperately tried to see the czar.

On June 23, 1872, a conference was held, and the assembly, not being able to agree on whether to send a delegation to St. Petersburg or to America, decided to ask for the advice of Pastor Hans.[80] He encouraged them to send some delegates to St. Petersburg.[81] On July 24 three delegates were chosen for this trip.

When, after returning, the delegates gave their report on August 7 indicating the fruitlessness of their exertions, mostly due to the czar's absence, a note was received from Governor-General von Kotzebue, asking that the same deputation which had been in the capital, come to the Crimea immediately, where the czar was sojourning for a short while on his way to Berlin. Ten days later they were back without having seen their sovereign.

While another delegation tried in vain to come to some results through the governor-general, the fourth deputation for the capital was prepared, which was to contact the Imperial council. Now they were told that the Imperial council would not begin to deliberate about the draft law before February, 1873, and again they were placarded with hopes and promises.[82] It became evident that they would have to accept sanitary service.

Delegation to America

The majority still hoped for the grace of the emperor, but a minority had been won for emigration now. The leaders of this smaller group had been holding a number of separate meetings, according to Dietrich Gaeddert.[83] He had been visiting Cornelius Jansen on May 10, 1872 to talk the problems over and to inform himself. Very early there had been an inclination for emigration in the Alexanderwohl congregation, the church in which most of the conferences were held, and to which Gaeddert belonged. At the end of June this congregation decided to spend three weeks collecting signatures of all those who were in favor for a deputation to America.

As a consequence of William Hespeler's visit the group favoring emigration gathered at Berdyansk on August 1. The deliberations, begun at the home of the Leonhard Sudermanns in the afternoon were removed to the home of Cornelius Jansen, and were continued until late in the night. Among the participants were Jacob Wiebe, Annenfeld, Crimea; Dietrich Gaeddert, Alexanderwohl; Heinrich Richert, Gnadenheim; and also Isaac Peters, Marienthal, all of whom seemed now to have been won for the emigration cause.

Dietrich Gaeddert does not give the topics of their conversation but one can imagine that it was not so easy for the representatives to decide, not only on some course of action but also to come to united decisions. A few weeks later the same group came together again and discussed for several days continuously, from September 22 until September 25 in the morning, in the homes of Sudermann, Jansen, and Bernhard Buhler. Again Elder Jacob Wiebe from Annenfeld, Crimea, and also Elder Jacob Buller from Alexanderwohl participated. They decided to send a deputation of three to America, but the time and the persons were not determined upon. This matter was to be brought first before the different congregations, and, according to Gaeddert's report, in December 1872, the Alexanderwohl congregation chose Dietrich Gaeddert as its representative in the delegation.

At the end of October 1872, a meeting at Alexanderwohl was held at which a delegation was appointed to see the czar or the Governor-

General von Kotzebue at Yalta, Crimea, if possible. Among the representatives of the various settlements were also the Bergthaler. They did not see the czar and the results were insignificant.[84]

On January 10, 1873, the emigration party met at Alexanderwohl at which meeting Jansen, of course, was present. On January 24, at a meeting held at the Pordenau church, Leonhard Sudermann was elected as the second delegate of the Molotschna settlement. The date of departure, February 21, was agreed upon. This date, however, was postponed, and in the place of Dietrich Gaeddert, who insisted that because of family circumstances he could not go at a later date, Elder Jacob Buller of Alexanherwohl was appointed.

A reason for this postponement probably was that a last effort was again made at St. Petersburg. On January 29, 1873, a conference had been held at Alexanderwohl where a letter of Pastor Hans was read. Pastor Hans gave a report on the situation and advised a petition in the Russian language. But the conference, at which the separation between the two groups had become more evident than before and the attitude between them becoming somewhat unfriendly, decided to send a delegation to St. Petersburg again.

This deputation, whose primary task was to see the president of the Imperial council, Prince Constantin, was no more successful than all previous ones. Due to this fact the emigration party gained more sympathizers.[85]

According to Elder Gerhard Wiebe of Bergthal, it was at this time that the "thread tore" which had united his group with these Mennonites who were still expecting a favorable outcome. They cast their lot with Cornelius Jansen, Leonhard Sudermann, Jacob Buller and Isaak Peters. The elder was supported by his brother Heinrich and by the Oberschulze, Jacob Peters. The latter two became the official delegates of Bergthal to investigate America. They also wrote a special letter to the czar causing some disturbance in the brotherhood.[86]

Spreading Literature

The whole development of the emigration move would have been different without the manifold and untiring efforts of Cornelius Jansen. As a means of influencing his fellow brethren, we have already mentioned before the ample correspondence Cornelius Jansen maintained, and which during the year 1872 became even more voluminous. The correspondence was continued with the Mennonite leaders in West Prussia and the Samara Mennonite settlements. Others to whom Cornelius Jansen sent frequent letters were Elder Jacob Wiebe, Annenfeld, the founder of the Krimmer Mennonite Brethren Church, the Mennonite settlements in Poland and Volhynia, and the Bergthal group. Besides distributing information about America, he kept the leaders of the distant settlements informed on the decisions of the emigration party in the Molotschna settlement and at Berdyansk.

We mentioned also that Cornelius Jansen saw the necessity of intensifying his work with the aid of printed material. Unfortunately few of these printings have been preserved. From the bills of the printers we can, however, establish the fact that Cornelius Jansen published seven different booklets or pamphlets.

The first one has been mentioned several times as *Sammlung von Notizen über Amerika.* The publication was delayed until April, 1872. During the delay Cornelius Jansen sent more letters to be included in the collection to his nephew at Danzig, Heinrich von Riesen, whom he had put in charge of the publication. Jansen's letter of April 22, with more material to be added if possible, came too late. The bill is made out on April 19, and paid on April 22. Three hundred copies of the booklet were printed for the sum of 26 talers[87] by the printer, Paul Thieme, at Danzig.

Some of the copies were distributed from Danzig on the orders of Cornelius Jansen, the larger part had to be sent to Russia.[88] All the information, however, which Cornelius Jansen was able to provide about America, was not sufficient for his fellow brethren to make their decision.

Cornelius Jansen described, in a letter to his Quaker friends,[89] what he experienced in this connection after he received official answers from America:

> With these encouraging replies I went to some of the villages to tell them of the hopes and expectations which had resulted from the action taken by some members of our Berdyansk congregation, but to my surprise I found much more mistrust than I expected, and although the governor-general, to whom I went in autumn as I think you perhaps know already, told me in the most friendly and sympathizing manner that there is no hope of our people being exempted from service at least in the hospitals, they—our Mennonites—continue, I am sorry to say, still to believe and hope that they will not be required to serve.[90]

Cornelius Jansen felt the necessity to explain to his coreligionists their situation in Russia and to point out the consequences which remaining in this country would involve. He also felt it his duty to arouse their consciences for the precious Mennonite heritage now threatened.

In May, June, and July, Cornelius Jansen sent more material to Danzig in order to have it printed. Five pamphlets appeared simultaneously in August, 1872, again at the printing house of Paul Thieme,[91] and again quantities of three hundred copies each. The titles of these pamphlets, as given on the bill were:

1. *Gedanken englischer und deutscher Friedensfreunde.*
2. *Gedanken über die Pflichten der Christen.*
3. *Gedanken über den indirekten Militairdienst.*
4. "American Paper."[92]
5. *Gedanken über Religionsfreiheit.*

None of these pamphlets are available at this time. But of two of them we have the English translation because they were probably fully quoted by Cornelius Jansen in his talk at Mt. Pleasant.[93] They are the second and the third of the above named pamphlets: *Thoughts on Our Duties Towards Magistrates,* and *Thoughts on Indirect Military Service, as that of Artisans, Train-Drivers, The Sanitary Service, etc.* On August 21 Jansen had not yet received the pamphlets but ordered his nephew to send them directly to Isaac Robson, to John F. Funk, to J. Braun at Hamburg and to Wilhelm Ewert and Abraham Sudermann in West Prussia. A few days later Mrs. Jansen objected to the many typographical errors in the pamphlets.[94] (See Appendix III).

In a letter to his English friends, Robson and Harvey, Cornelius Jansen describes how difficult the transfer of this material was: "As no one would print our leaflets here in Russia we had to send them to Prussia to be printed, whence perhaps some have been sent, as I ordered some time ago, to you. As the censor would stop leaflets of this kind, we are obliged to receive many of them from Germany . . . [addition on the margin illegible] enclosed in envelopes as letters, [crossed out: and costing very dear for postage]; others less conspicuous are sent to us by book post. In all we have already received and distributed about 900 copies."[95]

In spite of all caution some of the pamphlets came into the hands of the Russian authorities. *Sammlung von Notizen über Amerika* carried his full name, some however, had only his initials, and it is probable that already then his identity was discovered.[96]

The last and smallest pamphlet was printed in the beginning of 1873, again at Danzig, but by the printing house of Edwin Groening. Three hundred copies in octavo were made. The title, as given by the printer's bill, was: *Adressen an die Christenheit.* The contents of this last pamphlet are unknown.[97]

All these publications were printed at the personal expense of Cornelius Jansen, and distributed without charge. Jansen, though economical in his expenditures, felt obliged to sacrifice this much for the sake of his convictions. It is appropriate to take a look at his views and beliefs here involved.

Basic Convictions

From what we can gather from the preserved pamphlets and occasional passages in letters, the principle of nonresistance was not the central part of Jansen's belief, but it was a vital part of it, and being now in danger, it automatically moved into the foreground. It was important also that for this principle of nonresistance Cornelius Jansen found a confirmation of his convictions in the teachings of the Quakers.

For Jansen the revocation of the privileges gave to the Mennonites the opportunity to demonstrate their faith. It was his belief that Christians should witness to their faith wherever possible and as widely as possible. History now offered the Mennonites a unique occasion to bear witness. It was a great privilege that God held the Mennonites worth of suffering for the sake of peace.[98] Speaking of this period in the life of Cornelius Jansen, John F. Funk said in the obituary he wrote of him: "In after years he remembered these trials with joy and gratitude that he was accounted worthy to suffer for Christ and his Word."[99]

Cornelius Jansen's conception of the Mennonite emigration as an act of faith implied, on the other hand, his rejection of all other motives for emigration, and also his opposition to everyone who tried to use this migration for some other purpose. This should become evident, especially later in America.

It was valid also for Jansen's attitude toward the non-Mennonite colonists who were stirred up by the Mennonites and part of whom also planned to emigrate, though originally they did not object to warfare for religious reasons. As soon as he was convinced of the sincerity of their intentions, he was ready to cast aside all walls of separation. This is expressed in a letter to Robson and Harvey on November 13, 1872[100] where he wrote: "I hope that in not a long future I shall be able to make such an offer as now expressed to the Mennonites also to all colonists; because there are some among them more true to the Lord than many among the Mennonites."

These colonists, Germans like the Mennonites, were with the loss of their special status, threatened by Russianization. This was important in the motivation of the emigration movement. Yet, the allegation of P. M. Friesen, that for Jansen, Sudermann and others the terms "Mennonite" and "German" were identical, is an overstatement not founded on facts.[101] There was, in the whole movement, probably no German nationalistic motive involved although Mennonites may have lacked a full understanding and appreciation of the Russian culture. For most of the emigrants, of course, the matter of language was important, and they foresaw that with the loss of their cherished German language they would lose some vital part of their religious heritage.

But even this fear probably did not disturb Cornelius Jansen who distributed Bibles and tracts in many languages and had always felt the necessity of spreading the Gospel among his non-Mennonite neighbors. Jansen's concern was not the language, but the freedom of his church, and it is the latter which he saw threatened by the loss of the privileges to which Russianization was only a consequence.

Cornelius Jansen expressed his thoughts on this subject in an essay, probably prepared for publication, but which did not appear in print: "Etwas über unsere gegenwärtigen Zustände betreff dem Wehrdienst."[102] Jansen sensed dangerous possibilities in the fact that the Mennonite churches would not have equal rights with the Russian Orthodox Church which in a special way was protected and privileged by the Russian law. Again and again he stressed that in Russia religious freedom was not guaranteed to the Mennonites. (Appendix II).

The arguments used by Cornelius Jansen against noncombatant military service were contained in a German pamphlet distributed by him among the Mennonites in Russia, an English translation of which was published later in the Mount Pleasant, Iowa, newspaper on the occasion of some talks given there by Cornelius Jansen, *Thoughts on Indirect Military Service, As That of Artisans, Train-Drivers, The Sanitary Service*, etc. (See Appendix III).

He attacked sharply a pretended martyrdom which had to serve as an excuse for people who in spite of their scruples wanted to stay. Jansen rightly denounced these pretentions as untrue and selfish because those who now made their decisions would not reap the consequences of these acts, while their children and grandchildren would.

Jansen maintained that the Mennonites had no choice but to leave.

> The only testimony we can give, is to migrate like our fathers, and that I will do, my Lord and Savior helping me; and should I be deceived in my choice, and my children come into the same distress my testimony will make it easier for them to go on again. I did not teach them to strive after riches, but they also know well that nothing, nothing could press me to leave my good and comfortable position, except to preserve for me and for them the freedom of God's children, the freedom of conscience.[103]

Opposing Forces

To conceive more properly the achievement of Cornelius Jansen's in bringing about the emigration to America, we have also to take into account the forces which were fighting against him.

We already mentioned Pastor Hans and his attempts to influence the Mennonites in his way. He was favored by the general impression among the Mennonites that he was their sincere friend. A look into the books of the Russian Mennonite historians gives an impression of how successful he was. His appeal that it was a duty toward God for the Mennonites to stay in the country,[104] was especially welcome to the more well-to-do class who did not want to give up the comforts and those who had made more progress in adjusting themselves to the Russian environment.

On the other hand, the emigration was not seriously considered by many among the poorer groups, for the simple reason that they thought they could not afford the costs of transportation to America and did not have the means for a new start in a new country. We saw that Cornelius Jansen was concerned about this fact. The group responsibility, and the unity in the congregations not being very high, he tried to introduce a system by which the poor would be aided, and also applied for help to his Quaker friends in England. He believed that it could be worked out that everyone would be able to go.[105]

In order to understand the situation among the Mennonites fully, especially in their largest and leading villages on the Molotschna, we have to consider their inner conflicts and party strifes which divided the congregations into at least two groups of which the smaller one, the Ohrloff group, was somewhat more progressive, most positive toward the government, and consequently less inclined to leave the country. Belonging to this group, or at least closely related to it, were many influential and leading families, as the Cornies and the Philipp Wiebe families and others.[106]

More ready to emigrate was the small group of the so-called Friends of Jerusalem (Templers), but they had cast their eyes on Palestine. Among the Mennonite Brethren, who at that time were still more or less in the process of organization, there was very little inclination for emigration during the first years. Strangely enough, least receptive for the cause of emigration were the more-recently established settlements near the Volga River. The people settling there were often those who had left West Prussia specially for the principle of nonresistance, but were not willing to emigrate to America. Elder Toews, with whom Cornelius Jansen had been in correspondence, tried to influence his brethren in Prussia against going to America. Gerhard Penner complained about Toews' influence in a letter to Cornelius Jansen.[107]

Opposition also came from the Gnadenfeld congregation. Heinrich Dirks, at that time missionary in the Dutch East Indies, and as such highly respected by his fellow-brethren at home, did much to discourage emigration. His letters were copied and circulated widely. Dirks maintained that after the loss of all privileges, after the loss of the German language and the inherited customs and ways of living, even after giving up the principle of nonresistance, it would still be possible for the Mennonites to serve and worship God and Christ in the right way. He warned against any premature undertaking. All over the world the Mennonites would not find any place which could compare with Russia. Since Dirks had seen more of the world than most of the colonists, his warnings, no doubt, must have made notable impressions.[108]

Reviewing the emigration, as it actually developed in the following years, we find that the more conservative groups were more affected by this movement than the more progressive ones. Cornelius Jansen, in his endeavors, apparently was more impressed by the lack of information and the resulting distrust he met so frequently. "Cut off as we are from free intercourse with the outer world as regards religious and other books, it is but natural to expect that our people are ignorant, distrustful and timid.[109]

In his attempts to push the apparently inert mass of his people into action, Cornelius Jansen sometimes used rather sharp formulations, in his pamphlets as well as in the letters he wrote.[110] We are not astonished to find that occasionally people felt offended.[111] Jansen did not lack opponents, as we have learned previously from passages in the report of Dietrich Gaeddert. But in spite of all adversities he finally succeeded in his endeavors. And he could exclaim with an inner satisfaction: "Thanks be to God, our efforts have not been in vain.[112]

Expulsion

The first months of 1873 found Cornelius Jansen occupied with more direct preparation of the emigration, for himself and for others. To judge by his Emigration Letter File he was no longer primarily interested in influencing his friends. That was done and the stone was rolling. Now the correspondence with the emigration and transportation agents occupied more space. Besides his correspondence with Hespeler of Canada, he was corresponding with William Seeger of St. Paul, immigration agent for the state of Minnesota, and with H. Allardt, emigration-commissioner of the state of Michigan, at Hamburg. He inquired about price reduction on Canadian steamers with the agents of the Canadian line at Hamburg, Falk and Co.

It had been the intention of Cornelius Jansen to leave for America in the spring of 1873. In the previous fall he had written to his Quaker friends: "I have likewise begun to sell my property with a view to go to America next spring. My house, garden, stables etc., were sold in August, and gradually my other things are being disposed of.[113] Probably the disposal of his property required more time than Jansen had planned. Thus, he was not ready when suddenly he was forced to leave.[114]

On March 27, 1873, an officer in uniform accompanied by a soldier came to Cornelius Jansen to present to him an ukase from the czar which he read to him. It stated that he, Cornelius Jansen, and Wilhelm Loewens, Prussian subjects, who were spreading rumors and false ideas about the condition of the Mennonites in Russia and the emigration to America, were to leave the country and were prohibited from ever returning to Russia.[115]

After finishing reading the lengthy ukase the officer dismissed the soldier and sitting at Jansen's side asked him very cordially to ease his hard task and to prevent all curosity by going with him to the photographer. Jansen complied and was photographed. Afterwards he had to pay for twelve copies, which were sent by Imperial command to the inspections of the boundaries, where they were hung up among criminals, to whom access to the Russian empire was prohibited.

What Jansen resented most was that he was not given "the least opportunity for justification.[116] Since he was not a Russian citizen, the authorities did not dare to send him to Siberia.

The seven days' time given him were too short to get ready for leaving, especially since he wanted to take his family along. Therefore, he applied to the Prussian authorities for an intervention in his favor. It is doubtful, however, that he addressed himself to Bismarck, then the Prussian prime minister, or that Bismarck intervened personally, as it is reported by Peter Jansen.[117]

At two different times as far as we know, Cornelius Jansen himself wrote concerning this incident. Once in a letter to Falk and Co. at Hamburg, on May 1, 1873: "I protested at once and telegraphed to our Ministry as also to our Ambassador at St. Petersburg and through their united efforts and representations that I was the founder and for many years the representative of the Prussian and Mecklenburg consulate here, and a resident for seventeen years, I was allowed two months to arrange my affairs."[118] Even shorter as he reported in his Mt. Pleasant talk:[119] After relating the whole circumstance by telegram to the philanthropic Prince Henry von Reuss, at that time German ambassador at St. Petersburg, to whom I was known as the founder of the German consulate at Berdyansk, where I had held this official position many years, through his important influence I got a two-month prolongation of my time to stay."

Even two months was a short time. Though the house and other buildings were already sold, there was still farmland and the ranch to be disposed of. "People knew that we had to sell and naturally took advantage," writes Peter Jansen in his *Memoirs*.[120]

He also mentions that friends now were afraid of attracting the suspicions of the police if they associated openly with the Jansens. "Some of them came by night to say good-bye to us."[121]

III. *The Promised Land*

Last Days at Berdyansk

Into those last days at Berdyansk were crowded a number of important events. On May 4, occurred the Cornelius Jansen's silver wedding anniversary. In spite of the Russian government's attempt to discredit this family, an entry in Jansen's diary states that the anniversary was attended by "many visitors."[1] While we have discovered no other contemporaneous source about this event, months later, in a speech at Mount Pleasant, Iowa, the daughter, Helena, reported on some of the difficulties the children ran into before the event took place.[2] "One month before we left our home we celebrated the silver wedding of my dear parents. For this occasion we children wanted to get several copies of a hymn printed to be distributed as a remembrance of that day among our friends. To our disappointment it was said that no more than fifteen of these copies could be published as they were Christian hymns, which are not allowed to be published in a greater number."[3]

Moreover, the relatives of West Prussia sent the parents a gift package, among others, composed of "silved spectacles [placed] in cases of silver." The customs officials refused to give them up. The problem became so involved that finally, in order to obtain possession of them, Cornelius Jansen had to telegraph the Minister of Finance.

The auction sale lasted from May 15 to 18, omitting Ascension Day. To advertise the sale the family had printed one hundred large red posting bills.[4] It would be interesting to know how much the sale yielded, but the record is missing. The family destroyed all business papers and account books which they no longer needed.[5]

There is evidence, however, that the family was not without financial resources. Weeks before the auction sale, on April 4, Jansen had ordered a transfer of money from Russia to Germany through the banking house of Mahs and Company at Odessa. Five thousand ruble (silver) were ordered to Heinrich Schütt for the Jansen family, and an equal amount to a Braun at Hamburg for Rudolf Riesen, also a Prussian citizen who was permitted to leave. The Russian subjects experienced difficulty in obtaining their passports.[6] Jansen also instructed Schütt how to use the money entrusted to him.[7]

Early Saturday morning on the twenty-sixth of May the Jansen family bid farewell to their spacious Berdyansk home, where friends had gathered to spend a few last moments with them. At 5 a.m. a parting prayer was offered after which the Twenty-fifth Psalm was read and the family departed for the harbor, accompanied by many wagons and a group of former Russian laborers. As they reached the bridge approaching the harbor, they could see Grierson's steamboat waiting to take them to the ship *Mydridat,* which was anchored about a mile from the shore. Grierson, an English merchant and friend of Jansen, had insisted on taking this family to the ship. When the party reached the shore he called out to them: "Every one that loves Cornelius Jansen can come and accompany him to the large steamer," which many did. After more words of farewell, including those of their English friends, Grierson, Low and Wagstaff, the steamer set sail for Odessa, and with mingled feelings the exiled father of the family wrote "The waving of hats and kerchiefs were lost from sight and finally also our old Berdyansk sank beyond the horizon. And we all experienced what is meant when they speak of leaving a homeland."[8]

The names of those leaving were: Cornelius Jansen, his wife Helene (von Riesen), their children Margarete, Peter, Anna, Johannes, Helena, Heinrich later called Cornelius) and Mrs. Jansen's sister, Anna von Riesen, always referred to as "Tante Anna."[9]

By evening they had reached the harbor of Kerch and on the following day at Durandos, they were met by Entz, Heine and Goerz. Entz accompanied them to Sevastopol, arriving there on the twenty-eighth of May. As they approached Odessa they encountered a severe storm and all suffered from seasickness, especially "Tante Anna" became quite sick. They disembarked at Odessa and stayed for the night at the hotel London, probably visiting some of their friends in this town. The next day, May 30, they boarded the train which took them overland through Austria-Hungary, Poland, into Germany and finally to Danzig.[10] The children had never seen a railroad before, and it was the first new experience on their journey with many more to come.[11] Enroute they enjoyed the beautiful country scenes, the cedar forests and especially the snow-covered Carpathian Mountains to the left.[12]

Visit in Germany

Crossing national boundaries apparently did not delay them very much. Jansen remarks that their baggage was checked when they reached the boundary of Austria-Hungary but does not say that it caused any delay.[13] He doesn't even mention crossing the other national boundaries.

It was June 16 when they reached Breslau, Germany. There they devoted a day to visiting the zoological gardens and other places of interest, sent a telegram to uncle Johannes von Riesen of Weisshof, Mrs. Jansen's brother, and continued their journey. They reached Praust the next day where uncle von Riesen and Hans met them and together they proceeded by train to Weisshof, a village near the city of Danzig. They were now with their friends and relatives who gave them an arousing welcome. Johannes von Riesen, after his return from Berdyansk, had purchased a farm near Danzig and the Jansen family now made their stay with them.[14]

Mrs. Johannes von Riesen belonged to the Penner family group,[15] whom the Jansen family now learned to know and with whom they established an enduring friendship. This was especially true of the Andreas Penner family, a younger brother of Elder Gerhard Penner who also lived on a farm near Danzig. He had been a minister of the Heubuden congregation. While visiting with these people young Peter Jansen fell in love with Gertrude Penner, one of Andreas Penner's charming daughters. About this friendship Peter wrote later: "She was then a bright, handsome girl of nearly seventeen, with long, flaxen braids hanging down her back. In was a case of love at first sight, and I felt that she reciprocated my feelings."[16] While both were still too young to marry, their friendship had struck a cord that bound them together which neither the wide Atlantic nor the years of separation could sever.

This relationship established during their four weeks stay in the Danzig community helped to influence a small group of Prussian Mennonite families to look to America as their prospective fatherland. But there was another factor which strengthened this tie and influenced their decision to emigrate. On the question of nonresistance or military service the West Prussian Mennonites had divided into two groups. Only a minority group, led by Elder Gerhard Penner of the Heubuden congregation, was openly opposed to the forms of military service imposed upon the Prussian citizens. It was with this group that the Cornelius Jansen family now associated, celebrated communion with them, and no doubt used this time to strengthen each other in their faith.[17]

On the twelfth of July they held an emigration meeting at Koselitzke which was attended by Cornelius Jansen and his son Peter. It apparently was called for the benefit of this minority group. No detailed record of the meeting has been found. Cornelius Jansen merely referred to it and wrote that he, H. L. Zimmermann and H. von Steen arrived there with the early train but does not say what was discussed or agreed upon.[18] Years later, Peter Jansen wrote that they instructed his father to report to them his impressions of America.[19] That this meeting was attended by members of the deputation is doubtful. It was too late in the year.

The Jansens also utilized this opportunity to provide themselves with clothing and other necessities of life. While they lived in Russia they had frequently ordered items of clothing which they could not get in the Russian market, or if obtainable was of inferior quality. The family has preserved these purchase bills.[20] Peter Jansen reports that they purchased more fashionable clothes. They also had their pictures taken.

On the fourteenth of July they arrived in Danzig with all their baggage, ready to board the train for Berlin the following day. In the evening many friends and relatives had gathered for a farewell reception at the Louis Eduard Zimmermann home. The Elder Gerhard Penner gave the farewell talk, followed by prayer and the long dreaded words of farewell. Cornelius Jansen writes in his brief diary that this was a "sad parting."[21] They were leaving behind their close friends and relatives, to go into an unknown country facing an unknown future where as yet they had no home, no acquaintances, no relatives or friends. However, they fervently hoped that these dear Prussian friends and relatives whom they were leaving behind would soon follow them, and that this would be but an "Auf Wiedersehn." Early the next day they boarded the train and left for Berlin via Pomerania. Cousin Anna and Heinrich accompanied them, probably to the capital city.[22]

In Berlin they visited an art gallery, the mausoleum, the zoological gardens and other places. They left Berlin on July 19, reached Hamburg that same evening. They visited with Heinrich Braun and with members of the Baptist church in Altona, made the necessary business and travel arrangements, and boarded the steamship *Huddersfield* at 10 p.m., on the twenty-second of July, headed for England.[23]

Visit in England

Their ship landed in the harbor of Grimsby on the twenty-fourth of July and they boarded the train for Leeds, England, to visit their Quaker friends, the Isaac Robson's of Dalton, Huddersfield, England, and the Thomas Harvey family of Headingly Hall, Leeds, England. Cornelius Jansen had met and traveled with the men in Russia. They were cordially received and entertained by their Quaker friends. The Harvey and Robson families invited them into their homes and introduced them to their friends. Especially cherished among others was the Whiting family, who also invited them into their home. The Jansen family also attended the Quaker meetings and thus became better acquainted with their methods of worship.[24]

While the English language was not new to the Jansen family, they were far from proficient in the use of it. Peter later wrote that their "pronunciation and general foreign ways" must have given their English friends a "good deal of merriment." But he adds that the Quakers were "very tactful . . . not to let us see this."[25]

This renewal, deepening and broadening of friendship with the English Friends proved to be of great significance for the Mennonites as such. The English Friends rediscovered how closely akin they were in their religious beliefs and that those Mennonites leaving, practically sacrificing their comfortable homes in Russia and Prussia because of their opposition to war and military participation, were really on the frontier fighting for religious liberty. But equally important for the immediate future of Mennonite emigration was the fact that this visit gave Cornelius Jansen an opportunity to bring to the attention of the English Friends the immediate needs of some of the prospective Mennonite immigrants, who would not be able to emigrate without some financial assistance. It struck a sympathetic chord and later produced a sympathetic response.

Of great significance also was the fact that these English Friends now provided Cornelius Jansen with addresses and letters of recommendation to members of the Society of Friends in the United States whose contacts and influence were to prove valuable in Cornelius Jansen's later dealings with government officials.[26]

For the Jansen family these contacts supplied them with many a kind letter during the many lonely frontier days, and their relationship developed into a lasting friendship with the Friends in England, a contact kept up by their children and even by the grandchildren.

On the twenty-eighth of July Cornelius Jansen sent his son Peter to Liverpool, England, to make arrangement for their voyage to America[27] While still in Berdyansk Cornelius Jansen apparently had written the Allen Bros. & Co. about reduced rates to America. They agreed to give him "cabin passage at steerage rates" for five people, on the condition that he was going out "as a pioneer to recommend a route and place of settlement to his followers." Falk & Co. at Hamburg agreed to extend the same rate to the four other members of the Jansen family.[28]

On July 29, the Jansen family gathered at the Isaac Robson home for the farewell. Again friends had gathered to bid them adieu. Thomas Harvey read the Hundred Twenty-fifth Psalm, followed it with prayer and the Jansen family experienced a third parting from friends. On the thirtieth of July Mr. and Mrs. Whiting accompanied them to the depot where they boarded the train for Liverpool. Here they were met by a Mr. Ennis of the Allen Line who accompanied them to the ship *Circassian* also "of the Allen Line, at that time considered a very fine boat."[29] The following day at 3 p.m. the ocean steamer set sail and soon the skyline of smoky England disappeared from view. They reached Londonderry, Ireland, the next day, stopped a few hours for mail, and were off on the high seas, bound for America.[30]

Arrival in Canada

It was a beautiful ocean voyage for the family, except for Tante Anna. On the fifth day of August, also the fifth day of the voyage, she was still suffering from seasickness. By this time the family was fast getting acquainted with the passengers and officers of the ship, especially with Captain Wylie of Ireland. On the sixth day of their voyage they began to notice icebergs, which was interpreted as an indication that they were approaching Labrador. But they counted thirteen beautiful icebergs and traveled three more days before they skirted the coasts of Labrador on the right and Newfoundland on the left. They entered the St. Lawrence River August 10, just in time to enjoy the sights and heights of Quebec in the light of a beautiful sunset.[31] Peter later wrote about this: "As we floated down the broad, majestic St. Lawrence River towards the ancient French city, our hearts were full of anticipation of what the new world had in store for us."[32] This no doubt was literally true of Peter. You can imagine him standing on deck with mingled feelings, seeing a hundred and one strange things, and in his mind sharing them with Gertrude, whom he had left behind. However, other members of the family were filled with apprehension and anxiety as to what the future would hold for them. When no one was at the dock to greet them and bid them welcome to this strange new land, a feeling of loneliness and longing for friends and dear ones left behind overcame them.

The family disembarked at Quebec, stopped for the night, saw the city the following day and in the evening boarded the train for Berlin, now Kitchner, Ontario. Enroute they passed Montreal and arrived at Toronto on the evening of the twelfth. They had expected to be met by William Hespeler, agent of the Canadian government, but instead an immigration commissioner met them and took them to a hotel where they spent the night. They left Toronto at noon the following day and here were met by Hespeler and

Jacob Y. Schantz, who gave them a hearty welcome and took them to a hotel, but since there was no room in the town, Schantz invited them into his house and offered them his *Hinterhaus* with four rooms for an indefinite time. Peter later wrote that his father had corresponded with a Mennonite in America living near Berlin, Ontario and he had invited them "to stay at this house pending the selection of a permanent place of settlement." The Jansen family rented the house and the women folks at once began housekeeping.[33]

The Delegation from Russia

As soon as Cornelius Jansen had found a temporary home where the family could unpack, relax and live, he immediately telegraphed his address to the Mennonite delegation at Elkhart, Indiana. A message came back the same day, August 14, that the delegation was ready to leave America on the twenty-first and instead of Jansen meeting them at Elkhart as they had originally planned, they would meet him at New York City on the nineteenth. So it was decided on the same day they arrived in Berlin, Ontario, that Cornelius Jansen and his son Peter would leave for New York City on the eighteenth of August.[34]

The evening of the seventeenth Cornelius Jansen was sick and it was doubtful whether he would be able to leave as planned. But on the morning of the eighteenth he felt improved and they left on schedule. They reached New York City via Niagara Falls the following morning, went to the German Mission House where they had agreed to meet the delegates, but instead they met a Regehr from Rudnerweide, Molotschna. The deputation had not yet returned from Philadelphia.

The following morning the deputation arrived. "It was a happy and yet sorry meeting," wrote Cornelius Jansen, "for they [the delegates] were planning to leave the next day." Moreover, instead of meeting all the delegates he mentions meeting only three of them—Leonhard Sudermann, Wilhelm Ewert, and Jacob Buller.[35] The longing for each other was mutual. In his report on the delegation trip, written 1879, Leonhard Sudermann tells of the joy he felt when he met the Jansens, father and son.[36] His diary reveals, however, how anxiously he had longed and waited to see them. He had important decisions to make and desired to talk it all over with his friend Cornelius Jansen.[37]

To understand the statement of Elder Sudermann, it will be necessary to review briefly the accomplishments and conclusions reached by the deputies who had inspected the lands in Canada and in the United States.

C. Henry Smith divides the delegates into three groups. The Bergthal delegates, composed of Heinrich Wiebe, Jacob Peters and accompanied by Cornelius Buhr, not an elected delegate, had left Europe on the *Silesia* and landed in Halifax early in May, 1873. The second group was composed of delegates of the Kleine Gemeinde—Elder Cornelius Toews and David Klaasen—and the Hutterite representatives, Paul and Lorenz Tschetter. They also sailed on the *Silesia* but landed in New York City early in May, 1873. The third group was composed of representatives of the Molotschna settlement, Leonhard Sudermann and Jacob Buller; Tobias Unruh, representing the Polish Mennonite settlements; and Andreas Schrag, the Swiss Volhynian Mennonites. These four were later joined by Wilhelm Ewert who represented the Prussian Mennonites. They took passage on the *Frisia* and landed in New York City the latter part of May, 1873.[38]

While these delegates had planned originally to act as a unit and even to settle as a compact group in adjacent territory, consistent with Mennonite history, they soon discovered that their interests were fundamentally different. As a result the groups traveled independently of each other except that they met at Fargo, now North Dakota, to ascend the Red River territory into Canada to inspect the Manitoba lands, still an unsettled prairie wilderness. In this tour they were guided by William Hespeler, the representative of the Canadian government, and Jacob Schantz, both loyal boosters for Canada; by John F. Funk of Elkhart, Indiana, and by representatives of several railroad companies.[39]

Having traveled independently of each other, it was expected that their findings and conclusions would differ. So it happened that the Bergthal and Kleine Gemeinde delegates, who had traveled to Ottawa, had received a written assurance from the Canadian government that all their requests would be granted, including exemption from military service. Consequently they agreed to recommend Manitoba to their people. Paul and Lorenz Tschetter decided upon the Dakota territory, but the third group, representatives of the

Molotschna, Polish, Swiss Volhynian and Prussian Mennonites were more noncommittal, except that they agreed not to represent Manitoba to their constituencies. They would recommend emigration, but to the United States.[40]

The groups interested in the United States, however, had been unable to get any assurance from the national and state governments regarding exemption from military service, or reservation of compact land areas. In fact, the federal government in the legislation incorporating the various railroad companies reaching out into the unsettled lands, had given much of the available lands to the railroad companies under the term "alternate sections" and the rest was covered by the Government Homestead Act. It would require, therefore, a special act of Congress to make available to the Mennonites in the United States a compact area of land as well as to exempt them from military service.

However, since the delegates favoring the United States to Canada desired to present to their constituencies inducements equally as liberal and favorable as those of their fellow delegates who had decided upon Canada, they had entered into an optional contract with the Northern Pacific Railroad Company officials for the reservation of a large tract of land in the Dakota Territory along the Red River and had charged an agent of this company, Michael L. Hiller, with the responsibility and task of persuading the federal government to grant the Mennonites the desired land privileges. Contingent upon the success of this legislation the Northern Pacific Railroad Company agreed, August 20, 1873, "to reserve all its lands in Dakota within fifty miles of the Red River until March 1, 1874, for the Mennonites to choose from for settlement. By July 1, 1874, the Mennonites must say how many villages they want land for."[41] Apparently nothing was done about exemption from military service, but it appears that at least Leonhard Sudermann was convinced from his association with the Mennonite leaders who had lived in the States for years, that in this respect the Russian Mennonites would have nothing to fear in this country, that they could live a religious life according to their own convictions, even under the laws as they existed.

The important question which remains unanswered is, what did the three delegates—Sudermann, Buller, and Ewert—discuss with their friend Cornelius Jansen and his son Peter on the twentieth and the forenoon of the twenty-first of August, before they accompanied the delegates to the ship *Hamonia?* Both say that they had much to tell each other, but omit all details. Cornelius Jansen however, does say that on the twentieth of August he got acquainted with Michael L. Hiller, visited with some of the officers of the Northern Pacific Railroad Company and with Abbott, the director of the Erie Railroad Company.[42] Hiller, through Jay Cooke, New York banker and financier, had introduced Paul and Lorenz Tschetter and Tobias Unruh to President Grant on August 8. Thus the Mennonite concern had been introduced to the President and the Secretary of State, Hamilton Fish. John F. Funk and Amos Herr were also instrumental in making these contacts through Simon Cameron of Pennsylvania. No doubt Leonhard Sudermann told Cornelius Jansen about their agreement with the Northern Pacific Railroad Company and that they had asked Michael L. Hiller to press Congress for favorable legislation. Cornelius Jansen and his son Peter first spent some time in traveling over the states of Kansas, Nebraska, Missouri, Iowa, Wisconsin, Minnesota and the Dakota territory in search of land and then returned to the East to press Congress for legislation.

In Search of New Homes for Immigrants

They left New York City on the twenty-second of August, 1873, for Elkhart, Indiana. Enroute they visited with Carl Justus van der Smissen in Wadsworth, Ohio, and with Gerhard Wiebe and his brother-in-law, Krehbiel, near Cleveland. In the evening the Jansens took the train to Elkhart, Indiana. There they discovered that their friend, John F. Funk, whom Jansen had learned to know through his correspondence, was busy helping an advance guard of the Russian Mennonites who had left Russia early in 1873 without first waiting for the report of the deputies. Bernhard Warkentin had just left for Newton, Kansas, with several men of this group, apparently to help them select a place of settlement. Cornelius Jansen and Peter now decided to follow them.[43]

On the twenth-eighth of August, they reached Newton, Kansas, which Jansen describes as a "small prairie station of the A. T. & S. Fe Railroad Company." At noon the next day they met Bernhard Warkentin in company with Tobias and Daniel Unruh, David

Schroeder and Johann Fast. The Jansens now joined them in their travels to see the Santa Fe railroad lands. They traveled along the Missouri Valley, on the Nebraska side. At Council Bluffs a Calhoun, agent of the Canadian & Northwestern Railroad Company, showed them the lands of this railroad. After that they went to Chicago, where they met Funk and Seeger, and together they traveled through Wisconsin, Minnesota and into the Dakota territory. They reached Fargo, near the eastern border of the territories, on the eighth and spent four days seeing the lands of the Northern Pacific Railroad Company, with whose officers the seven delegates had made the provisional contract.[44]

True to his diary habits, Cornelius Jansen makes no comment about the Dakota lands.[45] But we know from other sources that he was not impressed, and not only did he decide against settling there himself, but apparently lost no time in telling Funk and Amos Herr about his impressions and advised his fellow Mennonites in Russia against the Dakota lands. Dietrich Gaeddert in his "Report on the Emigration from Russia to North America" directed to Peter Jansen and written in 1892, writes about this as follows:

> These delegates had decided upon Dakota as the land where the Mennonites should settle. But they had failed to make a thorough check into the water question. All immigrants to America, therefore, must thank C. Jansen, Berdyansk, for not settling on these chosen lands, for there the water level lies too deep. Friend Jansen was not satisfied with the evasive words of the agents: 'You people see water standing in low places everywhere along the railroad, and yet you ask for water.' C. Jansen wanted to see a well, and not rain water. But the agents could not be induced to drill for water, in spite of Jansen's suggestion that he would pay all the expenses connected with it. The reason why they refused is apparent. This experience friend Jansen relayed to Russia and the decision for Dakota fell into the 'water.'[46]

In a letter to Holden written sometime in 1873 or 1874, Jansen wrote, "that regarding the important water question in Dakota, he got his information from a Mr. Hebbart (?) who stayed with them in the Ebbott House."[47]

After seeing the Dakota lands they saw more lands along the St. Paul & Pacific Railroad Company, along the St. Paul and Sioux City Railroad, the Winona & St. Peter Railroad and they also looked at the lands of southern Minnesota. On the twenty-second of

September they returned to Berlin, Ontario, via Winona, Chicago, Elkhart, Cleveland, New York City, and Niagara Falls. They reached Berlin, Ontario, on the first of October, finding the lonesome family well, but anxiously waiting to receive them. Many letters were also waiting for them.[48]

Whether Cornelius Jansen and his son Peter made up their minds to settle in Nebraska as a result of this first journey westward is doubtful. But that this state appealed to them, we gather from what Father Jansen wrote in his diary when he referred to the Nebraska land bordering the Missouri River as "the beautiful Missouri Valley." However, at the time he wrote this he was traveling about seventy-five miles east of the place where they finally located their ranch. Later, in a letter written February 21, 1874, he expressed the desire to visit the lands of the Burlington and Missouri River Railroad Co.[49] Probably the only immediate results derived from this trip, therefore, were, first, the information he gathered about the vast extent of available lands in the United States, which information he sent to his brethren in Russia and Prussia, including his decision against the Dakota lands, and second the decision to sponsor legislation in Congress rather than to wait upon Hiller who was sponsoring the Dakota lands.

Petitions the United States Government

Cornelius Jansen had been back in Berlin, Ontario, less than a month when suddenly he and Peter again boarded the train, this time for Washington, D. C. Their aim was to petition the U. S. Government for permission to let the Mennonites emigrating from Russia and Prussia settle in a compact area where they would be exempt from military service. Already while visiting his Quaker friends in England and even in Berdyansk, Cornelius Jansen had selected names of influential men in the United States who might someday be helpful to him. Now his plan apparently was to first make contact with these men, learn from them, and then proceed to Washington and present his petition.

Jansen and his son Peter left Berlin, Ontario, for Washington, D. C., on October 29, 1873.[50] Enroute they stopped at New York City, Philadelphia, various places in Lancaster County, and Baltimore to discuss the problems of immigration, to gather suggestions from friends, and, if possible, get letters of introduction to the President of the United States. In New York City they met a Brown who was a personal friend of the President and whose son Cornelius Jansen had learned to know while still in Berdyansk. Brown showed great interest in the Mennonite cause and gave the Jansens a letter of introduction to the President.[51] In Philadelphia they visited, among others, Anthony and Francis Kimber of the Quaker faith, who apparently introduced them to a Forney, editor of the Philadelphia *Press,* also to another man, a personal friend of the President, whose name is unknown. Both gave them letters of introduction to President Grant.[52] Later correspondence with Forney reveals that he also gave the Jansens valuable information on how to proceed with the petition.[53] In Lancaster County they visited, among others, Amos Herr, an (Old) Mennonite, with whom he was to work in close cooperation after the matter reached Congress. In Baltimore they visited a King and a lady minister, Dr. Thomas, both of the Quaker faith. These also took great interest in the Mennonite cause.[54]

Armed with those letters of introduction and with a better understanding of American diplomatic procedures, the Jansens directed their steps to Washington, D. C., together with John B. Wood, one of their newly-found friends, to present their petition to the President.[55] They reached Washington on the fourth of November and went immediately to the White House where they were received by the President's private secretary, General Thomas S. Babcock, who took them to the President's room. President Grant greeted them with a friendly handshake and asked them to sit down. Cornelius Jansen presented their letters of recommendation and petition. The President took the petition and read it aloud. While he was reading, the Secretary of the Interior, Columbus Delano, entered. The President stopped to introduce him and they all participated in the discussion. The Jansens understood and spoke English. The President concluded that the request was reasonable, but that he could not decide the issue, that it was a matter of legislation. But he would use his influence on Congress by referring to their request in his opening address. He then turned them over to the Secretary of Interior, apparently to permit the latter to get the necessary detailed information so he could include it in his report to the President, for the petition asked for land reservation, a question under the supervision of the Interior Department of the government. They met with the Secretary of the Interior the next day and again on Monday and Thursday, November 17 and 20. Apparently Peter Jansen was struck by one of the questions the Secretary asked them, viz., whether they believed in the Godhead of Jesus Christ. When they told him that this was their only hope, he said that he was glad to hear it, for he had heard words to the contrary.[56]

Having learned that their request would involve legislation and that it would have to be brought before Congress, they spent some time in Washington to formulate a petition and to have it printed and sent to the various members of Congress. They finished this work on November 21, and boarded the train for Summerfield, Illinois, to visit their Mennonite friends, Warkentin, Goerz, probably Funk, and others, and discuss their accomplishments with them. They also wanted to stop at Wadsworth, Ohio, to look for a temporary residence.[57]

Enroute, while in Indianapolis, Sunday, November 23, Cornelius Jansen wrote a letter to Forney, the editor of the Philadelphia *Press,* to thank him again for his help and to report progress. He informed Forney that the petition, copy of which Jansen was inserting with the letter to him, had been printed and distributed to members of Congress. Cornelius Jansen asked Forney to keep up his "kind interest in this affair because your great influence is very valuable to us." The thinking which follows this statement, however, indicates that Jansen was still somewhat unfamiliar with U. S. governmental procedure. He wrote that "some people talk as if we want to have a new law, or destroy an old one," Jansen denied this and explained that what they really wanted was merely a guarantee that when a father's son is in distress, that he may send him to the United States, (apparently to avoid being drafted into the Russian military service). Meanwhile, the father could stay in Russia as long as was needed to sell his property gradually, thereby save a great deal of money, and yet have the assurance, when he is ready to follow his son to the United States that he will be able to locate on a piece of land in close proximity. By 1881, the date of the expiration of the period of grace for the Mennonites in Russia, those who wished to leave Russia would have emigrated.

Just how Jansen figured that the U. S. government would be able to grant the Mennonites this assurance without special legislation, remains unclear. Apparently he was still thinking in terms of a czar's decree. Or had he been mislead by the Secretary of the Interior's reasoning that somehow the Secretary could be authorized to withhold certain sections of land from sale, thereby giving the Mennonites the opportunity to settle in compact areas, without having to pass legislation legalizing the procedure. Cornelius Jansen closed the letter with the thought that if their request was asking for a special privilege, other denominations had an equal right to petition the government.[58] Again he did not see what effect this might have on future legislation, that a domestic government cannot engage in legislation favoring one class of citizens over another.

The Jansens had a very enjoyable visit with their friends in Summerfield, but their attempt to find a temporary home in Wadsworth apparently failed. They returned to Berlin, Ontario via Cleveland, Buffalo and Niagara Falls, and arrived there November 29, and to their surprise found the ground heavily covered with snow.[59]

Meanwhile, the Secretary of the Interior had sent the President his report in behalf of the Mennonite cause. His statement reads:

> I desire to invite the attention of Congress to a request from a colony of Mennonites, now and for several generations residing in Southern Russia, near the shores of the Black Sea and the Sea of Azov, for a modification of the existing land laws in certain particulars, to enable them to settle upon our public domain in a compact colony.
>
> (Then he discusses how the Russian Government deprived the Mennonites of their privileges and continues:)
>
> It is their desire to come to the United States and to occupy a portion of our public lands in a compact body, with no strangers to their religious faith within the exterior bounds of their possessions. Such exclusive occupancy they deem essential to enable them to carry out their peculiar system of farming, which to some extent involves a community of interest in the occupancy of the lands; and they also wish to avoid, as far as possible, the presence of any disturbing elements in their immediate neighborhood.
>
> The deprivation of the immunities heretofore enjoyed by them does not take effect until the expiration of ten years from June, 1871, the date of the imperial decree. Within that time it is their desire to dispose of their property in Russia, and remove to a country where they may enjoy civil and religious liberty, and they have selected the United States as a place where they can most fully realize such freedom.
>
> In order, however, to enable them to obtain possession of lands in a

> compact body, some concessions must necessarily be made from the present requirements of the land laws. I would respectfully suggest that the Secretary of the Interior be authorized to withdraw from sale or entry such lands as they may desire to occupy, for a term of years long enough to enable them to emigrate to this country and settle thereon, and to dispose of such lands to those persons among the emigrants who shall make the proper entry or purchase thereof in accordance with existing laws. Should they desire to settle within railroad limits, the authority should enable the withdrawal, in like manner, of the alternate sections belonging to the Government. It is possible that the entire body of emigrants may not desire to locate in one colony, but would prefer the selection of two or more colonies of locations. It would be well, therefore, to confer such discretion on the Secretary of the Interior as would enable him to meet their views in that regard. The entire area they will probably require will be about 500,000 acres.[60]

The President likewise kept his promise made to the Jansens and in his message to Congress asked that august body to give attention to the suggestions of the Secretary of the Interior. The section asking special concessions for the Mennonites reads:

> The expressed desire of the representatives of a large colony of citizens of Russia to emigrate to this country, as is understood, with the consent of their Government, if certain concessions can be made to enable them to settle in a compact colony, is of great interest, as going to show the light in which our institutions are regarded by an industrious, intelligent, and wealthy people, desirious of enjoying civil and religious liberty; and the acquisition of so large an immigration of citizens of a superior class would without doubt be of substantial benefit to the country. I invite attention to the suggestion of the Secretary of the Interior in this behalf.[61]

Meanwhile Cornelius Jansen had sent copies of the petition to the immediate supporters of his cause,[62] and kept J. F. Funk of Elkhart, Indiana, and Amos Herr, of Lancaster County, Pennsylvania, informed about his accomplishments. On the tenth of November he wrote Herr that the Secretary of Interior had asked him how many acres he should designate to be reserved for the Mennonites, whether 500,000 would be enough. Whereupon Jansen answered that it was not polite for a foreigner to specify any amount, but if the amount suggested was not too much, the Mennonites would have great cause to be thankful. "O no," replied the Secretary, "that is not too much." And Jansen wrote that the figure remained at that.[63] The Jansens had also spent some time meeting some of the leading representatives and senators of Congress.

Just how optimistic Cornelius Jansen was at this stage about the possible success of legislation is unknown, except for a statement left by Christian Krehbiel, who wrote:

> ... He (C. Jansen) wanted Congress to set aside a large tract somewhere in the West as a closed area to be reserved to Mennonites only. He received some encouragement, too; but Carl Schurz, who was then United States Senator from Missouri, flatly told him that his plan would never be approved. Jansen complained bitterly of Schurz to me when he visited Summerfield soon after; but I told him that Schurz was the only man who had told him the naked truth while others were sidestepping the issue. Congress, I said, to make sure that frontier lands went to actual settlers and not to speculators, had passed extensive and well-considered legislation and was not likely to reopen or alter it to fit special interests such as Jansen represented.[64]

That was a bitter pill for Jansen to swallow but he did not give up the cause.

Information as to who was to sponsor the introduction of legislation in Congress is missing from the Jansen collection, but fortunately C. Henry Smith comes to our rescue with the statement that "A petition bearing the signature of J. F. Funk and Amos Herr, and sponsored no doubt by Jansen was presented to the Lower House on December 8, by A. Herr Smith, congressman from Lancaster County, Pennsylvania. Smith, who represented a large Mennonite constituency, judging from his middle name, was perhaps of Mennonite ancestry. The same petition was presented by congressmen from Minnesota and Kansas the same day. On January 10 a similar petition was presented to the Senate by Senator Cameron, also of Pennsylvania."[65] Whether the petition was a copy or merely a modification of that which Cornelius and Peter Jansen sent to the various congressmen and senators, we are unable to determine, because no copy has been preserved in the Jansen collection. It is likely that Senator Cameron or even Funk and Herr may have edited it, but otherwise introduced it as they received it. For we know that Herr had contacted the Pennsylvania senators and possibly his representatives in behalf of this cause. The petition reads:

> To the Honorable, the Senate and House of Representatives of the United States of America in Congress assembled:
>
> We, the undersigned, belonging to the Christian denomination called Mennonites, of South Russia and Prussia, in our own behalf and that of our brethren, respectfully address the following to you:

For three generations our denomination has lived in Russia under their own control, free to enjoy, as a separate colony, government only interfering to punish crimes and collect its revenues. Now by a recent edict of the Russian government passed 4th [16th] June, 1871, we are deprived of all those rights, liberties, and privileges which had been granted to us forever, and the choice is presented to us of leaving Russia within ten years from the above-mentioned date, or after that time become Russianized in language and religion. In Prussia where we lived for more than two hundred years in the liberty of conscience the government has acted the same.

We have determined to emigrate to some country where we can enjoy civil, social and religious liberty.

By examining your constitution and country, we find the full assurance that under your constitution and laws, we shall find the liberty we so earnestly desire, and the sentiment expressed by President Grant in his Message of March 3, 1873, [This no doubt should read December,] gives us great encouragement.

Desirous of settling in your country in colonies, there is, however, one obstacle in the way: the unimproved lands which we would be likely to select for our future homes being owned in alternate sections by railroad companies, some of the sections belonging to the government would be taken up by persons who do not belong to our colony, and who are not in sympathy with us. Besides this our mode of farming is for fifteen or twenty portions of it set aside for common pasture where all the horses and cattle may graze together, kept by one herder. This saves much expense in fencing.

It will require time—no doubt the eight years yet open to emigration—before all property in Russia can be disposed of, business finally settled, and the last of our brethren brought to their new home.

In behalf, therefore, of our brethren, numbering between forty and fifty thousand, we would respectfully ask:

1. That if we select portions of railroad lands in different places suitable to our different wants as cattle-raisers, agriculturists, etc., we be allowed to take up and secure the sections of government lands lying adjacent thereto, either by purchase or under the homestead laws, and preserve the same until the year 1881.

2. If we find bodies of unoccupied land belonging to the government suited to our purposes that we be allowed the same privileges of taking up and securing a sufficient quantity of land protected from the interference of outside parties.

The Canadian government has offered to present us as much land as we would occupy within the before mentioned time, but a party of us would prefer to settle in the United States, if the opportunity is given us to locate in colonies.

Our only object being to care for those in distress, should there be anything in our petition looking like speculation, we beg you will prevent it. Justice exalts a nation, says the Word of God; and if you will use your great influence to promote this mission, and assist the emigration of those who are persecuted for conscience sake, you will have the deepest thanks of the sorrow stricken Mennonites of Russia and Prussia, and what is much more the blessings of Him who says that even a drink of cold water shall not be without reward.

We are with high estimation,

Some of the Emigrants from Russia and Prussia Called Mennonites

P.S. Our residence being transitory, if any reference should be required we beg to address to our brethren, Rev. Amos Herr, Lancaster County, Pennsylvania, and John F. Funk, Elkhart, Indiana, who are in sympathy with us and conversant with our movements.[66]

Cornelius Jansen was in Berlin, Ontario, when the petitions were introduced in Congress, devoting his time to assisting the family, writing letters and traveling in Canada with Jacob Y. Schantz in the interest of his people.[67] On February 9, 1874, he received a letter from the Secretary of the Interior suggesting that "if you desire the passage of this law, it would be likely to promote your wishes if you were able to come here and spend some time with the Committees on Public Lands and also with other influential members of Congress." Delano continued that while he was "entirely convinced of the propriety of this recommendation," he did not "feel at liberty to make any other expression on this subject, unless my opinion is called for by some Committee of one branch or of the National Legislature." But he would take the liberty of sending a copy of Jansen's letter of the third and his answer thereto to the Chairman of the Committee on Public Lands in the Senate, and in the House of Representatives.[68] Cornelius Jansen answered Delano's letter on the sixteenth or eighteenth, the writing is not clear, asking him to keep up the "benevolence" as he termed it, in behalf of the cause. He told him that when he received the letter his son Peter, together with other friends, had already left for Washington and they would come to him for guidance "to obtain the fulfillment of our petition to Congress." He wrote Delano to let him know through Peter if he still considered his presence necessary, if so he would "come without delay."[69]

Apparently the matter was not urgent at this time, for it was not until March 26, that Margarete Jansen wrote in her diary that "Father and Peter left for Washington," that her father had received a letter from the Secretary of the Interior asking him to come. Again we know but little of their activity in Washington, except that they traveled back and forth between Washington, Philadelphia and Baltimore. The family received occasional letters from Father and Peter but most of them are not in the collection. On the second of April they had a letter from Father Jansen written in Philadelphia, but Margarete does not reveal its content. On April 8, they received letters from Father and Peter in which Peter writes that they will soon go west to find a place to live. Father, however, wrote that the matter before Congress was still undecided, but apparently he did not have much hope that the bill would pass. Yet, he regarded it his duty to remain there as long as he could do anything to help the cause.[70] But on the thirteenth of April he again wrote the family from Philadelphia, saying that even though they had no definite promise that the petition would be granted, they were still hopeful. At least he had the peace of mind that "he had done what he could." He expected that the matter would be decided within a few days. He mentions having met Herr. Funk had also been expected, but did not come. However, he had been there earlier. All his supporters, however, had remained faithful. He gave the impression that he was the bill's sole promoter. He wrote that the past night he was at the home of J. Wood of Germantown, a Quaker, apparently the same man who accompanied them to the President's office in 1873.[71] Letters received by the family on the twenty-third of April said that they were still in Philadelphia but they apparently left for the West on the twentieth, two days before the question was definitely defeated in Congress.[72]

The Jansens had lost their first battle in Congress. While it apparently was a valuable experience for young Peter and may have unconsciously influenced his later life to enter politics, it was, according to Margarete, hard on her father who was suffering from lumbago (*Kreuzschmerzen*). She writes that they had to do much walking during those days.[73] That the cause of immigration suffered as a result of the defeat of the bill, is doubtful. For already plans were under way to help those poor Mennonites with funds who needed financial aid, as we shall see later. Moreover, it was probably fortunate for the future cause of the Mennonites and for the country as such, that the Mennonites settled in different states rather than all in one compact area as at first contemplated.

An important incident in connection with this undertaking is revealed by C. Henry Smith. It is the fact that Michael L. Hiller, who had been asked by the seven delegates to sponsor this legislation, was very much surprised when he discovered that Cornelius Jansen had beaten him to the draw. He expressed this surprise in a letter to J. F. Funk written December 1, 1873. Hiller went on to say that he had consulted with Jansen, whom he had met in New York the day before the delegates left, on all these matters but that he had not expected him to use this information in his own behalf. While he admitted that Jansen had made good progress, especially on the matter of land concessions, he was afraid that the petition would give the matter too much publicity and endanger the whole scheme. Funk, therefore, asked Herr to write Hiller a conciliatory letter to keep peace in the family. Apparently Herr did this, but on December 5, he also wrote Jansen a letter congratulating him on the favorable reception he had received in Washington and then told Jansen that he too had contacted the Pennsylvania senators, Cameron and Scott, influencing them in behalf of the cause.[74]

How Cornelius Jansen came to assume this responsibility of sponsoring this legislation, whether on his own behalf or instructed by Leonhard Sudermann and possibly even by Funk and Herr, we cannot tell. At any rate it appears that Funk and Herr were fully aware of what was happening. It is reasonable to conclude, however, that the shift was made from Hiller to Jansen and became necessary when they decided against the Dakota lands as the compact area.[75] For having decided not to designate the Dakota lands held by the Northern Pacific Railroad Company as the compact area for settlement, it would only be logical not to use its agent, Hiller, to sponsor their cause in Congress. Consequently Jansen replaced him.

Various reasons have been given for the defeat of the bill, but no doubt the main reason was the fact that it asked for a special privilege for the Mennonites, which if granted would have left Congress vulnerable to requests from any other group that might seek special favors. This is revealed time and again by the opposition in the legislative history.[76]

Why did not Cornelius Jansen petition Congress for exemption from military service, when this was one of the main reasons the Mennonites were leaving Russia and Prussia and seeking to establish new homes in Canada and in the United States? In the first place the United States did not have peacetime conscription as was the case in the two European countries. And furthermore, Paul and Lorenz Tschetter had included this request in their petition to President Grant, and the President's Secretary of State, Hamilton Fish, to whom the President had referred the question, had answered September 5, 1873 to this effect:

> They wish guarantees of exemption from military service and also jury service. They desire also to be free from the payment of substitute money in case of draft; and the right to govern their own schools.
>
> Since personal military service, citizenship obligations, jury service, and control over schools are all matters that fall under the jurisdiction of the various states in which they wish to settle, the President says that he cannot exempt them from the laws of the states and the laws to which other citizens are subject. As to the paying of substitute money for fifty years, that, too, is beyond his power of promising. It is true, however, that for the next fifty years we will not be entangled in another war in which military service will be necessary. But should it be necessary there is little likelihood that Congress would find justification in freeing them from duties which are asked of other citizens . . . [77]

While this answer was directed to Michael L. Hiller, there is little doubt that Hiller relayed it to either Funk or Herr and that by the time Jansen went to Washington to petition the President, he either knew about it or else the President informed him to that effect. Apparently they felt there was no point at this time in bringing the matter before Congress when the government officials felt that the question was not likely to arise within the next fifty years. Whether this was the explanation for Jansen's failure to press the matter before Congress, when we know from all his writings how utterly opposed he was to military service, the fact, nevertheless, remains that he did not press Congress for legislation to exempt the Mennonites from military service in case of a future war. The matter, however, was raised in Congress in connection with the land question by Orris Sanford Ferry, a Brigadier General of the Civil War, who opposed the land consessions on the ground that these people were pacifists.[78]

The matter of exemption from military service was particularly presented to President Grant by Paul and Lorenz Tschetter during an interview arranged by Hiller on July 27, 1873. To this petition Hamilton Fish, Secretary of State, responded in a letter dated September 5, 1873, in which it is stated that "the President says he cannot exempt them from the laws of the states and the laws to which other citizens are subject."[79]

Somewhat later Hamilton Fish made another statement regarding exemption from military service. This is dated November 15, 1873. The text reads as follows:

UNITED STATES OF AMERICA
DEPARTMENT OF STATE

To all to whom these presents shall come, Greeting:

I Certify, That the text of an act of Congress, approved February 24, 1864, entitled "An Act to Amend an act entitled 'An act for enrolling and calling out the national forces, and for other purposes, approved March third, eighteen hundred and sixty three," to be found on pages 6, 7, 8, 9, 10, and 11 of the annexed pamphlet of the Statutes at Large of the United States passed at the first session of the 38th Congress, is a true copy of the original amendatory act on file in this Department,

In testimony whereof, I, Hamilton Fish, [signature] SECRETARY OF STATE of the UNITED STATES, have hereunto subscribed my name and caused the seal of the Department of State to be affixed.

DONE at the City of Washington, this fifteenth day of November, A. D. 1873, and of the Independence of the United States of America the 98th.

Hamilton Fish (signature)

It is apparent that the Secretary of State or President Grant responded to a request by calling attention to the *STATUTES AT LARGE OF THE UNITED STATES* which were passed at the first session of the 38th Congress, dealing with the question of exemption from military service because of conscientious objection to war. It is likely that this copy was sent to the delegate Leonhard Sudermann in Russia. In any event it found its way to the Bethel College Historical Library through the heirs of Leonhard Sudermann.

The conclusion is definite, that in 1873 and 1874, the government of Canada was more liberal in its concessions to the Mennonites than the government of the United States. Nevertheless, the United States secured more of the Mennonites during this period than did Canada.

Influences Immigration

That Cornelius Jansen and his family influenced a number of Russian, Polish and Prussian Mennonites to leave their native country and settle in America is undoubtedly true. But to what extent this was the case is difficult to say. For too often it is impossible to credit the action of an individual to just one cause. Usually there are a number of factors that operate upon the mind of a person before he is driven to action. It is doubtful though, that there would have been a Mennonite immigration to the United States and Canada in the 1870's if it had not been for the threatened restriction of the religious and educational privileges of these people. Then again the question arises, to what extent did the expulsion of Cornelius Jansen and his family influence others to leave? One of the reasons given by the Russian government for his expulsion was that he was "spreading amongst the Mennonite inhabitants false ideas of their condition, and persuading the Mennonites to cease being Russian subjects and to emigrate to America . . ."[80] His own remark about the expulsion was, that the only good that could come from it was, that it would enable him "to operate from a foreign country the more energetically for (his) people.[81] That he lived up to this is revealed in almost everything he did during the first three or four years of his life in America.

The very nature of his departure awakened the curiosity of people. "Already at the first dinner on the small steamer," wrote Jansen "I had to explain to the captain, as well as to others, the reason of my leaving, and I can say that hardly a day passed without giving me an opportunity to witness for the Gospel of Peace."[82] At Berdyansk the Jansen family had many friends and he was considered a leader among his people, if not in the field of religion, yet his judgment and keen insight into conditions were highly respected. Naturally when he was forced to leave Russia there were many Mennonites who looked up to him and were willing to accept his word for its face value. When, therefore, he sent his observations to Russia and also to Prussia, they no doubt helped many people to decide to emigrate.

When the Jansen family left Russia and stopped for a number of weeks in Prussia, again there was a group of families that flocked around them and later followed them to the United States, and even settled in Nebraska in the same neighborhood where the Jansen family located.[83] Among them was that blond Penner girl whom Peter Jansen went to meet in New York City and whom he spied even before the ship docked. During three long years she had waited anxiously and impatiently, trying to hasten her parents' decision to emigrate, which in turn seemed to be dependent upon when the other families would be ready. There was a day in January of 1874, when she wrote Peter and asked whether she should risk it alone, for it might take till 1875 before her parents might be ready to emigrate. She had lost all interest in her fatherland. And yet, when she thought of venturing out alone, her tender mind was struck by so many unanswered questions that frustrated her decision to dare the risk. Yes, she waited two more years till she came with a group of thirty-three families.[84]

We have already noticed the close friendship between Leonhard Sudermann and Cornelius Jansen. They kept up a constant correspondence. We have also seen how Jansen influenced the Mennonites not to settle in the land of the Northern Pacific Railroad Company in Dakota. But in all fairness to Cornelius Jansen we hasten to add that while he had this ability to influence others, nevertheless, he was careful not to make decisions for them. He would give them the benefit of his observations and then let them draw their own conclusions. He wrote to Herr: ". . . even if they settle on the Northern Dakota lands, if they would only decide to come."[85]

The result of this influence was that many people asked Jansen to meet them in New York City, or wherever their ship landed, or else they would pass through Iowa via Mount Pleasant, later Beatrice, before they made their decision where to settle. Frequently, instead of meeting them personally he would send Peter to meet them. He did this, because of his health.

There were other ways in which Cornelius Jansen tried to help the Mennonite emigrants. He knew from experience as well as from what his friends wrote him of the ability of the Russian authorities to hinder the emigration of his religious comrades. The land was looked upon as crown property and thus the practical and often expensive dwelling houses practically lost their value.[86] Especially since they could sell those possessions only to Mennonites. And if almost the entire congregation planned to emigrate, who was there to purchase the property? Thus it happened that many sold their possessions for only a third, a fourth, or even a fifth of their normal value. After having accomplished this they often discovered to their dismay that the Russian officials on the spot would hold up their passports for months, adding one impediment after another to discourage them from emigrating. This was especially discouraging if the group had planned to leave early in spring so as to arrive in the States in time to get settled and prepare for the winter. The failure to issue passports in time, kept them stranded for months, forcing them to live on their reserves and in addition causing them to arrive in the States or Canada in the dead of winter.[87]

Aware of what was going on, Cornelius Jansen sought to help them. While still at Berdyansk he had written a letter to Falk and Co., shipping agency for the Canadian government in Hamburg, in which he explained that freedom of action in Russia was greatly impaired, that it would require energetic support and favor on the part of other governments to aid the emigration of the Russian Mennonites.[88] From Danzig he wrote a letter to the German Foreign Ministry in which he complained about the unjust treatment he had received in Russia and asked the ministry to help the colonists who wished to emigrate from Russia with their passports. But by the time the foreign ministry wrote back for more detailed information, Jansen had left for America. Moreover, it probably was he who had influenced the West Prussian Mennonites to ask the United States ambassador at St. Petersburg to intervene in behalf of the Russian Mennonites. Marshall Jewell, U. S. minister to Russia, wrote to Hamilton Fish, U. S. Secretary of State about this matter May 20, 1874. After mentioning General Todleben's efforts to keep the Mennonites in Russia, he reported that he had "received letters from Germany in connection with this matter, from parties, who I suppose, are either Mennonites themselves, or represent that people, asking my assistance in the matter, and stating that while the Russian government has ordered their officials to grant them the necessary passports, yet the agents of the government upon the spot appear to throw every possible impediment in their way, causing the intended emigrants loss both of time and money . . ."To this the Secretary of State replied, June 12, " . . . I desire to express my recommendation of the reserve maintained by you in regard to the subject."[89]

In a letter to Anthony Kimber, a Quaker of Germantown, Pa., which must have been written sometime in November or December

1873, Cornelius Jansen wrote that according to the latest news from Russia there were about one thousand families preparing to leave Russia in the spring of 1874, but that it seemed that the Russian government was refusing to issue the passports. Jansen then asked: "If the Russian government should use force in keeping them there against their own published law, should it not be possible to do something by a petition to the English and U. S. governments to ask their influence in the matter? Please let me know yours and you dear brother's [Francis] opinion on this object." Shifting his thought to the poor Mennonites, he added: "I think it very necessary to have by our work in assisting the poor amongst the Russian emigrants an intercourse with the Russian consuls in this country."[90] No answer to this letter has been found in the Jansen Collection. But we know that both governments, that of England as well as of the United States, in accordance with the prevailing international laws and practices, refused to interfere with the internal affairs of the Russian government. All efforts to influence immigration from the outside therefore, was checked as soon as they reached or came to the attention of the U.S. Minister and British ambassador to Russia.[91]

Mennonite Aid Funds

The efforts of Cornelius Jansen were more successful in soliciting aid for Mennonite families who needed help to emigrate and establish homes in America. These needs fell into different categories. There were families entirely dependent and would need money to purchase land, machinery, horses and cattle and food until they were self-supporting. Other families needed less help, enough money to purchase food until they could earn or until their own crops would support them. Jansen was determined that all should have the opportunity to emigrate and leave their oppressed lands of Germany and Russia.

Apparently Cornelius Jansen's mind was constantly working to help his fellow brethren. Barely had he reached Berlin, Ontario, when he was out traveling with Jacob Y. Schantz soliciting money to help the poor he had left behind. On August 16, 1873, his second day in Canada, he recorded in his diary that they held a meeting in Waterloo and collected money to help the poor Russian Mennonites come to America.[92] Ten days later, in a letter to

II. The Cornelius Jansen family at their home in Berdyansk, South Russia, about 1870. From left to right, rear, Peter, Tante Anna, Cornelius Jr., Mrs. Jansen, Father Jansen, and Margarete. Front row, Anna, John and Helena.

III. Dowry chest of Anna Jansen which was one of the 47 pieces of baggage with which the Jansen family landed at Quebec, August 28, 1873. (Cornelius Jansen Collection, Bethel College Historical Library.)

IV. The Jacob Y. Schantz home in Berlin (now Kitchener), Ontario. The Jansens lived in a small house in the rear of the larger house from August, 1873 to June, 1874.

V. Cornelius Jansen, Mrs. Jansen and Tante Anna (sister of Mrs. Jansen) at their home in Beatrice, Nebraska.

VI. The Cornelius Jansen family moved to Nebraska in November, 1876, where they spent the first winter on the ranch. In the spring of 1877 the family moved to Beatrice where they had purchased this home which they continued improving.

VII. In their home in Beatrice the Cornelius Jansens not only entertained their children and grandchildren but also their many neighbors and friends.

VIII. This is likely one of the last pictures of Cornelius Jansen who died on Dec. 14, 1894. Mother Jansen and Tante Anna passed away three years later. With them on the picture is Helena.

IX-X. Anna Jansen married Aron Claassen and lived on a farm five miles from Beatrice. John Jansen (right) first lived on the ranch near Jansen and later moved to Saskatchewan, Canada.

Children of Cornelius Jansen

XI-XII. Cornelius Jansen Jr. taught school in Beatrice and in California where he died in 1954. Helena Jansen lived with her parents and later moved to California.

XIII. Peter Jansen, the oldest son of Cornelius Jansen, after whom Jansen, Nebraska was named. This picture was taken about 1915. Pages 126-144 deal with the life and activities of Peter Jansen as rancher, businessman, and public servant.

XIV. Sheep shearing on the extensive Jansen ranch, Jansen, Nebraska.

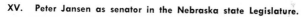

XV. Peter Jansen as senator in the Nebraska state Legislature.

XVI. Aron Claassen home near Beatrice, Nebraska. Aron Claassen married Anna Jansen. Their children were Cornelius, John, Aaron, Anna, Katharine, and Margarete.

XVII-XVIII. Cornelius Jansen Claassen (1883-1952), son of Anna Jansen Claassen, was a successful businessman in Jansen, Winnipeg and Omaha. He initiated the research project which culminated in the publication of this book. Aaron Jansen Claassen (right), also son of Anna Jansen Claassen, a successful farmer near Beatrice, Nebraska, also supported the research project and sponsored the publication of the book.

the Whitneys of Leeds, England, Peter Jansen spread the news to Quaker friends that the Mennonites in a small circle of about twenty miles had collected $10,000 "for their oppressed brethren in South Russia."[93] It is doubtful that the $10,000 had already been collected. He probably should have used the word promised. In December, 1873, shortly after the Jansens had returned from Washington and their journey westward, they continued this work, this time they solicited in Hamilton, Ontario, and remained there several days.[94] On the twenty-ninth of December, 1873, Cornelius Jansen wrote to Amos Herr that he and Schantz had traveled among the Mennonites in Canada in the interest of support for the "poor brethren," that Schantz was very active in this work. He also stated that the Mennonites in Canada had promised $10,000 for this cause, and if those in the States would contribute as generously, then all the Mennonites who would like to emigrate could be helped.

Two days later he wrote the same message to Francis Funk of Philadelphia and added, that he had travelled in Virginia, Pennsylvania and Illinois and that he could expect similar interest there for the cause, and closed with the thought that they are all working for it.[95] Apparently Jansen had prepared the ground also for these solicitations on his first and second journeys to New York and Washington. The January issue of the *Herald of Truth* now contained the news that about $10,000 had been subscribed by the Mennonites in Canada "for the Russian Brethren," but if need be they could double the amount.[96] J. Y. Schantz was active in Canada to help the Mennonites settle there. There is no doubt, however, that the presence of Cornlius Jansen and his son Peter helped Schantz to make the solicitations a success. Andreas Schrag and L. Sudermann had also petitioned for aid.[97]

Convinced of the importance of witnessing for peace, as Cornelius Jansen interpreted his efforts to help other Mennonites escape peacetime military service, he solicited the help of all his friends in behalf of the cause. We do not know what he and his wife told their Quaker friends when they visited them in England, but soon after, *The Friend, A Religious, Literary and Miscellaneous Journal* of the English Friends carried articles about the Mennonite emigration, quoted from the Jansen letters, told of the impediments the Russian officials put in the way of the emigrants in order to discourage their leaving, the tremendous financial sacrifice this movement imposed upon the Mennonites, and that many of them would have to be helped by outside sources to bridge the crises. These articles are written by the friends of the Jansens—by Isaac Robson and Thomas Harvey—whom they visited as they stopped in Leeds, England, en-route to America.[98] Before long they published extracts of Mr. and Mrs. Jansen's letters, and eventually, in March 1875, follows the "Appeal for Financial Help of the Russian Mennonites by the English Friends."[99]

Before they issued the appeal for contributions they had carefully pondered the question of raising funds to assist this emigration, but had "always felt a stop in the way." These reasons, which for a time thwarted their action, shows how thoroughly the English Friends considered matters before they acted:

> (1) because of the vastness of the need supposing the emigration to become general, and the inadequacy of any aid likely to be raised to meet it; (2) because such a fund would be likely to give an unhealthy stimulus to a movement which ought to spring from conscientious motives, requiring and deserving self-sacrifice; (3) that it would be offensive to the Russian Government, and give ground for representing the whole affair as one of foreign origin; (4) and, lastly, because such an interposition of Friends would have tended to check self-help and mutual aid, also the help of the American Mennonites, which has now been liberally rendered, and is likely to be sustained.
>
> The question has now passed into a phase in which Friends can assist, and in which their aid is urgently needed for the succour of temporary distress, which, without fault of their own, has overtaken numbers of those who have emigrated, and have been driven into the late autumn and winter for their first attempt to settle.[100]

The appeal mentions the efforts of the Emperor to calm the apprehensions of the Mennonites and induce them to remain, by sending his celebrated General Todleben to the colonies. While he was "extraordinarily condescending and sympathizing" he declined to put the terms he offered into writing. These were in substance that, "service in fire brigades, in military workshops, in the dockyards, and in the forests, would be accepted in lieu of the ordinary military service." But the Mennonite elders had little confidence in verbal promises, consequently the emigration continued. The Quakers were careful to defend the Europeans. Alexander II, they felt, had been a great benefactor to his country, and they pointed out that he was "surrounded by influences which he can very imperfectly control, and by which his own judgment is often unfavorably biased."

The article pointed out that in 1874 "not less than 5,000 Mennonites, emigrated . . . to Manitoba, in the Dominion of Canada, and to Kansas, Dakota, Nebraska, and other of the United States in the far West." It again mentioned the great sacrifices involved in the undertaking. And then came the important point in the appeal, that is that the "more affluent Mennonites have aided their poorer brethren, and the American, and the Canadian Mennonites have also raised as much as $80,000, which sum has been almost wholly absorbed in expenses of transport by sea and land." Now it was the Friends' turn to contribute.

The authors then wrote that the object of the present appeal was

> . . . to obtain pecuniary help, not for the purpose of stimulating the emigration, but to give relief in urgent cases to the sick and destitute among those already in America, or who may hereafter arrive in a desttitute condition; and to supply seed, implements and cattle for those whose means have been exhausted as described above. We believe the money contributed in America will, to a considerable extent be advanced on *loan,* of which congregations will guarantee repayment. We think it may prove advisable to do the same with a portion of the funds contributed in England, with the understanding that any repayments shall be used for the same purpose as the original advances, so long as required and in the end be applied to such charitable use as the Meeting for Sufferings may appoint.

They expected that the emigration for the year 1875 would again total about 1,000 families, or approximately 5,000 people. The appeal was signed by Isaac Robson, Treasurer of the "Mennonite Fund," and by Thomas Harvey.

The response was immediate. In the next issue of *The Friend,* April 1, 1875, Robson and Harvey thanked for the generous contributions already received. They had put the money to work immediately, rather than letting it accumulate in the bank. To Jansen they had sent £1,000 in three installments, and to John F. Funk £60. They again emphasized the fact that none of the money would be applied "to assist or promote the emigration" but to help those who had already reached America and had been plunged into distress "through delays and impediments put in their way by the authorities in Russia." Of Jansen and Funk they wrote.

> We think it a happy circumstance that, in our beloved friend C. Jansen, we have a disinterested and intelligent agent, who during his twenty years residence in Russia, had become, by frequent journeys, personally acquainted with the circumstances of the Mennonite people in the various provinces of Russia, and who is himself in full unity with Friends in their peace views, and other important points of Christian faith and practice.
>
> The funds entrusted to him will be chiefly employed in giving much-needed temporary aid to a class who are likely, with such help, to become in North America, as they were in South Russia, thrifty and comfortable farmers, able and willing to help others.
>
> The smaller amount sent to John Funk, will be employed for another class, who are more immediately objects of the care and succor of the Aid Committee of the American Mennonites.[101]

Funk and Jansen answered immediately to thank for the gift. Funk wrote that he had been able to sell the £60 for $333.97. He was sending provisions forward tomorrow for the needy to Kansas." Jansen figured on loaning a part of the money without interest, to some of the needy families. The remaining sum he was using to purchase "seed grain, ploughs, etc." He could buy them wholesale in the eastern states and the railroad companies had promised to haul the goods free of charge. By using this method he could buy twice as much for the money than if he bought the goods at the place where they were needed, meaning Kansas or Nebraska. The loan was to be repaid next year, "if the Lord giveth a crop next autumn. It can then be used by others." In case the Lord should call him, Jansen, before then, "the account of it will remain in the hands of trusted friends who know all circumstances." He concluded the letter by thanking them again for the money: "Dearest friends, I really confess that your gift for our people, and kind promise that this shall not be the last, encouraged me so much that I go on with new hope. . . . I see by your action, my dear friends, that you understand me when I plead for those 'bashful poor,' who in Russia declined assistance for themselves, and divided the little they had in helping poor relations to come over," expecting that they would be able to borrow money here without difficulty. Now they "suffer for need of the very necessaries of life." The smallest contribution was of great importance to them. For one dollar they bought two bushels of seed wheat. Without seed they had no prospect of a crop.[102]

The Jansens kept the Friends informed of their work. In the October issue of *The Friend* Robson and Harvey wrote that they had satisfactory accounts from Jansen and his wife. He and his eldest son Peter, were "giving up much of their time to visiting the new settlements of the emigrants, seeing how they fare, and giving them such encouragement and aid as they are able." Cornelius Jansen reported that during the first six months of 1875, 3,072 Mennonites had emigrated to Manitoba and about 1,000 to the United States. Leonhard Sudermann had written that they could expect the emigration to continue. Jansen feared that the last years, meaning those before 1881, would be the hardest, but he was comforted by the fact that the American Friends were also willing to assist with loans. Mrs. Jansen reported that her sister Anna and son Peter had visited the emigrants in Jefferson County, Nebraska, where nearly a thousand dollars of the English Friends' money had been distributed. The people were happy that they now had food to eat, also their cattle could be fed. They hoped that "with God's blessing, they will prosper in the coming years, and then be able to pay back that money they got through the kindness and Christian love of our English Friends.[103]

In the July issue of 1876, Robson published a letter from Isaac Peters addressed to him and translated by Mrs. Jansen. The Jansens were not afraid to use the English language if, thereby, they could help others, even though they lacked proficiency. Speaking of the sacrifices connected with the emigration, Peters wrote: "That such an emigration is connected with great sacrifices is not necessary to mention; not alone sacrifice of money must be made, for there are other privations, especially the giving up of our own will. To leave home, comforts, etc., is indeed a trial which can only be endured in faith on the promise in Matt. XIX. 29." He then spoke of the poor brethren who have been helped "through the kind and Christian sympathy of others: and also you, dear English friends, in helping them in this new country, for there are already many of them who enjoy to know their sons free from the yoke of slaughtering their fellow men. For all this kindness I feel induced to offer thanks to you, dear givers all, in the name of the members of my community here." Peters went on to explain that twenty families had received $791.97 through the kindness of Cornelius Jansen, which he had loaned them to purchase "seed and agricultural implements."

Besides that they had received from the Friends a gift of $50, sent them by J. F. Funk of Elkhart, Indiana, for which they expressed their "heartiest thanks." These gifts were especially meaningful to them because they knew that they were given "under prayer and supplication by a Society who, like we, witness for a kingdom of peace. . . ."[104] The feeling that they were witnessing for a "kingdom of peace" recurrs time and again in the letters of the Jansens.

The money contributed by the English Friends and sent to United States to Jansen and Funk, amounted to £1,200 of which Jansen received £1,000 and Funk £200. The rate of exchange varied between $5.53 and $5.57 in United States money totaling about $6,660. While the total amount contributed was small, it was valued very highly, and the Mennonites must thank the Jansen family for this help, for it was their intimate friendship with the British Friends that enlisted the sympathy of the Quakers for the Mennonite cause. The money was distributed among needy families in Nebraska and Kansas.[105]

To what extent Cornelius Jansen and his family helped to interest and solicit financial aid of the Mennonites in the United States in behalf of the poor Russian Mennonite emigrants is unknown. On the day the Mennonite Board of Guardians was elected in Summerfield, Illinois, November 7, 1873, Cornelius Jansen was traveling in Lancaster County, Pennsylvania, visiting with Amos Herr and the Quakers preparing to petition the President for a compact land area. Jansen had visited with the Mennonites of Elkhart, Indiana, and Summerfield, Illinois, on his previous travels in August 1873, several months before. No doubt at this time he discussed the problem constantly on his mind, how best to help the poor among the Mennonites to emigrate to United States. The members elected to this Mennonite Board of Guardians were Christian Krehbiel of Summerfield, Illinois, as director, David Goerz of Summerfield, Illinois, secretary, John F. Funk of Elkhart, Indiana, as treasurer and Bernhard Warkentin as business agent. The Board was to facilitate the emigration among the steamship and railroad companies, with the European brethren and also to sponsor the solicitations and distribution of funds. Whatever Cornelius Jansen did to help this cause was, therefore, in the nature of assisting the Board in its work.

IV. Settlement in Retrospect

First Temporary Home

When a person finds a home by correspondence, it may turn out to be a disappointment. In his *Memoirs* Peter Jansen wrote that his father had corresponded with a member of their faith near Berlin, Ontario, apparently while still in Berdyansk, and that this man had invited them to stay at his house, "pending the selection of a permanent place of settlement."[1] According to Cornelius Jansen, Jacob Schantz offered them this house—*Hinterhaus*—as it was called, the day they arrived in Berlin, after they discovered that there was no room for them in the hotel.[2] Now Kitchner, Ontario, Berlin, was then a small town with a population of about 500, but the railroad passed through it.

The house located in the backyard of the Schantz's place, had only four rooms and there were nine in the Jansen family, including Tante Anna. This crowded the family, yet they remained there until the middle of June, 1874. With this as the home base, Cornelius Jansen and son Peter made their journeys into the United States and also their travels in Canada. Mother Jansen and the rest of the family, therefore, were often alone. While they managed to get along, those were the days when they most noticed the loneliness and the absence of friends.

The accommodations of the house were meager. Apparently it

was furnished when they took possession. The cooking facilities were poor. Fifty-two days after they landed in Berlin, October 6, 1873, Margarete wrote in her diary that this was the first day they ate their own prepared noon meal in America. Mother had made very tasty beef soup (*Rindsuppe*), and how they liked it.[3] Seven days later she wrote that they would sleep for the first time on real bedsteads. Hitherto they had slept on mattresses on the floor.[4] That day Cornelius Jansen wrote in his diary that they had purchased two bedsteads for $1.60.

It must have been most thrilling for the Jansen family when they arrived in the new world, and noticed how differently the American people spoke, dressed, behaved, and worshiped. Probably it was equally amusing for the Americans to observe and hear the Prussian and Russian Mennonites when they first set foot upon the American soil, surrounded with their many trunks and baggage. Writing about the emigration of the Mennonites enroute, *The Friend* in October, 1874 reported that "at many a railway-station there can still be seen and recognized the homely luggage and boxes of occasional Mennonites almost uniformly labelled 'Über Hamburg-Amer' " which was misread by *The Friend* to read "Über Hamburg-Amen."[5] Five months later the same paper carried an article about an unfortunate party of 328 Mennonites stranded at Liverpool, England, because the germ of smallpox had been found among them. Notice the impression these people made on this Englishman:

> It is impossible to speak too highly of the conduct and behavior of the Russian emigrants, and of the fortitude and patience with which what must have been to them very grevious trials and disappointments have been borne; there have been among them neither murmurings nor discontent, and every direction given to them was most readily observed. In their moral discipline they appeared to exercise great vigor and severity, and both women and men avoided anything approaching ornament or elegance, maintaining a gravity and simplicity in gesture and clothing which was striking. An insight into their real character was given immediately after their arrival at the workhouse. Having been separated from the females and deprived of their luggage—to which they submitted without slightest complaint—the men were passed on to an apartment where tea and substantial food was in readiness for them; and it was supposed that they would very soon attack the good things provided. Had a party of Englishmen arrived at the workhouse under similar circumstances—after a long and tiresome journey of some 200 miles, on one of the very coldest days of

the year—very little ceremony would probably have been observed; but on this occasion, when the governor entered shortly afterwards to see that they were all doing well, he was astonished to find the whole party standing patiently by their seats, not one of them (as was explained afterwards) venturing to touch food until 'a blessing had been asked.' This incident immediately marked them as religious people. On retiring to rest they again all united in prayer and in singing a hymn. . . .[6]

First Impressions

And what were the observations of the Jansen family as they first set foot upon American soil? Peter, then twenty-one years of age, later wrote that one of the first things that impressed him was, "the light, spiderlike buggies we saw at the various places we passed through. They seemed so frail in comparison with the ponderous vehicles of Russia and Germany."[7] But what struck him more forcefully was when he discovered the absence of servants in America, that everybody was waiting on himself. There was no distinction. He became keenly aware of this the first day they landed in Berlin, Ontario, when he went to the station after their numerous trunks and baggage. He describes his experience in these words:

> They [the trunks] were all piled on the platform, to which a dray had backed up. The station agent came out while I was looking for the usual baggage carriers seen at European railway stations to load the trunks. The station master looked at me for a minute and then said: 'Look here, young fellow, you seem pretty husky. Take hold with me and be quick about it.' That was my first introduction to American independence, and it seemed very strange to me, in the first place that an official should perform manual labor, and also that he should have the temerity to command me to help him. Well, I soon got over my ideas regarding labor. [8]

The Jansen family noticed this time and again. They were shocked by it especially when they visited the White House and Secretary Delano and the President of the United States told them of their experiences on the farm. The Secretary casually remarked that in his younger days he had been in the habit of milking twenty cows mornings and evenings, and President Grant chimed in to say that he could still hitch up and drive a team of horses as well as ever. Later Peter Jansen remarked about this experience: "You, who never knew life in Europe, and especially in Russia, can hardly imagine our surprise when these gentlemen gave us the impression that it was the usual thing for the highest officials of the United States and the Minister of Agriculture to do manual labor."[9]

Peter, and no doubt his father, also, were equally surprised by the plain apparel of our state and federal government officials—the absence of uniforms with gold trimmings, etc. "In Russia," wrote Peter, "we associated a government official with a uniform and lots of gold lace and trimmings, and the higher ones would always have guards of soldiers at the entrances of their quarters and residences. Imagine our surprise when we reached the 'White House' to find its portals guarded by a single colored man, who not even displayed a sword."[10]

Cornelius Jansen, who regarded all things associated with religious worship as sacred, was surprised no end, by the behavior of the American people in church. In a letter to Amos Herr he wrote that in the United States and Canada people will enter the church buildings with their hats on and wear them even until they sit down, sometimes they keep them on even longer. And when friends meet they merely nod to each other with their head, only very seldom do they shake hands, and never remove their hats. " 'Help yourself,' says the host to his guest at the dinner table, and therewith he has invoked the blessing."[11] Margarete Jansen was annoyed by the behavior of children in Sunday school. She remarked how much better behaved the Mennonite children had been in Berdyansk.[12] While the Jansen family attended church very faithfully every Sunday, it is questionable whether they ever took part in the communion services while they lived in Berlin, Ontario. On April 12, 1874, Margarete wrote: "There were church services, also communion, but no one of our family participated. No, I had no desire. Oh, it was so different than at home." The following Sunday they attended the Lutheran church where the congregation also celebrated communion services but the Jansen children together with many others walked out.[13]

Peter made an interesting observation about the Mennonite farmers in America. Referring to those in Lancaster County, he wrote: "Here like everywhere in America, the Mennonites have the best farms, but do very little to educate their children." He remarked that an old Quaker had told him: "Your people in this land on the average have better farms than ours, but I think we do more for the education of our children. Your people take better care of their cattle than ours." While in Lancaster County, Cornelius Jansen and Peter also visited a school of about six hundred pupils and the elder Jansen was asked to speak to the pupils without having been notified beforehand. This also surprised Peter very much. He wrote that it is customary in America to expect people to speak extempore, that is not practiced in Europe.[14]

Berlin, Ontario provided the family with only a few interests. Peter had given Margarete a diary and she has supplied us with much information during the first years of their stay in America. Entertainments were few, except attending church, Sunday school, and revival meetings, of which there seemed to be a goodly number in the various churches. Peter wrote that they were entirely new to them, that his father, although a devout Christian did not believe in this kind of religion, "but we children had lots of fun."[15] With the Russian and Prussian Mennonites, religion was not so much an emotional and sensational adventure, rather an educational process—a spiritual growth in the way of Christian living, and a communion with God.

It appears that the family attended all the different churches in Berlin: the Baptist church, the Lutheran church, the Methodist church, and the men folks also occasionally attended the Young Men's Christian Association. Of all these Margarete liked the Methodist church the best.[16] Margarete and Anna also helped to teach Sunday school classes,[17] and before long they sang in the choir and Anna often played the piano during church services.[18] The (Old) Mennonite church, which they no doubt also attended, was very conservative at that time. J. Y. Schantz was a member of that church but joined the United Mennonites (later United Brethren in Christ) in 1875. Already at the time when the Jansens were his guests, he must have taken them to various churches.[19]

The churches had the preaching services on Sunday morning, Sunday school in the afternoon and then there were always evening services. Usually different members of the family attended all three services. At their first attendance at the Lutheran church, Margarete and Heinrich noticed the inscription on the altar-piece which read: "God's Word and Luther's teaching I will observe forevermore." Margarete wrote that in their own mind they soon changed that to read: "God's Word will I observe, Luther's teachings nevermore."[20] Was that a remnant of their past experience and feeling of Mennonites toward Lutheranism in Prussia?

The greatest disappointment to them was the manner in which the Americans observed the religious festivities. The Jansen family spent one Easter and one Christmas in Berlin. To them it seemed that even on the second holiday there were no church services. People were working in the fields as usual.[21] They were used to celebrating three holidays. But even more disappointing was the way they celebrated Christmas. Of this Margarete wrote:

> The lovely Christmas days have gone. Never before have we been so alone and felt so lonesome. Our thoughts so often went back to the years at Berdyansk. Here at Schantzens they think it is sinful to have a Christmas tree, and so we did not have one either, even though we could have picked a very lovely tree most any place. When we are fortunate enough to have our own home, we will again have a tree and place it in our large living room. Mother and I set dishes for each member of the family, but it really did not seem like Christmas, everything was so different. On the first holiday there were only the forenoon services, and none on the second holiday. Most of the people were out working.[22]

How disappointing it must have been to the Jansen children. A time of the year they had always looked forward to with such great anticipation, and then to find it robbed of so much of its former enjoyment. Was it only the absence of the tree? No, the absence of their many friends, the spacious home and its atmosphere in which they had always celebrated Christmas.

Even Cornelius Jansen wrote to the Quakers in England how out of place he felt among the Mennonites in Canada: "I feel myself yet very strange here, it is all very differently from my imagination among my own Mennonite friends; but I have my dear family around me, and expect this summer some relations."[23] Peter also wrote about this to the Whitings, August 26, 1873:

> I make use now of a leisure hour to write you that we are staying with the members of our society in this part of the country till we find a place to settle a new home. Although they are very kind, they have such different customs and necessities of life, from those we used to have, that we feel very strange indeed. And only the consciousness that we asked not for earthly profit by leaving our comfortable home and the trust that our dear Saviour who treated us with so much kindness all the time of our journey will not leave us, makes us content and happy again.[24]

Apparently Peter found it more difficult than the rest of the family to adjust himself to the conditions in Berlin, Ontario. Probably annoyed by the crowded and inadequate living conditions in the home, impatient with his father who placed the success of the Mennonite immigration above the comforts of his own family, but most of all worried about his fiancee, Gertrude Penner, who at this time was impatiently writing him whether she should brave the ocean voyage alone, or wait for her parents, which might take at least another year or two before they would be ready to leave.[25] The matter came to a head in March, 1874, shortly before Cornelius Jansen was called to Washington, to sponsor the legislation in Congress. Margarete, who repeatedly referred to these unpleasant events, wrote March 4, 1874:

> Yesterday and today were most difficult days for us. And even if I write nothing about them I shall never forget them. May God have pity on us, and in this foreign land, surrounded by strangers, give us at least peace and love in our own family. Oh how much we need this kindness and love! If only Peter would think less of himself and be more humble how that would change matters. We were so anxious to have him return and longed so to see him, [that was the trip he and Schantz took to Washington] and now he is only thinking of himself and thereby irritates father and makes him unhappy.[26]

On the tenth and especially on the twenty-first, she again referred to this subject. She wrote that for many days she had not written in her diary, yet she would never forget them. "They were days of many heartaches, worries and sorrow. Father's and Mother's hair have turned much grayer, and all because of our dear brother Peter, who wants to go his own way, and in his misconception of things even thinks that what he wants is God's will. Today is his birthday, but oh how he starts the new year."[27] Cornelius Jansen also referred to those days as having been very difficult.[28]

Such experiences of course come in every family, especially where there are active boys, and no doubt the conditions and circumstances during which they came helped to frustrate the active mind of Peter, whose solution probably was that he should return to Danzig, Germany, to bring Gertrude to the States, to which the parents objected. Peter was learning his first great lesson in self-discipline and was finding it a little difficult to subject his own interest and that of his loved one to those of the larger group of Mennonites of which he was a part, whose welfare his father was so patiently seeking.

But there were some things that they liked about Berlin, Ontario. They made friends with the neighbors and enjoyed them. The long winter with the deep snow made for good sleigh riding. And frequently the Schantz's and other neighbors took them out riding. This was fun and the family loved it. And in the fall and spring of the year they enjoyed the wonderful scenes of nature. Often members of the family, especially Father Jansen and his daughter Margarete, would go out walking into a small grove of trees, situated near a body of water and there watch the sun set. Of this Margarete wrote:

> . . . the sun was slowly disappearing, throwing its radiant crimson rays upon the water, leaving a picture indescribably beautiful; especially as the sun gradually disappeared behind the trees, and left us alone with those beautiful golden sunlit clouds. Oh! how I love such views, and father too. And occasions like this always remind me of Anna and Heinrich, [whom they had left in Prussia, but who had lived with them in Berdyansk] if only they too were here to enjoy this. But God alone knows whether we shall ever again have the privilege of all meeting together to enjoy such lovely views, like we so often used to do in Berdyansk.[29]

Moving to the United States

The absence of intimate friends, inadequate housing facilities, and the severe winter, often drove the family to letter writing and frequently they would gather around the piano and sing "old songs," especially on Sunday evenings.[30] And before long they began to long and look for a more permanent home. The desire to live in their own home cropped out time and again, especially in the spring of 1874.[31] But there were other reasons for leaving Berlin. The parents wanted the children to attend good schools. While the younger children and even Peter and John had started to attend classes shortly before they left Berlin, apparently the educational facilities were not what they were looking for.[32] Then too, there was Cornelius Jansen's health. After they had left Berlin, he wrote John Lowe, Secretary of Agriculture of Ottawa, Canada, that he had "to leave Canada for reasons of health, for a more southern climate." Yet Jansen was grateful for the liberal terms the Canadian government had offered the Mennonites and took a great interest in the Mennonite settlements in Manitoba.[33]

So on their journeys westward into Illinois, Indiana, and Iowa, Cornelius Jansen kept on the lookout for a place to live where the children could attend school while they were establishing their permanent home. They first expected to find such a place in Wadsworth, Ohio, where C. J. van der Smissen was teaching.[34] Peter Jansen wrote this in November 1873, in a letter to the manager of the Erie Railroad Company: "We intend to move before long from Canada to Wadsworth, Ohio, a little place on the Atlantic and Great Western Railroad, where we find a good college for my youngest brother, and where we can meet our friends coming in from Europe." Peter asked the Erie R. R. Co. for a reduction of rates, should they remove to this place.[35] Cornelius Jansen and son Peter stopped at Wadsworth on their second journey westward, but apparently were unable to find suitable living quarters. So on their third journey west, they looked again and this time found a place in Mount Pleasant, Iowa. The family lost no time in packing up their belongings and left for their new home.

The advance guard of the Jansen family—Peter, Anna, Tante Anna, and Barry (the large Newfoundland dog the family had purchased in Berlin,) left Berlin, Ontario, for their new home June 1, to prepare the house and make it livable. The rest of the family remained in Berlin until June 11 or 12. Margarete could hardly wait to leave, and forgot all about her diary until three weeks after they arrived in Mount Pleasant. She liked the new home, and the people were friendly. Cornelius Jansen was afflicted with lumbago (*Kreuzschmerzen*) and at times could hardly walk. This kept bothering him for some time.[36]

By the thirteenth of July he had regained his strength and he and Peter went to New York to meet a group of Russian Mennonites; which were members of the Kleine Gemeinde who settled in Jefferson County Nebraska, at the place which later became known as "Jansen." They brought these people to Clarence Center, New York, where they found temporary quarters for them. Cornelius Jansen and Peter returned to Mount Pleasant, Iowa, with three representatives to help them find new homes for the immigrants. Father Jansen stayed home with his family, while Peter left with the three delegates to show them the available lands in Kansas and Nebraska.[37]

The Jansen family had expected that among these immigrants would be their relatives, Heinrich and Anna von Riesens; for the dispatch they received read that the ship was bringing relatives. But they were disappointed. Thirteen days later, however, the Jansens received a telegram from Liverpool, England, which stated that Anna and Heinrich were waiting to take the next ship to the United States. They arrived on August 7, and Mr. and Mrs. Jansen went to New York to receive them. At last they were once more reunited with their intimate friends whom they had longed so much to see. On the fourteenth of August they happily remembered that it was a year ago when they first landed in Berlin, Ontario. But how different things were now than they had been. Some of their close friends were now with them again.[38]

On August 21, the immigrants whom Father Jansen and Peter had left at Clarence Center, N.Y., passed through Mount Pleasant on their way to Nebraska. Among them were "Uncle and Mrs. Friesen" who stayed with the Jansens for the time being, because Mrs. Friesen had a sore foot. They left October 1, to join their friends in Jefferson Country, Nebraska.[39]

Choosing Nebraska

Peter Jansen, who had taken the three delegates to see the Santa Fe Railroad lands in Kansas and the Burlington and Missouri River Railroad lands in Nebraska, had made progress. They had decided in favor of the Nebraska lands. The Burlington and Missouri River R. R. Co., whose western terminus at that time was Kearney, Nebraska, had a branch road from Crete to Beatrice. Peter discovered that this company had a compact area of 20,000 acres in Jefferson County, which although table land and therefore regarded by the natives as unfit for farming, was appraised, nevertheless, by his delegates, who were successful, experienced farmers, as good land, especially for sheep raising. Consequently they purchased the 20,000 acres at an average price of $3.75 per acre, payable in six annual installments, with 6 per cent interest on the deferred payments. This is the land on which the above mentioned Kleine Gemeinde Mennonites now made their settlement.[40]

Before Peter had left home, his father had instructed him to purchase two sections of land for the family, wherever the above-mentioned delegates selected a place for settlement. Peter did this and later wrote that he "selected a section and a half on the east side of the track where the colony was located, bordering on a wide range of prairie; which was rather hilly and rough, and which we expected would not be settled for a good many years. I selected this location with a view to utilizing the free grazing, as we had concluded to start a sheep ranch."[41]

The new settlers soon discovered that with their crude instruments they could not go down deep enough to strike well water, and for a time it seemed like the settlement might be abandoned. But A. E. Touzalin came to their rescue. He sent them experienced well drillers and set up twelve wells, free of charge. They found "sheet water" at a depth of "100 to 150 feet in inexhaustible quantity and of excellent quality."[42]

Kansas

That same fall there arrived the large Alexanderwohl congregation of some six or seven hundred souls on the *Cimbria* and the *Teutonia.* When the news of their coming reached Nebraska, Mr. and Mrs. Jansen went to New York to meet them.[43] They had many friends among these immigrants who had visited them in their home in Berdyansk, among them Jacob Buller and Dietrich Gaeddert.[44] Peter Jansen was also in New York when the immigrants of the *Cimbria* arrived, according to H. R. Voth's account, who was one of the passengers of this ship. Peter was acting as interpreter for Touzalin in the interest of the Burlington and Missouri River Railroad Company. C. B. Schmidt, agent of the Santa Fe Railroad Company, and A. E. Touzalin were both bidding for these immigrants. According to Voth the immigrants were first given a chance to inspect the Nebraska lands and then were taken by C. B. Schmidt to see the Santa Fe lands of Harvey, McPherson, Reno, and Marion counties. "When our committee returned from Kansas the 'palavers' with Touzalin and Jansen began," stated Voth who writes that he witnessed the affair. "In front of our barracks was seated the committee; in front of them in an open buggy stood Touzalin and Jansen—interpreter; and around stood the large crowd. It was a memorable moment, because it was now to be determined where our future homes would be." It was soon apparent, however, that the committee preferred the Kansas lands, for the following reasons: 1. They had found the Kansas lands covered with fine grass, which would give the settlers hay to winter their horses and cattle. 2. In Kansas they could find good well water at small depths, whereas in Nebraska the wells were deep. 3. A third objection to the Nebraska land was the sandy ridge between it and the nearest market place. While Touzalin met each objection with a generous compensating offer, the sale of the land went to C. B. Schmidt, representative of the Santa Fe Railroad Company, who stood among the emigrants from whence he quietly met all of Touzalin's offers with the statement that the Santa Fe would match any of the Touzalin offers.[45] Peter Jansen, therefore, did not come home until the ninth of October.[46]

In her diary Margarete frequently remarked that Papa and Peter were gone so often. Even when Cornelius Jansen was home, his time was often taken by immigrants, representatives of the railroad companies or steamship lines.[47] On July 26, when her father and Peter had returned from New York with a delegation of immigrants and Peter had to leave again that same night, she wrote: "It just makes me unhappy. Yet those poor people need help so badly, because they cannot make themselves understood."[48] When they were home she would go out walking with Papa, and Peter would take her out riding with his new horse, Coly, hitched to their newly purchased wagon. Their conversation would invariably drift to their loved ones in Prussia.[49]

Already on December 7, Margarete began to complain about her throat. Yet by the thirteenth it seemingly had improved. On the twentieth she attended a baptismal service and in her diary still described it with some detail. For Christmas they had decorated a small tree, which no doubt made her happy. On December 31, after a critical analysis of the past year, she wrote: "And now the year is almost past. How much cause we have to be thankful for all the good things we possess, which so many other people do not have. And yet we always want more and better things. If we could only appreciate how fortunate we are that our dear Saviour has kept us all together and protected us. How thankful we should be." Then thinking of the health of her parents, she added: "When I see how often dear Father and Mother are sick, I become fearful."[51]

On the third of January she was still attending church services, and had even accepted the responsibility of teaching a Sunday school class. But three days later, toward evening, her health began to fail, and by the tenth she was bedfast. She could not move her feet without severe pain.[52] And in spite of all available medical care they could provide, she passed away in the afternoon of January 19, at ten minutes of one. The cause of her death was diagnosed as inflamatory rheumatism. The last entry in her diary was completed by her *Papa,* her dearest friend. While we know her only through her diary, we are led to conclude that she had an admirable character. Although the entire family was grief-stricken and greatly mourned her loss, her father probably was most deeply moved. Peter later wrote about this:

> . . . She was twenty-four years old, and a girl of peculiarly good sense and sweet temper. It was a very hard blow to all of us, but particularly so to Father. There seemed to be a tender bond of love and sympathy between the two, which was really touching.[53] We buried her in the cemetery at Mt. Pleasant.[54]

Helping Immigrants

Mennonite immigration was still claiming much of Cornelius Jansen's time, during the years 1875 and 1876. Like in 1874, he still carried on heavy correspondence with the Prussian and Russian Mennonites, in an effort to induce as many as possible to emigrate. For he had lost confidence in the Russian government, which had exiled him and his family. But above all, he felt that this was an opportune time to witness for peace. He regarded this as a Christian duty. Even families without children could witness for peace by their emigration.[55] He also pointed out the advantages of conditions in one state over those of another. Of course he favored Nebraska, and was interested in establishing a large Mennonite settlement in that state. But he wanted the emigrants to make their own choice and warned against hasty and ill considered decisions. He wrote Aron Claassen, his future son-in-law, that most people purchased land without giving such an important subject due consideration. He was positive that many of them had given more thought and time to purchasing a horse (when they lived in Russia or Prussia) than they were now giving to the much more important factor of purchasing land, on which they planned to build their future home and where they would probably live the rest of their lives. He advised them to rent a house for a month or two. This would give them ample time to look around.[56] He advised those who were ready to emigrate, what to bring along. He asked them to itemize their baggage and list it as "goods only for family use." He also asked them to please be willing to comply with the requests of the immigration officers. It would avoid much trouble and delay.[57]

It was at this time too, that he corresponded with the British Friends, asking them to contribute to the cause of Mennonite immigration. After he received their generous contributions he was engaged in distributing the funds to elders of churches in Kansas and Nebraska, where he found the need to be most urgent. This also required some traveling on his part. We learn of this through his Quaker friends in England, discussed elsewhere.

In an article in the *Mennonitische Rundschau* of June 26, 1912 by Elder Jacob A. Wiebe, entitled "Von unserer Ankunft in Marion County, Kansas, Amerika," we find the following passage: "We were in need of oxen and plows to break the prairie sod, then our good friend Cornelius Jansen, known to all as Consul Jansen, loaned us one thousand dollars."

At different times Cornelius Jansen's daughter also referred to the fact that her father is continually occupied with correspondence. It seems to have affected his health. On March 13, 1875, she wrote: "Our dear Father has severe headaches. Oh that this daily writing might soon come to an end! It is entirely too much for Papa."[58]

When the newspapers printed false information about the Mennonite immigration, Cornelius Jansen regarded it his duty to correct them. Late in 1874, the Kansas newspapers had published the statement that the Mennonites were all settling in Kansas. Even the Chicago *Tribune* and other papers had carried the story. To set them right, Jansen came out with a lengthy article which was published in the Chicago *Tribune*. In it he pointed out that the Mennonites were "choosing Nebraska, Kansas, Dakota and Minnesota, though the two former states (were) receiving the majority of those coming to the United States." He also corrected the editors on a number of other historic points, saying: "It is a mistake to say that we were founded by Menno Simons, and so after him called ourselves. We claim to be only reformed and gathered by him, and trace our history back to the Waldenses, getting near, through them, to the earliest Christian congregations of the first centuries." Then he explained that the Mennonites were not coming to America to seek "better homes and to accumulate wealth." They were coming to seek religious freedom and to "carry out our principles of peace undisturbed." He went on to say that this had been the reason why years ago the Mennonites had left Holland, Switzerland, and Prussia, and added, that only "when our principles were violated and chiefly our religious liberty destroyed (did we feel) compelled to turn from our fertile farms and beautiful homes on the shores of the Black Sea and the Sea of Azov to this country and to the British province to commence anew . . . where our religious rights will be respected." He then ventured to predict that, "as our fathers made fertile their settlements in the wild region of South Russia, so we also hope to cover with wheat and flocks of sheep the prairie where our new homes will be."[59]

Boosting Nebraska

Jansen then returned to the discussion of the Mennonite settlements in America, saying that the first arrivals had settled largely in Minnesota and South Dakota, without first seeing the lands of Nebraska. Only a few of the emigrants that went to Kansas had actually settled there. Then he mentioned that 120 families had settled in Nebraska on some 50,000 acres purchased from the Burlington & Missouri River Railroad Company. This railroad, he pointed out, had built three large immigrant houses for the Mennonites, in addition to ones previously established. It had also sold them the land at a low price and given them cheap fare and freight rates. Jansen then predicted that a thousand additional families would emigrate to the States during the ensuing year and asked that they be given an opportunity to choose their own place of settlement, unhindered.

In his opinion, however, Nebraska was by far the best western state for the Mennonite people. It offered splendid agricultural opportunities, which could not be said of all localities west of the Missouri River. Furthermore, Nebraska was a good wheat state, had good markets with three railroads leading to Chicago, and offered religious and social freedom.[60] In another article he pointed out that the climate in Nebraska was decidely healthier than that of Kansas, not so much adapted to fever and ague, nor did it have such droughts and sickening heat as Kansas.[61] But like a good salesman and booster for Nebraska, he did not mention the number of Mennonite families that had actually settled in Kansas, nor did he mention any of its good points.

Mrs. Jansen also took time out to write her friends about America. She told them about the good characteristics of the American people, how the Temperance League had been successful in keeping the liquor dealers out of Mt. Pleasant, Iowa. The ministers were fighting these dealers, holding them responsible for crimes committed by their drunken patrons.[62] She too was sold on Nebraska. She told Aron Claassen, who had visited them in Mt. Pleasant, Iowa, the previous year, that in New York nobody knew anything about Nebraska. Emigrants landing there were sent directly to Kansas, via St. Louis and Atchison.[63] She wrote how an Abram Peters family had found their way to Nebraska *via* Kansas, and added: "Whom the Lord wants in Nebraska, he will get there, even though it is *via* Kansas, Iowa, Dakota, Minnesota and Manitoba."[64]

During the years 1875-76, Cornelius Jansen and Peter traveled much, as referred to above. In May 1875, Father Jansen and Peter were gone for eight days. They were probably in Nebraska planning the ranch buildings, for they brought with them Abraham Friesen from the new Nebraska settlement.[65] In August, Cornelius Jansen went east to meet some emigrants from Russia.[66] In October he again left for Nebraska, this time to inspect the lands of Webster and Franklin counties, apparently working under the direction of Touzalin.[67] In February, May and June of 1876 he was with Peter and John on the ranch.[68] This place was beginning to occupy more and more of the family's time.

Arrival of Prussian Mennonites

In March and April of 1876, the Jansens spent some time finding temporary living quarters for some of the Prussian Mennonites contemplating emigration. These immigrants had followed Cornelius Jansen's suggestion to take time to find a home, and had asked the Jansens to help them find temporary living quarters for them.[69] The Jansens were successful in locating a number of houses in Mt. Pleasant, varying in rates from $7 to $20 a month per house, but they were all somewhat dilapidated and dirty. "But ours looked just like that when we first saw it," wrote Anna.[70] She knew because she had helped clean it.

Finally, on August 28, 1876, the long looked-for steamer with the Prussian Mennonite families arrived at Hoboken, New York. This was the group of immigrants Peter had impatiently waited for. Using good psychology, Father Jansen let Peter have the whole show with these immigrants, for his fiancee would be among them. Peter arrived at New York several days ahead of time and had planned to see the world's fair, which was held that year at Philadelphia. But he soon discovered that on occasions like that even a world's fair could not hold his attention, and he left for New York where he waited a whole day for the arrival of the steamer. Is it any wonder that he saw Gertrude smiling through a porthole before the steamer landed?[71]

Peter had secured a special car on which he now took the favored immigrants to Mt. Pleasant, where they stayed for the winter. But as soon as the families were quartered the leading men started out to select a location to build their homes. Peter, of course, was anxious to have them settle in Nebraska and describes his anxiety in these words: "It was up to me to see that they came to Nebraska. I was kept on the anxious seat for some time, as they examined lands in Kansas and other states. However, Nebraska suited them best, and I felt very much relieved when my present brother-in-law, John Penner, signed the first contract for this land purchase."[72] They settled in Gage County, the adjoining county of Jefferson, where the Kleine Gemeinde Mennonites had settled. Peter regarded these as "probably the best immigrants that ever came to the West in a large body." Most of them were well-to-do; some had large fortunes; they were well dressed and had good manners, quite different from the usual class of immigrants then coming to this country by the thousands. Peter was proud of them. In the spring of 1877, they moved to Gage County, Nebraska, to establish new homes in this land of opportunity. The Cornelius Jansen family left its temporary home in Mt. Pleasant in November, 1877, and settled in the little town of Beatrice, Gage County, Nebraska, where Cornelius Jansen had purchased a stone house on South Second Street.[73]

Mt. Pleasant, Iowa, had been quite an improvement for them over Berlin, Ontario. True, there they had buried Margarete and still missed her very much, but they knew that she was removed from all earthly sorrow and suffering. Mt. Pleasant too, had brought them one step closer to Beatrice, their permanent home. Cornelius and Helena had attended school, and Helena had progressed to the point where she was ready to start teaching. Their Russian and Prussian friends had finally arrived and had decided to make their homes with them in Nebraska. Anna wrote that that had changed everything.[74] It was all like a dream to her. The ranch land had been purchased and the boys were working hard to build it according to their dreams.

The Ranch

Cornelius Jansen helped his sons, Peter and John, establish the ranch. In the spring of 1875, the three went to their newly-purchased land in Jefferson County, Nebraska, to select the building site, plan the sheep sheds, the corrals, and other establishments. Peter later wrote about this: "I shall always remember how Father took a piece of board and wrote on it with pencil: 'With God's help, we will here build our new home,' and stuck it in the ground."[75] On this virgin prairie they built a large sheep shed, for they anticipated raising large flocks of sheep, and in Russian style, partitioned off a room in one end of the building where the two brothers batched the first winter. But they often came home, and when they did, Mother Jansen, like all good mothers, would send along a generous supply of well-cooked food. Roasted ducks, baked *Zwieback,* potatoes, and apples was the portion she sent along December 30, 1875.[76]

Peter indicated in his *Memoirs* that his father had the idea of starting a cooperative sheep ranch in which they would buy the sheep, furnish the sheds, corrals, and shepherds while the new settlers were to furnish the hay and grain necessary to keep the flocks during the winter, pay half of the other expenses and divide the profit at the end of the year. Peter Jansen and his brother John went to Wisconsin and New York, bought the sheep and started the venture. He states further that this plan seemed plausible in theory but did not work out in practice, so they bought out their partners and ran the ranch independently.[77]

Life on the ranch fascinated the Jansen brothers. It was pioneer life on the "wild, open prairie," and they enjoyed "ruffing it," and loved to watch the changes wrought by the hard labor of this Mennonite settlement. Although the wild prairies were no longer inhabited by the wild buffalo, it still had the dangerous rattlesnake, and wild game was abundant, including flocks of wild ducks, geese and prairie chickens. This gave them plenty of wild meat, even to the point where they had "quail on toast" for breakfast.[78]

The boys fell victim to some pioneer habits. Peter regretfully relates an interesting story of his experience with the "filthy American habit of chewing";

> . . . One day we had gotten in a new supply of groceries and also a big plug of what was known as 'Star' chewing tobacco. Next morning I started out on my pony with the sheep, the plug in my pocket, anticipating a good time. Soon a severe thunder storm came up; lightning was striking all around me. I felt sure I would be hit and they would find me dead with the big plug of tobacco in my pocket. My mother knew nothing of my bad habit, and I also knew that it would nearly kill her to find out, so I threw the plug far away and felt better—for a while. The clouds soon passed away, however, and the sun came out brightly and soon found me hunting for the plug, which to my great disappointment, I never recovered.[79]

It is just possible that a part of the story about this event found its way to Mt. Pleasant, Iowa, for one day in February, 1876, Anna wrote in her diary: "Peter and also Johannes, with God's help, for some reason or another have entirely given up the use of tobacco."[80]

During the first few years both Peter and John worked on the sheep ranch and farm for their father, apparently sharing in the profits, with the father retaining supervision. In June, 1876, they sheared the first crop of wool from the 1,500 sheep and 500 lambs they had on their ranch.[81] Peter wrote that they sold the wool for twenty-five cents a pound, which netted them "a handsome profit."[82] Thus they got off to a good start, and kept increasing the flock from year to year.

The Beatrice Weekly Express carried a description of the Jansen sheep ranch which account was based on a visit to the ranch by three Nebraska sheep-growers. The visit was made on January 7, 1876, approximately twenty months after Jansen settled in Jefferson County. These men reported:

> Here we find indications of such prosperity as we had in our mind's eye to be our own some time in the future. Substantial shed on the north and west with gable roof 360 feet in length. Yards are large and numerous giving separate space for different ages, sexes and conditions. On a gentle slope to the south is a lot of ten acres enclosed with a five-board fence with cedar posts where the flock can be turned for feeding

> and exercise. Here are the wells for the use of the stock. Just below this lot on one side we saw a dam across a ravine, which when filled will do away with the labor of watering. The flock numbering 1,500 to 2,000 sheep is made up of selections from some of the best flocks of Wisconsin, Iowa, and New York.[83]

Even though the sheep industry grew into large proportions, the Jansen family believed in diversified farming. In line with this, Cornelius Jansen sent to Russia for seed of the Russian mulberry which he distributed among the Mennonite settlements with the purpose of establishing the silkworm culture as practiced in Southern Russia. However, it was found that the climate of the plains was not suitable for this. A letter announcing the shipment of lots of mulberry seeds from Tiefengrund, Russia, is in the Jansen Collection. One of the trees planted for this early silkworm industry in the Jansen community is still growing today (1955). It is located on the Peter E. Friesen residence, on the north edge of the Jansen village, just across the road from the Evangelical Mennonite Church.

In a few years after the Jansens had started their ranch they had several hundred acres of land under cultivation. From the beginning they had their own registered cattle,[84] and raised spring wheat, but soon changed to winter wheat, with corn and oats to feed their stock. They also planted an orchard including fruit trees and grape vines, one hundred catalpa and two hundred mulberry trees; like the Mennonites used to do in Russia.[85] They improved the front yard, and before many years the "Jansen's Ranch," as it came to be known, became a landmark and had the reputation of being the "finest in the country."[86]

About this time too, the telephone lines were built, connecting the ranch with Beatrice. The mail service came about a year later, giving the ranch, as well as the settlers the daily mail service, which was a great improvement. Thus Beatrice and the ranch, eighteen miles distant, became closely linked with each other.[87]

Father Jansen frequently visited the ranch, especially after they lived in Beatrice. For him it soon became a place of real relaxation from his immigration and routine work at home. It also must have given him a feeling of deep satisfaction to help build up a new settlement—to see the vast fields of wild prairie lands changed into fruitful farms dotted with beautiful homes, surrounded by fruitful orchards, herds of cattle, with horses and sheep grazing in the pastures; and in spring and summer to see the vast fields of wheat and corn swaying in the wind. The whole family enjoyed going to the ranch, even *Tante* Anna. For all of them, it was a happy diversion from the daily routine of homelife. But with the arrival of the Prussian Mennonites, things began to change on the ranch, especially as Peter's and Gertrude's dreams were translated into reality.

On the twenty-fourth of February, 1877, the Cornelius Jansens and the Andreas and Catharina Goossen Penners celebrated the betrothal of their respective son and daughter, Peter and Gertrude. As was then customary among the Mennonites, the young bride and bridegroom visited their friends and relatives, presenting themselves as an engaged couple. It was always a jolly, festive occasion, made merry with elaborate meals. Peter had prepared for this occasion by purchasing a beautiful black mare for the then exhorbitant price of $200. The nice Studebaker buggy, he had secured as a commission from a company for procuring wagons for the Jefferson County settlers. In this "rig" he proudly sported his beautiful bride. The event was climaxed by the marriage which took place on the fourth of May in Beatrice, Nebraska.[88] The day following the wedding Peter and Gertrude moved on to the ranch, but before they got there, his spirited span of horses had upset the vehicle and spilled both of them, but fortunately, nobody was seriously hurt.[89] And on the eighteenth of July, Cornelius Jansen gave the management of the ranch into the hands of Peter and Gertrude. That night Anna wrote in her diary, "May God grant him the necessary wisdom."[90] This business relationship lasted until Peter's brother, John was married in 1882, when he replaced Peter, who by this time had saved enough money to purchase his own land, had built buildings on it, and had become a prosperous farmer. God had given him "wisdom" and he profited by it.[91]

Peter, although vivacious, was good at heart, and was willing to risk his life to save that of another. An event which showed his courage took place on the ranch several years after they were married. Peter also tells this story:

> . . . One Sunday afternoon, wife and I were sitting on the porch of our small frame house, while our baby was playing a few feet away at a pile of sand. Our attention was attracted by her loud and gleeful crooning. Looking up, we saw her poking a stick at a big rattler, coiled, ready to spring, about three feet away. I have always detested

> snakes and would have given even a harmless bull snake a wide berth. However, on this occasion, I took one big jump and landed on Mr. Rattler with both feet, while my wife snatched the baby out of harm's way.[92]

But they had other frontier experiences on the ranch. One December evening in 1877, shortly after Peter's marriage, two men on horseback came riding onto the yard, soon followed by two others. Sometime later a wagon drove up with drunken men who talked with the men on horseback. It looked like they were all members of one gang, trying to conceal their ulterior motives. Peter and his hired man Kunkel were not at home. This left John with a second hired man alone, together with the women folks, Anna and Gertrude, Peter's wife. The men on horseback asked to stay for the night. John and Jacob were afraid to let them stay for fear that they might be horse thieves. They looked suspicious to them. The women folks were of little help. Anna, who had come there to help Gertrude, was suffering from a bad toothache and was of little moral support. Gertrude, a new arrival from Prussia and unfamiliar with frontier life, was frightened to the point where she shook all over. It was dark before the men on the wagon left the yard. Still the other men lingered. Before long, fortunately, Peter and Kunkel came home. After observing the strange men carefully, Kunkel admitted that they looked and acted very suspicious, and agreed that they might be horse thieves. So Peter ordered them off the yard, and showed them the way to the nearest town.[93]

Nebraska, like Kansas, was occasionally visited by severe snow blizzards. Peter wrote that those early winters seemed to be more severe than later "and the snow storms or blizzards were much fiercer, probably because the wind had an unrestricted sweep over the vast prairies." In the dead of winter of 1880, the early settlers experienced one of these severe blizzards. It started with a gentle fall of snow, lasting for a day, then suddenly the wind veered to the north and the next moment the air seemed like "a sea of milk," wrote Peter, limiting visibility to less than three rods. The Jansens had built a corral and sheep shed for the wethers about a mile and a half from the house, and placed it under the care of a herder. Peter describes how they were caught in an effort to reach the corral:

> . . . We were very anxious to know the fate of our herder and his band of sheep, and towards noon I attempted to reach them, hitching

> a pair of horses to a sleigh and taking a man along. We got lost and drove around in a circle, blinded by the snow, for hours, my companion giving up and resigning himself to death. We probably would have both perished had it not been for the sagacity of my near horse, to which I finally gave the rein, being benumbed myself. He brought us home, and you may believe the barking of the shepherd dogs sounded very musical to me as we neared the barn.[94]

Peter also recounts the historic blizzard of February 1888, with its terrible drifts. It was this blizzard that brought such terrible destruction of livestock to western Kansas. He describes it as one of the worst ones he ever experienced. It had been snowing steadily since morning that day, without wind, covering the ground to a depth of about twelve inches with loose snow. The temperature was just below freezing. Suddenly the wind whipped around to the north and soon obstructed visibility to less than a rod. The blizzard kept on for twenty-four hours without abating. Transportation was unthinkable. In the excitement of trying to shelter his flocks, Peter had momentarily forgotten that he had sent Carl Bernhard, one of his trusted helpers, a native of Württemberg, to the village of Jansen, to get the mail. Although very accommodating and trustworthy, Peter writes that he was "not very bright." About eight o'clock that evening, Peter talked with him over the telephone and told him to leave the mules at the livery stable and stay at the hotel at Jansen for the night. But the faithful mail carrier, disregarding Peter's advice, had slung the mail pouch over his shoulder and in the blinding snowstorm walked for four miles, "feeling his way from one telephone pole to the next one, floundering through drifts of snow six feet deep, often losing his way but never giving up." When finally he reached the house door at midnight, "looking like a veritable Santa," he was all exhausted and could hardly stand. But he brought the mail to Peter, even though under the hazard of his own life.[95]

The ranch was always operated in an atmosphere of bigness. There were nearly always a large number of hired men about the place. Tenant houses and a public school building were standing near the ranch home to form a little village at this spot. The tenant houses were occupied by the families of the regular workers, and during corn-husking season or sheep-shearing time there was always a host of additional men around.

The central operation headquarters were at the ranch home. A scale house served as the headquarters for the foreman and was located west and slightly south of the house. Farther out around the periphery of the farmyard and located on a gentle slope away from the house were the barns, sheep-sheds, corrals, corn cribs, granaries and four windmills.[96] Some of the tenant houses were situated across the road north of the house and others on the south side next to the ranch house but all spaced so that one did not have the feeling of being crowded.

Ranch operations were highly organized. Peter Jansen had a private office in his ranch home with two doors, one leading into his living quarters and the other an outside exit. A special bell on the outside door was to be used to gain entrance from the outside. Jansen used his office for interviews with railroad representatives, government officials, businessmen, the ranch foremen, and others who oftentimes traveled great distances to see him. Also, he had a special telephone line from his office to the foreman headquarters in the scale house so that efficient contacts were always possible.

Jansen's work took him away from the ranch quite frequently and occasionally for an extended period of time. The ranch operations continued just the same in Jansen's absence under the capable and experienced management of the long-time foreman, Frank Penner. Penner, who served Peter Jansen for over twenty years, was in time entrusted with almost complete authority to operate the place according to his own judgment. His position as head foreman was highly respected by the workers and also wisely administered.

Each morning the workers would get their teams ready and come to the foreman's office at 7 o'clock for instructions. Activities would then continue in almost regimental fashion. The teams in good harness and shining buckles, curried and sleek and with a fresh appearance, were lined up one behind the other, and each worker stopped to receive his order for the day's work from the foreman. After instructions were given the drivers started the teams down the land to the fields in an orderly and almost dignified fashion. According to the testimonies of those who saw or engaged in this procedure, this was an unusually interesting sight. Each driver had a well-matched, four abreast team. Each animal in itself was a fine specimen and to see the team combinations marching in an orderly procession to begin the day's work was enough to arouse a sense of pride among the workers themselves.[97]

Jansen and his associates were extremely successful financially, particularly in the early years of the sheep raising enterprise when grazing resources were abundant and at almost no cost. Jansen gives an interesting response to what was apparently an interrogation as to his financial worth after nine years of living in Nebraska. This reply was addressed to R. R. Randall, implement agent.

> I send you my report for the 1882 crop. I am not able to tell you what I am worth, or what I have made in the nine years I have been in Nebraska but I will say we have done very well and would not swap my sheep ranch today for the Russian emperor's whole empire.
>
> I raised 320 acres of corn, 12,800 bushels, worth 38 cents per bushel; 100 acres of oats, 3,000 bushels, 30 cents per bushel. The corn was cut down by hail June 24, 1882, or my average would have been 15 or 20 bushels more per acre. My oats were badly damaged from the same hailstorms.
>
> —Peter Jansen, Fairbury, Jefferson County, Nebraska[98]

Another brief news item in the paper supports further the fact of Jansen's financial success with the ranch operations. It states, "Mr. Jansen is a shrewd and successful speculator. His sheep sales this spring yielded him a handsome profit.[99]

In the latter 1880's Peter Jansen formed a partnership with Charles Owen, another sheep raiser from Colorado. This partnership was formed because it became necessary with the changing times to change the methods in the sheep business. After settlers moved in and people were confined to their own land, it became impossible to graze the sheep on the open prairie. It was for this reason that Jansen changed from "raising" to "fattening" sheep. This partnership was called "Peter Jansen and Company." They would buy sheep from the west in the fall of the year, feed them corn, oats and hay in the winter, shear them in the spring, then ship them to the Chicago market. In their big years they would feed in the neighborhood of twenty-five thousand sheep. It was while in this partnership fattening business that they had their record season of 25,800 head.[100]

Peter Jansen summarizes the extent of his sheep business in a letter to the editor of the *Fairbury Journal*.[101] This letter is headed by the editor's title "Peter's Valedictory." In this letter he states:

> During the 35 years since I came to Jefferson County and started raising and fattening sheep, I have handled over 350,000 head, shipping a great many as far west as Oregon. I have shipped into my feed lots

at Jansen and on the home place as high as a hundred double-deck cars in the fall, shipping out a hundred and twenty in the spring, the increase being caused by the gain in weight and the wool.

The sheep consumed over a million bushels of corn, about 35,000 tons of rough feed, besides oil cake and bran.

In all of these shipping operations I have been lucky enough not to lose a single man nor even have had a bad accident.

I have produced and shipped during this period over a million pounds of wool . . . .

When I look back over my 35 year's career in Jefferson County, I have abundant reasons to feel thankful. I have made a good many mistakes, like all mortals, but I hope they were mistakes of the head and not the heart.

Jansen pays high tribute to his hired men, particularly to the two who remained with him for an extended period of time. Frank Penner in time became the manager of the ranch or home place, and P. A. Buller, "P. A." as they called him, was manager of the "Peter Jansen and Company" sheep feeding and fattening business. The headquarters for this latter business was located near the village of Jansen, across the tracks a short distance southwest of town, approximately four miles from the ranch. Peter Jansen calls these men his faithful lieutenants. He states in "Peter's Valedictory," mentioned above, and in his *Memoirs,* that it was seldom necessary for these men to report a loss of an animal, and that only through their capable and efficient management were they able to operate the ranch and the feeding business successfully.

The ranch, of course, was the chief source of income for the Cornelius Jansen family. While we do not have the detailed information about the financial income derived from it, there is ample evidence that they greatly benefited from it and built up a nice fortune for the family. Peter Jansen's property alone, for the years 1885-1887, increased in value from $37,000 to $56,000, respectively.[108] There is every reason to believe that Father Jansen's ranch was equally productive and over a period of years netted the family a handsome profit.

Peter Jansen continued operating the ranch until 1909. On February 20, of that year the land was deeded to Charles Caldwell[109] and Jansen moved to Beatrice. The later years of Peter Jansen's experience are often spoken of with some feeling of remorse. It appears that he was confronted at times with financial difficulties in that later 1890's and up to the time he sold out in 1909. Some of this difficulty was caused by his son who was in business in Canada and who was faced a number of times with embarrassing financial obligations which he was unable to meet and Peter Jansen, the faithful father, continued to help his son as long as he was able.

The Early Jansen Community

The Jansens purchased land and established a home in the area which is today the Jansen Community. They were also instrumental in influencing other immigrants to settle here. The Jansen community was consequently the recipient of a part of the flow of migrants which left Russia in the 1870's.

The first larger group of Mennonite settlers in Jefferson County was comprised of thirty-six families, all of the Kleine Gemeinde. Cornelius and Peter Jansen (Mrs. Cornelius Jansen was related to some members of the Kleine Gemeinde) contacted the group in New York and informed them of the possibilities of the choice land in Nebraska. Leaders of the group were issued passes by the railroad company to tour the states of Minnesota, the Dakotas, Nebraska, and Kansas. The prospective settlers selected Nebraska as the best location because here they could get a large solid block of good fertile soil at low cost and it was considered to be a happy medium so far as climatic conditions were concerned.

The Kleine Gemeinde Mennonites settled in the following villages: Rosenhof, Rosenort, Rosenfeld, Rosental, Heuboden, Neuanlag, and Blumenort. The two villages at the south edge of the settlement, Rosenhof and Rosenort, included nearly nine sections of land, forming a rectangle two by four and one-half miles. Shortly after the first settlement was made, Rosenhof was extended one-half mile farther west which then made the combined east-west section length of the two villages five miles. A road cut through the central east-west section line and was lined on both sides by the residences of the Russian immigrants. This road later acquired the name, "Russian Lane," and became a popular road for sight-seers.

The early settlers in the Jansen community brought along with them the culture they had developed in the old country. They developed economic patterns which were similar in nature to those of their former homelands. This cultural transplantation was reflected in various phases of their living.

They settled in compact villages. Residences were established close together, usually along both sides of the section lines. The farm for each family extended in a long narrow strip back of the residence, usually to the next section line. Thus, in general, the farms were one mile long and varied in width from perhaps a few hundred feet to one-fourth mile or occasionally a greater width. The one-fourth mile wide farm would contain 160 acres, and many of the narrow farms were eighty acres and some only sixty acres, but in mile-long strips. Thus one might well visualize the unusual pattern by the large number of narrow strip farms.[110]

The largest settlement was along the section lines running east and west at the north edge of present-day Jansen. This settlement extended four and one-half miles in length, two miles east and one and one half miles west of the section on which Jansen is located today. This settlement included both Rosenort and Rosenhof.

Along this four and one-half miles of "Russian Lane" there had been erected at some time since 1874, a total of thirty-seven dwellings, three church buildings, two schools, and three cemeteries. Thirty-six of the thirty-seven dwelling houses were standing at one time. Also at this time, two of the churches, one school and three cemeteries were serving their various functions. At the peak of this "Russian settlement," there was a total of forty-two dwellings, churches, schools and cemeteries in use simultaneously along a road four and one-half miles long. According to the opinions of the older residents in the community, this peak occurred in the years between 1890 and 1900. (See map, Appendix VII.)

Worship services of the Kleine Gemeinde congregation were organized immediately after their arrival in 1874. They first met in homes but in a short time began construction of their church building near the center of their settlement located two miles west and three north of the present site of Jansen.

This congregation operated and increased in number in Jefferson County until the year 1906. By this time certain pressures were bearing upon the group and migrations to Meade, Kansas, were begun. For some time they had been feeling a need for more land in order to accommodate their young people with farms. The families were large and available land scarce and becoming more costly. Because of the increasingly crowded conditions in the rural areas around

Jansen, isolation was becoming more and more difficult and even impossible, while the Meade, Kansas, area which had been inspected in view of a new location, was still relatively unsettled and an abundance of land was available at a low cost. The infiltration of new religious views, causing the disintegration of the traditional way of life was also an important factor causing dissatisfaction among the more conservative element. Consequently they sold their land in Nebraska, bought new land at Meade and migrated again. Within a period of three years—1906, 1907, and 1908—the entire Kleine Gemeinde group migrated as a body from the Jansen community to Meade, Kansas, with the exception of those that had joined other Mennonite groups.

Town of Jansen

The town of Jansen was started in 1886, after the Rock Island Railroad was surveyed from St. Joseph via Beatrice to Fairbury. The railroad company erected a depot at the south edge of what was to be the site of Jansen. This is still standing and serving its function today. Peter Jansen took an active part representing the railroad in buying right-of-way, voting bonds, and so forth. He purchased eighty acres (S½ of NW¼ of Section 34), forty acres each from Peter Isaac and Martin Barkman. Isaac and Barkman had purchased this land from the Burlington and Missouri Railroad in 1874. Jansen acquired it August 28, 1886, planned the town and the railroad officials named it "Jansen" in his honor and to his great satisfaction. On October 1, 1886, it was deeded to the "Town of Jansen."[111]

The railroad ran diagonally almost directly through the middle of Jansen's eighty-acre plot of land. It entered approximately one hundred yards south of the northeast corner and came out at the southwest corner. The land to the north of the tract was considered the "Town of Jansen."

Peter Jansen used various methods to attract prospective businessmen to the town. He had circulars printed which mapped the layout of the town with the streets and lot numbers. This circular also indicated the location of Jansen in relation to Fairbury, and stated that "lots for improvement are offered at low prices and on favorable terms."[112] These circulars were distributed, ads were run[113] and news accounts appeared in the papers which were intended to encourage people to settle and start businesses in town. The following are some excerpts from the first column entitled "Jansen Items" that appeared in *The Fairbury Gazette.*

> Our town is booming. . . . Friesen Bros. have their shop completed and are doing a big pump and windmill business. . . . Henry and Coatsworth bought two more lots to have more room for their lumber yard . . . elevator is paying highest prices for all kinds of grain . . . hotel is ready for the plasterers . . . Thiessen's hardware store is progressing rapidly. . . . Everybody invited to invest in Jansen before it is too late, and all lots gone.[114]

The Jansen town plot was laid October 1, 1886. Lots were sold and buildings were begun immediately thereafter. A few discrepancies appear as to the actual beginning of the first building or business. This, no doubt, is due to the fact that when the railroad came through, the town was planned and the early developments moved rapidly. Several stores, business places and residences got underway within the first months of the town's history. Construction on several places was in progress and reached completion at approximately the same time. Within the first year after the town was platted there were thirteen distinct businesses operating in Jansen. These early business operations, with the year and month in which each is first referred to in print, are listed below. (It should be noted that the date given for each is not necessarily the date this business was established, but is only the date on which first reference was made to it in the paper.)

Thiessen's Hardware & Implement (March, 1887)
Friesen Bros. Implement (March, 1887)
Henry & Coatsworth Lumber (March, 1887)
Elevator (March, 1887)
Hotel (March, 1887)
Carpenter Shop (April, 1887)
Drug Store (May, 1887)
Medical Doctor (May, 1887)
General Store (June, 1887)
Bank (August, 1887)
Barber Shop (August, 1887)
Shoe Shop (August, 1887)
Koop Bros. & Barkman Store (September, 1887)[115]

The *Fairbury Gazette* (1886-1906) makes some reference to each of the businesses mentioned above and also to twenty-three other businesses which were begun in this period.[116]

When the original town lots were sold, the deed for each lot contained a clause stating that

> Intoxicating liquors shall not be manufactured, sold or given away in any place of public resort as a beverage on said premises and in case this condition be broken or violated this conveyance shall be null and void.[117]

It was apparently Peter Jansen's intention that liquor would never be sold in the town of Jansen. Even though the prohibitive clause was effective on the town lots for a period of time, there was no prohibitive clause on the lots which were conveniently located just outside the city limits. In effect, the town of Jansen never went without a saloon. In May, 1892, there were two saloons operating, both located across the road north of the town's original boundary line, one on each side of the main (Broad) street and actually very centrally and conveniently located. This property on which these saloons were located became a part of the town of Jansen on November 5, 1887. It is known as the "Heidelk Addition."

The first saloon was operating prior to August, 1888.[118] At this time it was ordered to close its doors because of "license elapsed." In 1892, the second saloon was erected and on May 28, 1892, the paper reports that "two saloons are more hilarity than one."[119] Several months after the two saloons were operating, one of them featuring a monkey which was purchased in Beatrice and brought to the saloon to offer added attraction and entertainment.[120]

In September, 1896, a saloon was opened within the boundaries of the original town. It is reported by residents of Jansen that one lot (lot 7, block 8) had been sold without a deed containing the prohibitive clause. A saloon was then set up here, and Henry Fette was the first liquor dealer in the town.

The reason for this one lot being sold without the prohibitive clause, as explained by individuals interviewed, is as follows. When Peter Jansen began selling lots for the town, he had special forms prepared for the deeds in which provisions for the clause were printed on each form. As the story goes, Peter Jansen was in Fairbury one day and contacted a prospective shoemaker who was willing to buy a lot to start the much needed shoe store in Jansen. Peter Jansen did not have his special form on hand at the time. Consequently, rather than losing the sale, he transacted the deal on a standard form thereby omitting the clause. Shortly after this deal, the shoemaker sold the lot and later it was leased to a brewing company which in turn was responsible for starting the saloon in town.[121]

In summarizing the discussion on the Jansen village, we might say that, as the traveler speeds along today on State Highway No. 3, between Beatrice and Fairbury, he will perhaps hardly notice the small town of Jansen. However, in spite of its small size (pop. 250) it is an active town which does a big volume of business over a wide trade area, considering its size. The chief businesses in the village are electrical appliance sales; farm machinery, equipment, hardware and lumber sales; mill and elevator; grocery stores; dine and dance taverns; and, the bank which was founded by Peter Jansen (1887) and which has operated continuously ever since its beginning. However, Peter Jansen's activities were not restricted to business and the building up and developing of the town of Jansen. He also played a significant role in the public life of the state of Nebraska and beyond. In this respect he followed in the footsteps of his father who was active in public affairs, such as the consular service in Berdyansk.

Peter Jansen in Public Life

Many of Peter Jansen's trips took him to Chicago, Denver, St. Joseph and Kansas City, where he usually purchased or sold his sheep. His sheep business grew into quite an enterprise. In July, 1891, on one of his many trips to Denver, he purchased ten thousand head of sheep.[122] That same year in November, he brought home from the reserves twenty-one thousand sheep and lost only two on the road.[123] He made most of his money by fattening the sheep, and then selling the wool and sheep. Yet Peter was a diversified farmer. During that same year, 1891, he sold eight thousand bushels of wheat and raised corn. The yield of his wheat the following year averaged thirty bushels to the acre.[124] Much of the money he made off the ranch he invested in real estate. By August 1894, he had purchased 1,631.30 acres of land in Nebraska and Kansas; plus four city lots in Jansen and two in Diller, Nebraska.[125] But the year 1894-95 proved to be less profitable. The dry summer of 1894 with the accompanying hot winds withered and ruined the corn crop. Also, the price of sheep, suffering from the panic of 1893, dropped to a new low where the industry practically lost its profit.[126] But the Peter Jansen family had made their fortune and Peter could devote his attention to other interests.

Peter's active and dynamic personality, influenced by the numerous contacts with his business friends, awakened in him desires which at times somewhat strained the tenets of his Mennonite upbringing. Among others, he tugged with such questions as life insurance. The unfortunate name attached to this type of investment gave the impression to many Mennonites, when first they came in contact with it, that the thing was unbiblical because by taking out a policy you were relinquishing your trust in God and placing it in a life insurance company. So one day when Leonhard Sudermann from Kansas was visiting at the home of Peter's parents, Peter asked him about it. No doubt to his disappointment he found him also opposed to it.[127]

But when Peter visited the Kansas Mennonites, that same month, he returned with the information that those people in Kansas all had their own wine, and in general he had found them to be more liberal.[128] Mrs. Jansen had no comment to make, at least she did not enter it.

Peter's interest in politics grew with the passing years. He became a staunch Republican and remained so to the end. He was an advocate of the "gold standard," and a supporter and personal friend of President William McKinley. A statement from his *Memoirs* indicates quite clearly his political views. It was made in regard to the Cleveland administration which came into power in 1893.

> For over a year we have had genuine democratic times; banks failing right and left; business failings doubled; money scarce, high and hard to get on the best of collateral; factories shut down; freight cars idle . . . and the worst is yet to come.[129]

His first experiences in political activity began shortly after his arrival in America. He and his father arrived in Canada in 1873. They immediately devoted themselves to the task of preparing for the arrival of more immigrants from Russia. In 1874, he and his father had an interview with President Grant regarding public lands that might be available to large bodies of Mennonites. In 1884, he was chosen as alternate delegate to the Republican National Convention in Chicago at which time James G. Blaine was nominated on the fourth ballot. In 1888, his neighbors in Jefferson County elected him without his knowledge to the office of justice of the peace. In 1896, he was delegate-at-large to the Republican National Convention which nominated William McKinley. Jansen was elected to the state Legislature representing the thirty-fourth district in the State of Nebraska in 1898. In 1899, he was named by President McKinley and approved by the Senate to become United States Commissioner to the Paris Exposition to be held in 1900. When McKinley was assassinated in 1901, Jansen was delegated by Governor Mickey to represent Nebraska at his funeral. In 1904, he represented Nebraska at the Louisiana Purchase Exposition in St. Louis, and in 1910, was elected to the state Senate in the state of Nebraska.[130] Jansen assumed the responsibilities of these various roles and performed them in a very capable and determined manner. In controversial issues he stood by what he believed even if that required standing alone.

While in the state Senate, Jansen made a blistering attack on the liquor interests when a "county option" bill came up for consideration in 1911. He favored county option and wished to eliminate the liquor interests from state politics. Excerpts from his speech are as follows:

> I want to eliminate the pernicious influence of the brewers in our state politics; they are becoming more obnoxious than the railroads ever were.
>
> We had a strong man in the governor's chair; a man, although a Democrat, who had the courage of his convictions, and who, in spite of the threats of my friends from Omaha placed his signature under the eight o'clock closing act. What was the result? The liquor interests got his scalp, as they said they would, and (I blush to say it) by the aid of Republicans, nominated Dahlman and would have elected him if he had been sober enough to stay at home.
>
> What did they do to that former idol of democracy, William Jennings Bryan, when he saw the need of delivering the Democratic party from the demon of rum? Why, they simply eliminated him from politics and relegated him to Texas.
>
> They claim county option is a step toward statewide prohibition, and I hope to God it is. But in the same breath they tell us that prohibition does not prohibit and that more liquor is sold in prohibition states than in those that have not this law. Mark their convincing logic!
>
> Before God and this honorable body, I impeach the saloon. I charge

it with the murder of the bodies and souls of innumerable thousands. I charge it with being the cause of almost all crime, almost all poverty, and almost all the ignorance afflicting our land.

Gentlemen: I implore you for the sake of the fair name of our state; for the sake of the thousands of wives and children whose husbands and fathers squander their hard-earned wages in squalid, reeking saloons; for the sake of generations still unborn—yes, on behalf of the sacred memory of your mothers, vote for this bill. I VOTE 'AYE.' [131]

In the election of 1912, Jansen lost the senatorial race to his Democratic opponent. His reactions to the loss are expressed well in an open letter to the paper. Parts of this letter are quoted below.

It seems fashionable at this season for defeated candidates to issue what you might call "post-mortem" statements, giving the why and wherefore of their defeat. The only reason I attribute mine to, is that I lacked a few votes. But after all, I find myself in very distinguished company.

However, I desire to thank my many friends for their loyal support and to assure them that I deeply appreciate their efforts on my behalf; their friendship is worth more to me than any paltry honor I might have obtained.

As is generally known, sickness in my family prevented me from making an aggressive personal campaign. I did not attend a single political meeting, nor did I attempt to make a single political speech, and under these circumstances, to be beaten by a few votes out of some 7,500 in the district is certainly nothing to be ashamed of. . . .

Thanking my friends again, I am very sincerely, Peter Jansen.[132]

In his *Memoirs* he states "Theodore Roosevelt delivered the Republican party bodily into the hands of the Democrats, and I was defeated for a re-election by thirty votes out of a total of seventy-five hundred in the two counties of Gage and Pawnee."[133]

The story is told of a rather humorous incident that occurred to Jansen during one of his political campaigns. When he was campaigning for the office of state legislator in 1898, he would go around in the community making speeches in schoolhouses. At the close of the meeting he would shake hands with and pass out cigars to the people as they filed out. On one such occasion a stout old lady was in line and as she approached Jansen she lowered her hand and with a forceful swing slapped the bottom of the box of cigars knocking it from Jansen's hand and scattering cigars in every direction, and shouted angrily, "That much for your dirty Republican cigars."

Later Jansen would jokingly comment on the assistance he had received on one occasion in distributing his cigars.[134]

During his prosperous years, Jansen was compared by some writers, with "James J. Hill and other great North Western business luminaries." This was indicated in a news story reprinted from *The Daily Province of Vancouver,* British Columbia and reprinted in one of the local papers. It stated that Peter Jansen was vice president of the Frazer Lumber Company in Canada, and that a steamship was named "Senator Jansen" in his honor.[135]

Jansen was urged at various times by his political friends to become candidate for state governor. Because of his pronounced opposition to the state militia, he refused to seek this honor. There was also the factor that he was opposed to the death penalty which the governor was required at times to execute. Thus Jansen's personal scruples prevented him from submitting to the wish of his party so far as becoming candidate for governor was concerned.

When Jansen was at the International Exposition in Europe he visited his native homelands in Russia. Being a special envoy of the United States, he visited Moscow. When he presented his credentials to De Witte, the Premier of Russia, he was standing, intimating that the interview was to be brief. When Jansen approached him with a dignified salutation in the Russian language the premier was surprised and asked him how he had learned the language. Jansen replied that he was a native of Russia and was exiled when twenty years old. De Witte then said, "How can a Russian exile come back to this country as a special representative of the great government of the United States?" Jansen, knowing De Witte to be a liberal, replied, "Because of our free institutions under which any man may become whatever he has the power to become." De Witte pointed to a chair and the interview lasted two hours.[136]

Peter Jansen was invited by the Quakers to visit the Dukhobors in Saskatchewan. This led to some settlement and business undertakings in that province.[137] At many occasions Peter Jansen helped the Mennonite constituency with advice and through mediation. In 1921, sixty-two young Russian refugees were detained at Ellis Island, New York, and it seemed almost certain that they would be deported. Jansen intervened and through his political connections and influence he was able to contact the President and numerous senators and representatives, some of whom were his personal friends, and, it is said that largely through influence and negotiations of Jansen the young men were granted permission to stay.[138]

Interested in securing a good hospital for Beatrice, Peter Jansen gave one of his plots to the Beatrice Mennonites for the building of the Mennonite Deaconess Hospital and also contributed heavily to the building fund.

During his remaining years, he continued to serve his people and community in every way that opened before him. After a lingering illness, he passed away at his home in Beatrice, June 6, 1923. Cornelius J. Claassen said of him: "His passing is well described in the poignant phrase he once used in speaking of a friend, 'God's finger touched him and he slept.' "[139]

At Home in Beatrice

The Cornelius Jansen family had moved to Beatrice, Gage County, Nebraska, in the spring of 1877.[140] They had left Mount Pleasant, Iowa, on November 16, 1876, but spent the winter and Christmas at the ranch with Peter and John. Anna wrote that they liked their new Beatrice home very much and that they now had more room.[141] But for years they worked to improve the place. Among other things, they built a porch, added an addition to the house and improved the bath house.[142] In April of 1880 they purchased the adjoining lot to the south and the following year they added four more lots to their estate, including a large tree on the Blue River, apparently somewhat of a landmark.[143]

The Jansen house in Beatrice soon became more than a family home. They were surrounded by many Mennonite friends, Russian and Prussian, whom they had encouraged to come to the United States; many of whom sooner or later found their way to the Jansen home. They came from Kansas and Nebraska, either for advice, to get help during the early years, or just to visit and reminisce. And in the Jansen home they were always welcome. It was fortunate that this family had a large ranch to support them and their many visitors, or else they might have eaten them "out of house and home." There was seldom a day in which this family did not entertain guests. Yet in those days families were large and the best time to visit was around the dinner table or over a cup of coffee or tea. No wonder Cornelius, the youngest in the family, wrote that June 26, 1883, had been an unusually quiet day because no visitor or stranger had stopped at the house.[144] Yet the family enjoyed their many friends. They were no longer lonesome. Anna wrote, January 2, 1877: "Now there are many here, and among them our most intimate Prussian and Russian friends. Oh how much more enjoyable this is than when we were so lonesome and alone."[145] But this necessitated having a maid servant, a practice which the Jansens now resumed in Beatrice, as they had had it in Berdyansk.

Probably one of the most welcome guests in the Jansen home was Leonhard H. Sudermann, formerly of Berdyansk, but later of Newton and Whitewater, Kansas. His coming to Beatrice always created a sensation and seemed to thrill the entire family. Even Peter found in him a man with whom he could discuss his most intimate and confidenctial problems, and feel that he profited by it.[146]

The Jansen family's church attendance was not limited to the Mennonite church. While on Sunday morning they usually worshiped in the church of their own faith, on Sunday evenings and week days different members of the family, including the parents, often attended the different non-Mennonite church services. In this way they became acquainted with the various Beatrice church people.[147] The result was that the little town of Beatrice found in this family not only staunch supporters of those things that made for a wholesome life, but also leadership in the Christian way of life. They had taken this same position the year they lived in Berlin, Ontario, and again when they lived in Mount Pleasant, Iowa.

When in 1881, the Mennonite congregation of the Reverend H. Zimmerman decided to build a large country church building, Cornelius Jansen, Sr., apparently was not in sympathy with the building program nor with the way in which they had decided to raise the money. This information we gather from a written statement of Jansen. The congregation's decision apparently was to raise the necessary funds by taxing the church members according to the amount of land they owned. Cornelius Jansen reasoned that this was unbiblical and even unjust. Contributions for this purpose should be voluntary. He referred to the Old and New Testament to support his position. Moreover, he felt that this would work a hardship on the poorer people, and be unfair. For example, if John Hamm paid $10 because he owned 20 acres and Heinrich Zimmerman $250 because he owned 500 acres, in reality, Hamm was worth only $500 whereas Zimmerman was worth $50,000. To be fair to Hamm, Zimmerman should pay $1,000 instead of $250. Moreover, Jansen also felt that instead of building one large country church building, they should build two smaller buildings and locate one in Beatrice. In that way they would accommodate more of the people. He also objected to the decision that only heads of families should be solicited to give, and thereby interest all members of the congregation. Above all, however, their contributions should be voluntary. To begin with, the Jansen family therefore preferred to remain guests of the church, until such a time they would decide to make the change.[148] The writer does not know whether this was the Jansen's final decision regarding this matter or whether they contributed to the building fund. It should be mentioned that in 1890 Jansen expressed a willingness to make a contribution to the church.

Nevertheless, the country church building was built about four miles west of Beatrice. The first building built in 1879, burned down December 21 of the same year.[149] The congregation then decided to build a new building and apparently it was the discussion over this building which caused the dissention.[150] While there was agitation for a Beatrice church building, it apparently was not until some years after the death of Jansen when it was built.[151] In the meantime church services were held in Beatrice on alternate Sundays in the spacious Jansen and J. G. Wiebe homes.

As stated before, this group of Prussian immigrants brought with them considerable wealth. Some of them built up, for that time, rather pretentious homesteads, with extensive operations in raising sugar beets, cheese making and cattle feeding to the extent of going in debt beyond their means. Cornelius Jansen warned against such over-expansion in a new and untried economy and country. He was succintly asked, *Sind Sie denn allwissend?* (Do you know everything?) However, many who did not heed his advice lost everything in the depression of the early 1890's.

The Jansen family continued their sympathetic feeling for the sick, the needy and homeless people. Through their broad interest in religious work in Beatrice they made many contacts even with non-Mennonites and entered wholeheartedly into social service work in behalf of the many sick and needy people. Non-Mennonite ministers would stop at their house to talk over problems and conditions of the poor in their care and often before they left they would receive money or other gifts to help the cause of their unfortunate people.[152] For example, in June of 1892, they helped to find temporary living quarters and work for three Baptist and two Lutheran Russian families. Mrs. Jansen found them an eating place and also interpreted for them as they did their shopping.[153] Service kindred to this was always freely given by this family. Always being prepared for unheralded mealtime guests, there often was food left after meals. This was taken to the sick and needy, often by the grandchildren. Thus, Grandmother Jansen in her homespun, Christian way taught her grandchildren to share with others what the Lord had provided for them.

Closely related to their interest in social welfare was the Jansen's genuine interest in temperance. Father Jansen and his daughter Helena, and later his son, Cornelius, were active members of the local temperance organization. Father Jansen was a vigorous advocate of his convictions of what was right, and opposed with all his might the use of spirituous liquor and tobacco.[154] Mrs. Jansen, although probably not a member of the organization, was no less interested and active in the cause.

Above all else, however, the Jansens were absorbed in living and promoting the Christian way of life, as they interpreted it. The Beatrice *Daily Express* wrote that Jansen "abhored shams and hypocrisy and was the incarnation of every good and noble thought and action."[155] The Jansen, Nebraska, correspondent of *Der Christliche Apologete* wrote that even though Cornelius Jansen was not a member of their church, he was very dear to them. In his home, next to the Bible, religious papers would be found. These he purchased in large numbers and distributed them among his friends. The correspondent wrote that often he had seen Jansen in the railroad stations distributing religious literature among immigrants, extending to them a helping hand or giving advice.[156] The *Christliche Bundesbote* referred to him as a man deeply rooted in the Christian principles of peace of which his daily life witnessed alike before friend and foe.[157] It might well be said of him as so many did, that "he lived not for himself and that his hopes were not placed on the things of earth, but on heavenly things."[158] Having this deep religious concern for others, Father Jansen was above all else interested in the religious and general welfare of his own children and grandchildren. Since his ill health constantly reminded him of what might happen to him any moment, it no doubt was his desire to spend the last years of intimate fellowship with his children, helping them wherever and in whatever way he could.

During the late seventies and the early eighties, most of the Jansen children had reached the age of maturity and some of them had established their own homes. Peter and his wife Gertrude were working hard on their own sheep ranch. Gertrude was busy rearing her children—Trude, Hans, Anna, Margarete and Katarienchen.[159] On her shoulders rested by far the major responsibility of this family work. Peter's ranch and his political interests took him away from home rather frequently. In fact, so often that on one occasion Father Jansen warned him to be careful that his frequent travels would not foster in him the desire to be on the road rather than at home. This rather irritated Peter and he did not like the implication. But he soon forgot, especially when his kind mother assured him it was just the advice of a loving father.[160]

Aron and Anna Claassen

Barely had the Cornelius Jansen family moved to Beatrice, Nebraska, when Anna, the second daughter of the family, became engaged to Aron Claassen, a young Mennonite from Prussia, who had visited the Jansens already in their home in Berdyansk. He had made a previous trip to America and returning to Germany he was chosen as leader of the large group of Prussian immigrants to whom Peter referred to previously. We find him corresponding with the Cornelius Jansens on immigration matters and deciding to locate in or near Beatrice, Nebraska, perhaps for obvious reasons.

Although rather different from her deceased sister, Margarete, Anna had this in common with her, that she would often stop to study her own behavior, words and thought. She often was a severe critic of her past conduct. Shortly after Margarete's death she wrote: "Margarete always got up early in the morning to make the fire, leaving the rest of us asleep in bed. Often she had finished milking before the rest of us came downstairs." Anna therefore concluded that she was not living up to her responsibility, like her sister had done. Six weeks later she wrote in her diary: "Once a person is satisfied with himself, he soon begins to find fault with his neighbor." It was not easy for the lively, fun-loving Anna to make up her mind to marry this quiet young farmer, but once she decided she was happy in her decision. On November 24, 1877 she wrote in her diary: "For me this day is especially significant, for in the presence of my parents I promised Aron Claassen that within another year I will become his wife."[161] She now felt that she would never regret her decision and hoped that God too might approve of it. She prayed God that in the ensuing year He might give her much wisdom and keep her from faltering, as she had so often done in the past. It would help her to become worthy of her bridegroom's true love. Anna had asked Aron Claassen for a year's time to prepare for the great event in her life. He was willing to wait. She interpreted this as an indication of his true love.[162]

Anna planned to keep her new relationship with Aron Claassen rather quiet. But apparently she found this somewhat difficult. When, two weeks later, she had occasion to tell Peter and Gertrude about it, they were greatly surprised, but pleasantly so.[163] When Aron Claassen came to court Anna, it seems that the boys in the neighborhood watched their opportunity to tease the newcomer. At any rate, one Sunday night Aron had difficulty in finding his horse when he was ready to leave. It was finally discovered tied in front of Müller's store.[164] On another evening when Aron came to see Anna, she was at the ranch, so Mother Jansen met him at the door. When, true to his European custom, Aron stooped to kiss her hand, Mother Jansen politely told him that she did not expect him to do that. Anna was somewhat annoyed by her mother's attitude.[165]

It was not until November 29, 1878, that Aron and Anna celebrated their engagement. It was a festive occasion and many Kansas friends were present. H. Zimmerman, Peter Claassen and Abraham Sudermann spoke. The words of advice Peter Claassen gave the young couple would be appropriate for any engaged couple even today, namely: They should not think that the person they were marrying was perfect, as though a pair of angels were about to be married, but be realistic and remember that they are but imperfect human beings subject to mistakes, which would have to be forgiven when made.[166]

The engaged couple spent the interim period of about six weeks prior to the wedding in visiting friends and relatives, as was then customary. Since Anna's time was now taken up with more urgent matters than keeping a diary, she discontinued that task after her engagement. It was her brother Cornelius who now assumed that aspect of the family's responsibility.

Anna's wedding took place January 9, 1879. Of this period we have only the record left by Cornelius, which is rather brief. Five days before the wedding Cornelius wrote that the parents were making purchases for the occasion, and he also added that they had started to bake.[167] About the wedding he merely wrote: "January 9, 1879, Tuesday—An important day for us—wedding of Anna and Aron—promised each other at 4:23 p.m. Wedding was at Claassens; We came home at 12:30 the next morning and went to bed at 3:30."[168] We therefore know less about the wedding than about the engagement.

Aron Claassen, a Prussian Mennonite, was born in the year 1850. He visited the United States in the early 1870's, returned to Prussia and immigrated to Nebraska in 1877 with the Prussian Mennonite group whom Peter Jansen went to meet in New York. He purchased land about five miles west of Beatrice, where he and his young bride now made their home. Since we have no diary of the Aron Claassen family life we learn of them only through others.

Anna's first two children died in infancy. The first one, born November 20, 1879,[169] was a still-born baby. The second child, Lena, was born October 11, 1881.[170] She died when she was ten months old, August 10, 1882. "Just when she was beginning to be so cute," wrote Cornelius. Apparently she was sick only a few days, for the news of her illness reached the grandparents only the day before her death. Grandfather Jansen was at the ranch, so Anna's sister Helena went along with Doctor Grabe to help Mrs. Claassen. The funeral was on the eleventh of August.[171] Their third child was a little boy, Cornelius, born May 6, 1883.[172] Anna had five more children before the death of her father in December, 1894. They were Hans, Aaron, Anna, Danny and Katherine. Margarete, the youngest, was born after his death. Mother Anna Jansen Claassen died October 17, 1924.

John Jansen

Johannes Jansen, born at Berdyansk, October 16, 1857, was the fourth oldest child in the family. When the parents moved to

Nebraska he was nineteen years old, helping Peter build up the ranch. Apparently John (Johannes) never kept a diary, but Peter, Mrs. Jansen and Cornelius have left information about him. Like Peter, John did not always live up to the expectations of his parents. Living with Peter, he too could not resist the temptation of tobacco. On July 5, 1879, Cornelius wrote: "Today John smoked a cigar."[173] Apparently it was a surprise to Cornelius. Since John was at the ranch and Cornelius lived with his parents in Beatrice, they saw each other only occasionally.

John's interest in girls was also first mentioned by Cornelius. It happened in the spring of 1882 when one day Cornelius wrote that Peter suddenly came to Beatrice, but left almost immediately for H. Zimmermans. He soon returned with a "Yes." Cornelius then added: "Now Johannes and Albertine (Penner) are as good as engaged. May it be God's will, is my wish."[174] Peter was still playing the old roll of a middleman, probably getting the permission from the girl's parents. About a week later Cornelius wrote again that "Today John got the consent of Albertine."[175] A week later, June 1, they celebrated their engagement. It rained all afternoon.[176] Like Peter and Anna, the engaged couple used the interim period between their engagement and the wedding to visit relatives and friends.

They were married on the twenty-fourth of August, 1882, at the Zimmerman home. Cornelius merely wrote that he enjoyed the afternoon and that the bride and groom received a great variety of presents.[177]

For some time John and Albertine lived at the ranch with Peter and Gertrude, but before long an arrangement was reached whereby John became manager of the ranch and Peter and his family moved on their own farm,[178] apparently not far from the ranch. The two brothers continued to work together very nicely. When one was sick, the other would take over the added responsibility. Peter often remarked how thankful he was that he had John close by, for on him he could depend.[179]

John and Albertine had their first child June 21, 1883. It was a boy whom they christened Willie.[180] However, before Father Jansen passed away they had four more children, Helena, Henry, Gertrude and Betty. On December 24, 1894, shortly after the death of John's

Father, they had another son whom they named Cornelius, after his deceased grandfather.[181] Charles, born in Beatrice, was the youngest of this family.

In January and February of 1884, John was seriously ill. The sickness had settled on his lungs and for several days his sputum showed blood. The family was rather worried about him. But by the middle of March he had practically regained his strength.[182]

John was a great lover of beautiful horses, and soon his farm bore evidence of his interest. He had, of course, built the necessary stables for them. Then one night in May, 1893, the stable in which he had tied eighteen of his best horses, burned down. He had kept them in the stable that night because he had planned to help Peter plant corn the next morning. The fire was discovered at 1 a.m., by a Mrs. Schulz, who was staying with the Jansens for the night. When her child became restless and she got up to take care of it, she noticed the bright light flashing into the room and saw that the barn was on fire. Excited and bewildered, John and his family rushed out to rescue the whinnying horses, but were able to save only seven out of the eighteen.

Included among the dead was *der alte Peet,* the old faithful family horse whom the children used to drive to school. The loss of those horses was a terrible shock to John. His wife, Albertine, remarked how relieved she was when the last stable wall crumbled and she found her husband safely outside, so anxious was he to save the suffering animals. For some time the thought and memory of the event haunted him and he could not forget it. When he telephoned the news to his parents in the morning, and mother Jansen heard his sobbing voice, she sighed: "Oh poor, poor John! Why must it always strike you." For several hours the family kept the news from Father Jansen, who was ill at the time. But when he finally heard about it, he said, with tears filling his eyes: "I must go and comfort John." He took the three o'clock train that same afternoon. Fortunately he met Peter on the same train, returning from Colorado. Father Jansen told Peter of what had happened and together they now proceeded to John's home to comfort him.[183]

The cause of the fire was never discovered. John said that none of his hired hands smoked, and he had discontinued smoking that previous August.[184] Sometime later a man from Crete, Nebraska, apparently an old frontiersman, asked John whether he had checked to see that the bones of all the horses could be accounted for. He then remarked, that frequently horse thieves would steal the best horses, and then set the barn on fire to distract the attention of the owner and to cover up their own tracks.[185] Mrs. Jansen's diary does not give John's answer to this question.

In the beginning of this century John Jansen moved to the Quill Lake district, Saskatchewan, Canada, where he broke the prairie and started farming and ranching. When the railroad was built through that area, the town and station near his land was named Jansen. He died in 1932.

Helena Jansen

Helena Jansen, born November 14, 1858, also in Berdyansk, was the youngest of the three daughters. Her diary covers the years 1888 to July, 1892. She was never married, and helped take care of the household until after the death of her parents. In Berlin and Mount Pleasant, Iowa, she attended school, and continued this the first years in Beatrice. According to Anna's diary, Helena completed the requirements for a teacher's certificate and was supposed to start teaching the second week in January, 1877.[186] She left on the eighth of January to be gone for two years, wrote Anna.[187] But nothing more was ever said about her teaching. She was at home in July, 1877, and was on the springwagon returning from the ranch, July 14, when suddenly the rear seat tipped over backwards and spilled her sister-in-law, Gertrude, and Aunt Anna. Both fell over backwards. While they suffered severe shocks and bruises, apparently they were not seriously injured, although laid up for a number of days.[188] Helena is mentioned again in August of 1881, when she, her father and Aunt attended a lecture on Poland given by Mr. Sobieski.[189] The Jansen family was intellectually alert and interested, and always attended lectures, chautauqua programs, religious and temperance meetings when they had the opportunity. In August, 1882, Helena helped her sister Anna, when her daughter Lena suddenly passed away.[190] The following year in August, Cornelius wrote that Papa, Mother and Helena went to Peter's to celebrate his birthday, a custom the family always observed for members of their family.[191] Helena and her father frequently visited Peter and John, and Anna on their farms and she usually helped out when there was sickness in these families. Like her father, she was an ardent temperance worker and was an active member of the local W.C.T.U.

She organized and was the leader of a children's temperance club, known as the "Band of Hope." They met weekly in local churches and learned temperance slogans and pledges such as: "When asked to drink we'll smile and turn our glasses upside down," "If I never drink the first glass of brandy, gin or wine, I will never fill a drunkard's grave," and "Habits are like cords of steel, binding us for woe or weal, to be careful we will try, how we form them, you and I." Also, "Tobacco is an Indian weed that causes much of want and need, 'twas the devil sowed the seed." The children were taught that their bodies were temples of God to be kept clean, pure and sanctified (1 Cor. 3:16, 17). They learned and recited Scripture verses warning against the use of wine and strong drink. The temperance stand of the Jansens, as their other endeavors, was based on their interpretation of the Bible. Father Jansen held the conviction that as in Christ's own words, "A drunkard shall not enter the Kingdom of Heaven" anyone offering or enticing a fellow man to strong drink thereby exposing him to the danger of becoming a drunkard was himself in danger of committing the unpardonable sin, that is, being the cause of a fellow man's soul going to perdition.

Helena enjoyed the many friends of the family and shared actively in the responsibility of letter writing. She also took great interest in her many nephews and nieces who always looked forward to a vacation at the grandparents', and often helped Grandmother take care of them.

She also was active in Sunday school and city mission work. Her hobby was china painting of which many pieces are in the family. In 1917 Helena Jansen moved to Pasadena, California, continuing her activities until her death November 9, 1937.

Cornelius Jansen, Jr.

Cornelius, the youngest member of the Jansen family, was also born at Berdyansk on April 30, 1863. At the age of sixteen, in the year 1879, he started to keep a diary and continued it till January 1, 1884. Cornelius probably was even more educationally minded than his brothers and sisters. This may have been due to the fact that he arrived in the United States in time to enable his parents to give him the advantage of these schools. His sister Helena, who was four years older than he, was seventeen years old when the parents moved to Beatrice, and therefore somewhat past the formative school years.

Just how much education Cornelius had acquired before the death of his father is not too clear. Apparently he had finished the equivalent of a high school education and had taken some special courses in Latin and Greek, and attended Haverford College at least a year. On April 10, 1879, Cornelius wrote that he was taking algebra, general history, physical geography, zoology, and botany.[192] He was then almost sixteen years old. While some of those courses appear to be first year high school, others would seem to belong in the second or third-year group. On the third of March, 1882, he wrote again: "Today I quit school because of my health." During that school year he was reading Cicero's *Select Orations.* He reviewed his school work and concluded that he had attended school in Beatrice for almost six years.[193] Before long he was back in school again, but this time it was the Normal Institute. He enrolled on July 17, 1882, for five weeks in the following subjects: history, physiology, reading, arithmetic, geography, civil government and grammar. It was a full program and at first he felt rather discouraged, but soon began to like it.[194] He came out with a third-grade certificate with an average of 80%.[195]

By October 2, 1882, Cornelius was teaching school. It was a country school, located close to the Jansen ranch. It was only a three-months term, October, November and December. He started out with four pupils, all boys.[196] But the enrollment continually increased, both boys and girls, until November 10, when he had twenty pupils. That day the county superintendent visited him for three hours. Before he left he had told Cornelius that his work was equal to that of John Fast. Cornelius interpreted it to mean that the superintendent was pleased with his work.[197] Anxious for the school to close so he could go home, he wrote: "Today I finished my last day of school. After many anxious days of longing and waiting, this day is finally here and is now past. And now I may go home, home—to my parents. . . . I think it was destined to be so. If only my work will have been of some value, even though only small."[198] His salary for the three months' work was $105.[199]

Cornelius now prepared to attend Haverford College in fall. This was a Quaker school in Haverford, Pennsylvania. He got out his

Greek textbook and together with Abel Wagner they began studying it under the tutelage of his former professor, Schryock.[200] Meanwhile he corresponded with a Thomas of Haverford.[201] In November of the same year, still in Beatrice, he was studying Latin and some Greek under W. Ebright, whom he liked very much.[202] The last entry in his diary, January 1, 1884, shows that he was still planning to attend Haverford, but he had postponed it to the fall of 1884. He was reviewing for the entrance examinations, hoping that he might pass them.[203]

That Cornelius did attend Haverford College we learn from a letter written by James E. Rhoads of Bryn Mawr, Pennsylvania. He wrote Cornelius, December 24, 1894, following the death of Father Jansen: "I recall thy stay at Haverford and only wish that the absorbing character of my duties had allowed me to see more of thee."[204]

The record is silent about what Cornelius did in the meantime. Peter's diary, although it covers this period, gives us no information about him. From Mrs. Jansen's diary we learn that in the summer of 1892 the school board of Mansford, Nebraska, literally begged him to teach their school again the coming year. They offered him an increase of $100 over the past year. Thus he apparently had taught their school during the previous school year, 1891-92. But Cornelius was not interested in the position. His mother was almost as anxious as the board that he should accept the position. But it appears that Cornelius made his own decision, which Mrs. Jansen failed to record.[205] We know, however, that the following year, 1893-94, he taught German and Greek in the Beatrice High School.[206]

Like the rest of the Jansen family, Cornelius showed a wide range of interest. He manifested a lively interest in politics, favored women's suffrage, and supported the temperance movement.[207] He attended the Republican County Committee meeting in July, 1882, and when Iowa voted prohibition by a 40,000 majority, he wrote: "Thank God for that. Hallelujah! Amen. God's cause will win, even if all devils oppose it!"[208] He also showed interest in bee culture. At one time he took care of thirty-two hives for his parents. They produced a lot of honey, much of which his parents gave away.[209]

Cornelius Jansen married Christine Fossler of Lincoln, Nebraska. Both taught school in Los Angeles, California, where Cornelius

Jansen died on August 22, 1954. He was a staunch promoter of the principles of his father and associated closely with the Friends.

It was in these carefully trained, intelligent children and grandchildren that Father and Mother Jansen now found great interest and satisfaction. They had given them a Christian home where they could cultivate their own interests, and enough of earthly possessions so that they would not be handicapped in following their chosen profession. On their birthday or on other occasions, the parents would often remember them with gifts which would enable them to learn more about their vocation. For example, on one occasion Father Jansen gave Peter the *Library of Universal Knowledge,*[210] on another occasion he gave Cornelius the six volumes of Bancroft's *History of the United States.* No doubt John and the daughters received equally appropriate gifts, even though they have not been recorded.

Mother Jansen frequently had the grandchildren at her house for several days, or even a week. On those occasions she would often take them along to the market or go out walking with them. Her diary has many references to their reactions to what they saw, and their clever remarks. One stormy Sunday morning the parents stayed home from church. As he always did on such occasions, Father Jansen read a sermon to the family, they all sang songs and he prayed with them. This time he read one of Moody's sermons. On this occasion little Cornelius Claassen, Anna's son, was staying at the home, listening to Grandfather read. When he finished reading little Cornelius remarked: "Grandfather should read from the Bible. This sermon is just a story." Later in the evening Father Jansen read from one of Paul's letters about baptism and then remarked that Leonhard Sudermann held that we should not baptize a person because he believes in a general way in God, but upon his personal confession of faith in God. On the other hand Isaac Peters believes that the candidate for baptism should quit smoking before he is baptized. Jansen then questioned whether after all the latter view was not correct. Again the silence was broken by the voice of little Cornelius interposing his answer, "Yes."[211]

In contrast to his great activity in the eighteen seventies and early eighties, Father Jansen spent the later years of his life in quiet retirement with his wife and children in Beatrice and on the ranch. Much of the time was spent in reading, attending church services, chautauqua lectures, temperance meetings, visiting the sick and helping the needy, and writing letters to his many friends. The family had kept up the correspondence with their Quaker friends in England and Pennsylvania, with their Mennonite friends still living in Prussia, Russia and those that had emigrated to Canada and the United States.

The Passing of a Generation

There were several reasons why Cornelius Jansen was less active in public affairs than he had been. In the first place, the great immigration movements had ceased and the period of adjustment during which they needed help so badly, was past. Moreover, the Mennonite Board of Guardians was taking care of what immigration problems still were left. But the main reason for his withdrawal from public service apparently was the condition of his health.

Almost immediately after his arrival in North America Father Jansen was troubled with lumbago. The much walking he and Peter had to do when they traveled so frequently in 1873, 1874 and even in 1875, apparently made this illness more acute.[212] Father Jansen apparently attributed his sickness to the severe climate in Berlin, Ontario, for as stated before, he wrote that his reason for leaving Canada was his health.[213] And yet when they lived in Mt. Pleasant, Iowa, Margarete continued to worry about the condition of her father's health. His lumbago continued to bother him[214] and in addition he now also had frequent headaches. The years of uncertainty, before they finally settled in Nebraska, apparently were very hard on him. On April 6, 1874, Anna wrote: "Papa's hair has turned entirely gray in America. He looks tired and exhausted. The last four to six weeks I do not wish to relive, nor do I want to write about them. I'll remember what happened without recording it."[215] During the years 1875 and 1876, he suffered from severe headaches and paralysis. Anna blamed the headache on his daily writing.[216] In December, 1875 she wrote that her father had little appetite, his right arm was cold and his legs would shake.[217] In March, 1876 she wrote that he was losing weight.[218] The last time she mentioned the condition of his poor health was in January, 1877.[219] After they settled in Nebraska his health apparently improved, for not until July, 1883, when he was severely ill with Cholera Morbus during several weeks, is there any further mention of his illness.[220] He soon regained his strength and apparently enjoyed near normal health until the early nineties.

It was in 1892 when Mrs. Jansen began to be worried about the condition of her husband's health. His hips bothered him, apparently some more rheumatic pain. But what worried Mrs. Jansen much more was the fact that he would get dizzy spells and slight paralytic attacks.[221] On June 9, 1893, she wrote: "Father is still troubled with pains in his hips, but what gives me greater concern is that since yesterday he has had difficulty controlling his tongue. When he reads he often hesitates as though he is struggling how to express himself."[222] She prayed God to save him from a paralytic stroke. This illness continued for several weeks and it seems that the dizzy spells never entirely left him. On the eleventh of June he perspired so profusely that the mattress was soaked to the straw. While a week later he felt somewhat better, on the twenty-fifth he apparently suffered from a relapse. In November, 1893 he had frequent coughing spells and for several days remained in bed mornings till ten and eleven o'clock.[223]

For the last year of Father Jansen's life we are dependent upon Peter's dairy, and since he lived miles from Beatrice, we read only occasionally about him. On March 20, Peter wrote that his father was really sick, and when he met him at his sister, Aron Claassen's, on the twenty-third of March where the family had gathered to celebrate Anna's birthday, Peter wrote that father looked very tired and exhausted.[224] While the Peter Jansens visited their parents rather frequently, Peter never again mentioned the condition of his father's health until December 13, 1894. That evening while the Peter Jansen family was sitting around the table, following the evening meal, suddenly the telephone rang twice and the Jansen telephone girl said, "Beatrice is calling." It was 7:30 p.m. Peter writes: "I recognized sister Helena's voice at once and heard that she was crying. I asked, 'It is Papa?' She answered, 'Yes, our dear father cannot live longer than a few hours.'" Peter immediately telephoned John and within an hour they had left for Beatrice and arrived there at 10 that night. They found Father Jansen unconscious but still breathing. He lived till 1:30 the following morning and then quietly passed away, apparently without pain.[225] Peter writes that the last time he and his family visited with their father was December 1, when they celebrated his mother's birthday. Little did they realize that it would be their last visit with him.[226] Anna was more fortunate; she visited with him shortly before he had the attack. The spring-like weather of December 13, had induced the Jansens to drive out in the afternoon to visit the Aron Claassens, about five miles from Beatrice. Father Jansen returned in seemingly good spirits, but about half an hour later, he had the attack.[227] The cause of his death was diagnosed as apoplexy.[228]

The funeral was held on Sunday afternoon, December 16, 1894. A preliminary service was held in the family home, where Elder Gerhard Penner spoke in the German language and Elder Yother in the English language. The main service, however, was held in the Mennonite church of which he was a member. It is located three miles west of Beatrice. As the funeral procession wended its way from Beatrice to the country church it was followed by nearly one hundred vehicles of relatives, friends and neighbors who wished to pay the last measure of love and respect to this man who had meant so much to them. J. H. Zimmerman preached the funeral sermon. Peaceful and smiling as if asleep, the deceased rested in the casket. The sun was casting its slanting rays through the church windows when the pallbearers (John H. von Steen, Peter Penner, J. G. Wiebe, Peter Claassen, H. V. Riesen, Johann Zimmerman, Gerhard Wiebe and Andreas Wiebe) removed the body and carried it to the cemetery near the church. Just as the sun cast its last shadow on the earth below, the body was lowered to its final resting place. Evening services were held in the bereaved family home by Leonhard Sudermann and Isaac Peters.[229]

Friends and relatives from near and far attended the funeral services. Many paid tribute to his life with their presence and wreaths of flowers. Many others who could not attend expressed their respect for the life of the deceased in letters addressed to the bereaved wife and children. These letters have been preserved in a scrapbook.[230]

Mother Jansen lived three more years when she, too, passed away and was buried by the side of her husband. Her death came December 2, 1897. Letters of tribute to the life of Mrs. Jansen came from many who had had the privilege of visiting in the Jansen home. C. B. Schmidt, land agent of the Atchison, Topeka and Santa Fe Railroad Company remembered the "always genial hospitality of (this) parental home, the friendly and sympathetic faces of (their) father and mother."[231]

Tante Anna had passed away only several months earlier, for J. Hume of Great Britain, remembered both Mother Jansen and Tante Anna in his letter of January 10, 1898: "They were lovely and pleasant in their lives, and in their death they were not long divided. How many timeless memories crowd upon my mind as I think of their unvarying kindness in days and years that are past."[232] Before the turn of the century, the Jansen children had been made orphans. But they were old enough to shift for themselves in the land of their adoption, the land of opportunity, freedom of religion and conscience their parents had chosen for them.

In Appreciation

The formal education of Cornelius Jansen seemingly was limited to the village school at Tiegenhof, Germany, and like most German youngsters at that time, he served as an apprentice and journeyman before he took up his profession as merchant and farmer in Berdyansk. Nevertheless, his intellectual growth did not end there. He kept an open mind throughout his life. That he must have read widely and with understanding, his whole attitude and life bear ample testimony. His stay at Gerhard Penners, later the elder of the Heubuden Mennonite Church, probably helped him to learn to put first things first— to put Christian principles in his own life above other interests.

His outlook on life no doubt was broadened by the many contacts he made as merchant of Berdyansk. But especially important as a contributing factor was his service as consular agent of Mecklenburg and of Prussia. This gave him rank and prestige, and with it came the opportunity to learn more about the national and international affairs and the opportunity to exchange ideas with men of other nations. It also prompted him to learn the English language, which was of such great help to him in his later dealings with the United States government officials.

But what probably was of especial help to him and to other Mennonites is the fact that it opened the door for his intimate friendship with the English Quakers, whom he learned to love and admire for their Christian principles, especially their peace principles. In this

Christian fellowship both the Mennonites (for these contacts were enjoyed by other Mennonites) and the Quakers found a common denominator in their religious outlook on life, and strengthened and supported each other in the struggles that confronted them. It deepened their religious convictions and gave them added strength to remain firm and steadfast in the days of trial and in the hours of temptation. From their correspondence and through the Quaker publication, *The Friend,* we get a glimpse of how much their fellowship meant to them.

William and Annie Graham of Suffolk, England, wrote December 16, 1894: "How many memories crowd up into our minds of kind words and acts received from the departed one, in fact from each and all of you, both in Berdyansk and in after years, since you have been in America."[233] Anna M. Harvey of Heathfield, England, wrote January 2, 1895: ". . . The part he (Cornelius Jansen) took some few years ago in assisting his persecuted and poorer brethren in Russia will make his memory honored and beloved by very many."[234] George Hume of London, England, wrote: ". . . His was no ordinary life. Vicissitudes of a most painful character, had often been his lot, and it will be interesting to those of your friends in your new Fatherland to preserve the remembrance of one who in so many ways recalled the staunch faith and undaunted courage of the Pilgrim Fathers." Hume knew many of the Russian Mennonites personally, among them Cornelius Reimer, Leonhard Sudermann, Jacob Dick, and others.[235] Cornelius Jansen's friendship with the English Quakers carried over to those in America. William G. Hubbard, President of the Peace Association of the Friends in America, Columbus, Ohio, wrote about Jansen: "The world is better and happier because he lived in it."[236]

The admiration for the life of Cornelius Jansen found expression also among the writers of his time. Thus wrote Ludwig Keller of Münster, Germany, author of many books dealing with the Anabaptists: ". . . In his death the world lost an exceptionally fine man. A man like the early Mennonites of centuries ago, yet now seldom found among them. He saw clearer than many others the far-reaching significance of the present intellectual struggles that began with the publication of my writings, and he fully realized how difficult it is in the present generation to successfully cope with them.

For his constant sympathy, understanding and participation in my struggles, which I so deeply appreciated, I now wish to commemorate him in my publication." Keller therefore asked Peter Jansen to send him a brief history of his father and asked Peter whether he could not make him a member of the Comenius-Gesellschaft (a historical society) so as to commemorate the family name in this organization. He then added: "If it is possible to arouse the interest of the Mennonites in my publication (*Monatshefte*), it will enable me to realize my long desired hopes, namely, to clarify and publicize through my paper more fully the Mennonite principles and the history of your forefathers who were so unjustly mistreated and persecuted." In his commemoration Keller wrote, among other things, "Cornelius Jansen was an exceptional man. Although not a member of the learned societies, yet he studied and followed with intense interest all the spiritual movements, and out of it built his own Christian philosophy of life. . . . In him lived the old spirit found in members of the earlier Christian churches who were so severely persecuted. . . ."[237]

Cornelius Jansen was equally admired by the railroad land agents with whom he had many contacts; even by those from whom he did not purchase land. On December 20, 1894, C. B. Schmidt, formerly the Kansas land agent of the Atchison, Topeka and Santa Fe Railroad Company wrote to Peter Jansen: "The death of your father must have caused great sorrow, especially among the Mennonites. For was it not he who started the great emigration movement from Russia, and who in the interest and for the welfare of his people made the greatest sacrifices?"[238] Years later, in 1915, in a public address given at Topeka, Kansas, C. B. Schmidt recalled his travels with Cornelius Jansen over the Santa Fe lands and emphasized the role which Cornelius Jansen played in the migration of 1874-84.[239]

Letters and telegrams of sympathy and condolence came from all over the United States and Canada, from England, Prussia and Russia. Jansen's friend and co-worker in the great immigration work, Jacob Y. Schantz, wrote comforting the family, particularly Mrs. Jansen. The American Bible Society and the National Women's Christian Temperance Union, as well as railroad companies and other business enterprises wrote sincere letters of appreciation, stressing the great help which they had received through Cornelius Jansen.[240]

John F. Funk, another early co-worker in the immigration work, wrote Peter Jansen about his father: "But it is a pleasing and a comforting thought that he lived not for himself and that his hopes were not placed on the things of earth, but on heavenly things. This will be a great consolation for your mother, your brothers and sisters and yourself."[241]

Wilhelm Hespeler, at that time in the German consular service at Winnipeg, expressed his Christian sympathies to the family. Isaac Peters of Henderson, Nebraska, who participated in the funeral service, wrote a long letter dated January 15, to Mrs. Cornelius Jansen and the family, in which he states that he had read the biography of Cornelius Jansen in *Der Christliche Bundesbote*. He was most impressed by the fact that Jansen "devoted so much time during his stay in America to the welfare of his fellow believers. How pleasing was it when he helped us here in Nebraska with counsel and through means, since we were here in a strange land without credit. How disappointing is it, therefore, when we experience that so many people take advantage of this and do not repay their debt."[242]

Bernhard Warkentin of Newton wrote on January 3, 1894 to Peter Jansen relating that Wm. A. Barkameyer, who had been in business with him for nearly nineteen years, had passed away. Warkentin states: "He was one of the noblest Christian characters I have ever known and often reminded me of your good kindhearted benevolent father whose aim in life was to do good. I assure you my heartfelt sympathy in your bereavement, as I have had the same experience in the year just past to lose my father, whom I was so anxious to see once more when I undertook my trip last year to Europe, but providence prevented me from reaching there in time.[243]

Many more of the 112 letters and telegrams and 12 articles contained in the *Cornelius Jansen Memorial* book could be quoted to illustrate the significant role which Jansen had played in the great migration of the 1870's, and the contribution which he had made in helping many thousand Mennonites to establish new homes in a land of freedom and plenty. He had indeed become a Moses for many, who himself was privileged to live two decades in the land of his choice.

Even in his own home town the tribute to Cornelius Jansen is no less pointed. The *Beatrice Daily Express* wrote about him:

> Few men were more generally known or deeply beloved in this city and county than Cornelius Jansen, Sr. He was the perfect embodiment of a courtly gentleman of the old school. He was possessed of the deepest religious convictions and carried all the elements of a pure Christian character into every act of his life. Pleasant, affable and deeply sincere in the love of his fellow men he occupied the most affectionate and loving place in the hearts of all who knew him.[244]

Cornelius Jansen had reached the age of 72 years, 5 months and 8 days, and left to mourn his passing, his wife, three sons and two daughters, one son-in-law, two daughters-in-law, sixteen grandchildren, two sisters-in-law, two nephews and four nieces.[245]

"And I heard a voice from Heaven saying unto me: Write, Blessed are the dead which die in the Lord from henceforth: yea saith the Spirit, that they may rest from their labours; and their works do follow them" (Rev. 14:13).

NOTES and APPENDIXES

NOTES

I. PREPARATION FOR A TASK

[1]Cornelius Jansen changed his name from Janzen to Jansen when he came to America. His grandfather spelled the name "Jantzen." Places where some of the bearers of the name originally came from are: Amsterdam, Friesland, Barbant, Westphalia, Holstein, etc. The origin of the name is as follows: Jan (John) is a common name in the Low Countries. "Zen" or "sen" or "zon" is the equivalent for "son." The combination "Janzon," "Janzen," "Jansen" means the "son of Jan," which gradually became a family name.

[2]*Memoirs of Peter Jansen,* (Beatrice, Nebraska, 1921) p. 16.

[3]According to Helena Jansen (daughter), *Der Herold,* (June 11, 1931), C. J. had a *gute Schulbildung.* Her brother, Cornelius Jansen Jr., however, in answering the questionnaire, wrote: "Had the usual village school at Tiegenhof," i.e. only an elementary education.

[4]In the von Riesen families the erroneous tradition exists that his family once came from Sweden and was of nobility. The name seems to indicate that they originally came from Rijssen, a town in the Dutch province of Overijssel.

[5]Concerning the ancestors of Margaretha Harder more details are available in *Mitteilungen des Sippenverbandes Danziger Mennonitenfamilien,* (1941) p. 74.

[6]These are the nine children:

1. Johann, born April 27, 1819. Died in infancy.
2. Heinrich, born May 5, 1821. Was married, but died early. His widow later was married to a Quiring. Probably no children.
3. Helena, born Dec. 1, 1822. Mrs. Cornelius Jansen.
4. Elisabeth, born Dec. 2, 1824. Probably died in childhood.
5. Abraham, born April 24, 1827. Married Johanna Hamm. Both died early, and left two children, Heinrich and Anna, who were educated partly in the Cornelius Jansen home and partly by relatives in West Prussia.
6. Anna, born January 14, 1829. Was not married. Lived all her life with her sister, Mrs. C. Jansen.
7. Johann, born March 6, 1832. Died in infancy.
8. Johannes, born March 25, 1833. Was married to Marie Wiebe, a niece of elder Gerhard Penner. Was first with the Jansens at Berdyansk, later stayed in West Prussia and farmed at Wickerau, Altenau, Weisshof and migrated in 1876 to Beatrice, Nebraska.
9. Maria, born Oct. 18, 1835. Probably died in infancy.

[7]*Abschrift vom Abstammungsnachweis.* Copy belongs to Mrs. P. S. Goertz, North Newton, Kansas.

[8]When deacons were elected in 1807 he got one vote out of 128: Archives of the Danzig Mennonite Church, Bethel College Historical Library. (Bethel College Historical Library will hereafter be referred to by the initials BCHL).

[9]Helena Jansen (daughter) in a letter (Pasadena, May 17, 1928) to C. J. Claassen, said that he at one time was a member of the city council of Danzig. See also Peter Jansen, *op. cit.,* p. 14.

[10]P. Töws, *Eine seltsame Begebenheit,* (Hochstadt, Man., 1911).

[11]Each of his children was to have three sets of the Menno Simons *Fundamentbuch,* and also three copies of the *Geschichte der Martyrer* by Isaac von Dühren (Königsberg, 1787). (See note of Anna von Riesen in M272 Dg Copy 3, BCHL).

[12]When Jansens were exiled from Russia in 1873 he destroyed many of his account books and business papers but kept those of his sister-in-law.

[13]Letter in Cornelius Jansen Collection, dated May 17, 1928.

[14]Peter Isaak, *Stammbuch meiner Voreltern,* appendix by Johann F. Friesen.

[15]". . . weil mir die dortigen Verhältnisse der Gemeinden und unsere Verfassung zum Staate nicht zusagten, und wir in Russland als Ausländer im Irdischen jedem andern gleichgestellt werden," *Mennonitische Blätter,* 1870, No. 7 (September).

[16]Leonhard Sudermann, "Wie und auf welche Weise eine Mennonitengemeinde in der Seestadt Berdjiansk in Süd-Russland gegründet wurde," manuscript, BCHL.

[17]The only information concerning this is given in *Memoirs of Peter Jansen*, p. 18, who writes that during the Crimean War "one of my father's warehouses was struck by a cannon ball."

[18]*Gesamt-Ausgaben für Anna und Johannes von Riesen und C. Janzen*, 1850-1852, Cornelius Jansen Collection. (This collection will hereafter be referred to by the initials CJC).

[19]Sudermann, *op. cit.*

[20]In October, 1856, the part of the property of Anna von Riesen, handled by C. H. Zimmermann, Danzig, and consisting of bonds and securities, amounted to more than 5,000 Prussian talers.

[21]Jacob Buhler paid, from September, 1852 to July, 1953, a total rent of rubles banco 942.60. *See Verwaltung der Berdjiansk Wirtschaft*, CJC.

[22]Autobiography of Bernhard Buhler, manuscript in BCHL. Bernhard Buhler was a younger brother of Jacob, later Mennonite minister at Berdyansk and elder at Buhler, Kansas. J. Prinz, *Die Kolonien der Brüdergemeinde*, (Moscow, 1898) p. 87.

[23]Peter Jansen, *op. cit.*, p. 18 f.

[24]This and some other data for this time we find in some of the 17 volumes of the diaries of Louis Eduard Zimmermann (in BCHL): *Tage-Buch No. I.* 1852-1853, Nov. 24, 27 and 28, 1852, March 3, and June 6, 1853, etc. At one place we read: "Herr Jantzen wusste von seiner Reise und dem Aufenthalte in Russland vieles zu erzählen und wusste uns dadurch nicht nur die Zeit zu verkürzen, sondern auch höchst angenehm zu unterhalten."

[25]Anna von Riesen's share (one sixth) from Nov. 28, 1852, to Dec. 31, 1853, was talers 116.

[26]Sudermann, *op. cit.*

[27]*Nachweis gegenseitiger Verrechnung der Anna von Riesen mit C. Janzen*, 1848-1856, CJC.

[28]P. Töws, *op. cit.*, p. 7.

[29]Leonhard Sudermann, *op. cit.*; H. Ediger, *Erinnerungen aus meinem Leben*, (Karlsruhe-Rüppurr, 1927) p. 9.

[30]Bernhard Buhler, *op. cit.*

[31]Peter Jansen, *op. cit.*, p. 19.

[32]*Ibid.*, p. 23.

[33]*Conto für die Berdjiansker Wirtschaft*, 1856-1861, CJC.

[34]*Ibid.*; see also *Mission Cto. and Colportage* book.

[35]This 2 per cent is sometimes called *Mäklers Commission*, or also sometimes *Unsere Commission*, or also *Unsere und Mäklers Commission*. It depended probably whether he sold it directly to the buyer or through a broker.

[36]Peter Jansen, *op. cit.*, p. 23.

[37]*Ibid.*, p. 24.

[38]*Ibid.*, p. 19.

[39]*Ibid.*, p. 26.

[40]"Russischer Unterthan, resp. Colonist gleich meinen vielen Bekenntnisgenossen hier zu werden, habe ich aus vielen Gründen nicht die Freudigkeit, und beschäftige mich dieserhalb mit dem Gedanken, ob es nicht besser wäre, um wenngleich mit Verlust an irdischen Gütern, die Geistesfreiheit zu bewahren, fortzuziehen . . ." *Mennonitische Blätter*, 1870, No. 7 (September). Helena Jansen asserts that some of his brethren blamed Cornelius Jansen for not taking out Russian citizenship. *Der Herold*, June 11, 1931.

[41]Later on in a pamphlet, "Thoughts on Our Duties Towards Magistrates" he defined his position, CJC.

[42]Letter of Helena Jansen to C. J. Claassen, Pasadena, May 17, 1928, CJC.

[43]"Deutsche Pioniere in Russland und Amerika." Etwas gekürzt nach den Aufzeichnungen seiner Tochter, Helena Jansen, Pasadena, Calif., U.S.A. Eingesandt von (Abraham) Kröker. *Der Herold*, (June 11, 1931).

[44]"1856 wurde er zum preussischen Konsul ernannt, welches Amt er 9 Jahre

bekleidete. Als er dann aus verschiedenen Gründen dieses Amt aufgab, erhielt er vom Fürsten Bismarck ein persönliches Dankschreiben, in dem er ihm Anerkennung für seine uneigennützigen Dienste aussprach."

[45]*Op. cit.*, p. 25.

[46]Answer to Questionnaire.

[47]George Hume, *Thirty-Five Years in Russia,* (London, 1914) pp. 51, 64, 109.

[48]*Narrative of the Visit of Isaac Robson and Thomas Harvey to the South of Russia,* etc.

[49]George Leibbrandt, "The Emigration of the German Mennonites from Russia to the United States and Canada in 1873-1880: I., *Mennonite Quarterly Review,* (Oct., 1932) p. 205.

[50]*Reminiscences of Foreign Immigration Work.* Address by C. B. Schmidt at the Fourth Annual Convention of the Colorado State Realty Association held at Colorado Springs, Colorado, June 20 to 23, 1905, p. g. C. Henry Smith obviously followed C. B. Schmidt in his presentation. See *The Coming of the Russian Mennonites,* p. 49.

[51]"Der Kaufmann Cornelius Jansen wurde 1859 von dem Preussischen Konsul in Odessa zum Konsularagenten in Berdjiansk bestellt. Seine Funktion als solcher endete 1862, weil in Berdjiansk ein Konsulat errichtet und dieses einem andern übertragen wurde." Letter of the Germany Embassy, Washington, D. C., Sept. 16, 1933. This was all the information they had about Cornelius Jansen except for a letter he wrote to the German Foreign Ministry in 1873. Since the Berlin Archives were completely destroyed in World War II, there will be no way of getting more details from this source. Another place for inquiry would be the State Archives of Mecklenburg-Schwerin at Schwerin, Mecklenburg, now Russian zone of Germany.

[52]"The Mennonites" *The Free Press,* (Mt. Pleasant Iowa, Dec. 2, 16, and 23, 1875, and Jan. 6, 13, 20, and 27, 1876).

Henry VII Prince of Reuss (1825-1906) became Prussian ambassador (*Gesandter*) at St. Petersburg in 1867 and Botschafter in 1871 from which post he retired in 1876.

[53]Cornelius Jansen to Falck and Co. shipping for Canadian government in Hamburg, Germany. Berdyansk 7/19 April, 1873. Ernst Correll Collection, Goshen College.

[54]Interview Mrs. G. C. Wiebe and A. J. Claassen, Beatrice, January 2, 1950.

[55]*Op. cit.*, p. 25.

[56]George Hume, *op. cit.*, p. 35.

[57]Jansen, *op. cit.*, p. 35.

[58]Interview Mrs. G. C. Wiebe and A. J. Claassen, Beatrice, Nebraska.

[59]*Immigration Letter-File* 1871-1873, esp. Dec. 11, 1871, Feb. 15, Dec. 22 and 29, 1872, Feb. 28, 1873, CJC.

[60]Hume, *op. cit.*

[61]With William Wagner, Odessa, Cornelius Jansen maintained a correspondence mostly on financial matters. See *Immigration Letter-File* 1871-1873, CJC.

[62]Hume, *op. cit.*, pp. 37, 55, 109.

[63]Diary of Margaretha Jansen, esp. June 14 and 15, 1866. Later W. Graham moved to Rostov. *Immigration Letter-File,* April 22, 1872, and May 3, 1873; Hume, *op. cit.*, p. 64. See also letters of condolence at the death of Cornelius Jansen in *Cornelius Jansen Memorial.*

[64]Apparently brother and sister. Wagstaff was often a dinner guest at the Jansen home. Occasionally he would be so bold as to ask Margaretha for a dance, which she refused. Diary of Margaretha Jansen, 1866, April 29.

[65]*Ibid.*, January 14, 21; Feb. 1, 11; June 24; Aug. 2, etc.

[66]*Ibid.*, July 13, Aug. 23, etc.

[67]*Namenverseichniss der Ältesten, Lehrer und Diakonen oder Vorsteher der Taufgesinnten Mennonitischen Gemeinden, etc.* (Elbing, 1843) p. 54. He is, however, not mentioned in the following edition of the *Namesverseichnis,* (Danzig, 1857). According to a remark made by P. M. Friesen, *Die Alt-Evangelische Mennonitische Brüderschaft* etc., (Halbstadt, 1911) p. 188, he joined the Gnadenfeld congregation, known for a more active religious life.

[68]P. M. Friesen, *op. cit.*, p. 87.

[69]Not to be confused with his nephew, Jacob Reimer, Gnadenfeld-Wiesenfeld, born at Felsenthal as the son of David Reimer, and later one of the leaders of the Mennonite Brethren.

[70]Always small in number, they existed already in West Prussia: Gustav H. Reimer, *Mennonitische Geschichtsblätter,* (April, 1949) p. 30. Though classified as "Gichtelianer" by P. M. Friesen, *op. cit*., p. 132 f., and Neff, *Mennonitisches Lexikon,* Vol. I, p. 638, the direct origin of this movement among the Mennonites is still unknown.

[71]A letter of Jacob Reimer is preserved, written on July 10, 1858, to Cornelius Jansen which contains some characteristics of writer and time. Cornelius Jansen is addressed: "Geliebtester Freund," Diary of Margaretha Jansen, August 19, 1866, CJC.

[72]Letter of Jacob Friesen to Cornelius Jansen, Blumstein, October 22, 1861.

[73]P. M. Friesen, *op. cit.,* p. 186.

[74]Leonhard Sudermann, *Wie und auf welche Weise,* etc.

[75]Draft of a letter of H. P. Krehbiel, without date, Leonhard Sudermann Collection, BCHL.

[76]Interview Mrs. S. K. Mosiman, Bluffton, Ohio, Dec. 5, 1949.

[77]Letter from Herman E. Suderman, Newton, Feb. 13, 1950. Concerning a possible competition he mentioned that it was "on a friendly basis—each had his own particular friends among the Mennonites of the various Mennonite villages."

[78]Family notes of Mrs. P. S. Goertz, North Newton, Kansas. Franz Isaak, *Die Molotschnaer Mennoniten*, (Halbstadt, 1908) p. 227.

[79]Helena Jansen, *Der Herold,* (June 6, 1931). Probably Cornelius Jansen had better relations to Wüst's more considerate successor, Pastor Bentel, whose name appears in the *Account-Book* in 1862, and to whom he wrote a letter after Bentel's return to Württemberg (*Letter-File*, May, 1872). Cornelius Jansen, in answering the questionnaire, writes that his brother Peter attended Pastor Wüst's boy's school. This is unlikely, since Wüst died in 1859. It could be Pastor Bentel instead, though this is not mentioned in the *Memoirs of Peter Jansen.*

[80]Notes, October, 1873. His selection of names here gives a good picture of his preferences. Literally he says: "Die unsichtbare Kirche. Es ist, so viel ich weiss, in der Bibel von keiner unsichtbaren Kirche die Rede. Die Kirche Christi soll eine durch ihre Werke 'sichtbare' sein.

Die streitende Kirche. In allen Gemeinden gab es einzelne streitende Glieder, wie die Geschichte der alten Kirchenväter bis in die Neuzeit (zeigt) bis a Kempis, Hus, Arendt, Symons, Zinzendorf, Roos, Paul Gerhard, Gossner und zuletzt Hoffacker neben vielen, sehr vielen nicht so bekannt geworden und doch nichts weniger treuen Zeugen. Unter diesen weniger sichtbaren und, wie ich fürchte, durch unserer Schuld *zu wenig sichtbaren,* gehört auch unsere Gemeinschaft."

[81]In an article in the *Chicago Daily Tribune*, (January 5, 1875), he wrote: "We call ourselves 'defenseless Christians'."

[82]*Ibid*., His friend, Leonhard Sudermann expresses himself very similarly when he says: "Unsere Gemeinschaft datiert sich nicht wie die übrige protestantische Kirche nur von der Reformationszeit, sie zieht sich viel mehr von der Apostelzeit durch all Jahrhunderte der Christlichen Zeitrechnung hindurch und ist wegen dieser ihrer Glaubenslehren immer bis auf die neusste Zeit ein verachtetes und unterdrücktes Häuflein gewesen." Draft of a letter, August 4, 1844. Leonhard Sudermann Collection, BCHL.

[83]*Memoirs of Peter Jansen,* p. 17.

[84]Answers to Questionnaire, (CJC).

[85]An den Enthaltsamkeits-Verein in Berlin, Ontario, Canada, von dem russischen Emigranten P. Janzen, 1873.

> "Meine Freunde, wenn ich so über das Verderben, das Alkohol verbreitet, spreche, so geschieht es leider aus eigener Erfahrung an meinen nächsten Verwandten, von denen einige diesem Laster (erlagen) ein junger blühender Mann im Besitz eines liebendes Weibes und Geschwister, er wurde gefesselt vom Alkohol; er sank tiefer, er hörte nicht auf die vermahnende Stimme eines Vaters, sein Vermögen ging dahin und er starb im. . . . (?) auf dem Felde, fern von aller menschlichen Hülfe und als man ihn nach 4 tägigem Suchen fand, hatte

sich an ihn die schreckliche Drohung Gottes wörtlich erfüllt; Ein Auge das der Mutter nicht gehorchet und verspottet des Vaters Gebot, das sollen die Raben am Bache ausshaken und die jungen Adler fressen. Ein anderer kam von Wein berauscht in seine Dampfmühle, steigerte den Dampf bis zu einer solchen Höhe dass der Kessel platzen musste in dem ihm ein Splitter desselben in den Kopt drang, als ein Opfer vom Alkohol vor den Richterstuhl Gottes gefordert."

It is believed that these two "closest relatives" were the brothers of Mrs. Jansen, Heinrich and Abraham, who both died young.

[86]*Account Book; Mission Cto. and Colportage.* (Written in the handwriting of son Peter, therefore use of plural "wir.")

[87]*Mission Cto. and Colportage.* —Johann Gerhard Oncken (1800-1884) was the founder of the Baptist Church in Germany. For many years he operated a publishing house and bookstore in Hamburg. For his connection with the Mennonite Brethren in South Russia see P. M. Friesen, *op. cit.,* pp. 281 and 382.

[88]*Mission Cto. and Colportage.*

[89]This Bible is a part of the Cornelius Jansen Collection.

[90]According to a form sheet in the German language: "Bibel-Magazin von J. Watt im Hause mimi, Preobrashenskaja-Strasse, gegenüber der Kathedrale in Odessa." As sub-agents for Watt a certain Rügel and also a Rempel are mentioned, (CJC).

[91]Ottobald Bischof, *Geschichte der christlichen Kirche in Bildern.* Leipzig, 1865. J. Prinz, *op. cit.*, p. 81; P. M. Friesen, *op. cit.*, p. 238, Fn. 1.

[92]*Correspondenz* (1871-1873), p. 2: "Empfohlene Bücher: 1. S. Kierkegaard, *Christenthum und Kirche,* Hamburg. J. G. Oncken." Under March 22, 1872, Jansen asked for the book of Kierkegaard in a letter to J. Wiehler, Odessa. The book he mentioned must be a very early translation into the German, since Kierkegaard's writings in general were not translated before the 80's.

[93]Papers and magazines from abroad at that time usually did not reach their destination in Russia on the direct way. They had to be ordered through special houses. Cornelius Jansen in this respect was served by the firm of Deubner, located at Riga as well as at Odessa. On November 17, 1871, he ordered from Deubner, Odessa: *Sunday at Home, Sendbote, Mennonitische Blätter;* On the same day he ordered from Deubner, Riga: Children's paper, Barth's *Jugendblatt, Kinderfreund* (Bremen), (*Correspondenz,* 1871-1873).

[94]*Memoirs of Peter Jansen,* p. 33.

[95]Helena Jansen said in a letter to C. J. Claassen, Pasadena, May 17, 1928: "As the Public Schools in South Russia were exceedingly poor and deficient, at that time we children received our education from private tutors, and from governesses, who came there from Prussia for that purpose."

[96]Diaries of Margaretha Jansen, and C. Jansen, Jr., Answer to Questionnaire.

[97]Interview with Mrs. S. K. Mosiman, Dec. 5, 1949.

[98]*Account Books,* also a bill by jeweler Stumpf, Danzig, April 8, 1873, where they pay Reichsthaler 6 for two pairs of glasses but 18 for the cases.

[99]These diaries are preserved for the periods from January to October, 1866, November, 1871 to October, 1872, and from October, 1873, to January, 1875, CJC.

[100]*Diary* of Margaretha Jansen, 1873.

[101]May 16, 1866, April 5 and 18, 1874, etc.

[102]Called by Margaretha (1866) *der grosse Heinrich* for distinction from the "Little Heinrich," or *Heine* as the youngest son was called then. Anna was called *Cousin Anna* for distinction, since there were two more Annas in the home, Aunt Anna and Sister Anna.

[103]Margaretha Jansen, *Diary,* March 22, 1874.

[104]*Ibid.*, Jan. 18, Feb. 15 and July 13, 1866.

[105]Isaac Robson and Thomas Harvey, *The Mennonites of South Russia* (1872) and *Narrative of the Visit of Isaac Robson and Thomas Harvey to the South of Russia, etc.* See also Owen Gingerich "Relation between the Russian Mennonites and the Friends during the Nineteenth Century," M.Q.R. (Oct., 1951) p. 283.

[106]Benjamin Seebohn, *Memoirs of the Life and Gospel Labours of Stephen Grillet* (London, 1860).

[107]*Narrative, ibid.*

[108]See also the chapter "Mennonite Friends."

[109]*Narrative*, p. 25.

[110]The original with Cornelius Jansen's translation into the German is preserved in CJC.

[111]Helena Jansen, "Value of Liberty in Religion and in the Press," and Cornelius Jansen, "The Mennonites etc.," *The Free Press,* (Mount Pleasant, Iowa, July 22, 1875 and January 18, 1876).

II. GREAT ISSUES

[1]"The Mennonites," *The Free Press,* (Mt. Pleasant, Iowa, Dec. 16, 1875).

[2]Up to 1861 this is done extensively by Wilhelm Mannhardt, *Die Wehrfreiheit der Altpreussischen Mennoniten,* (Marienburg, 1863). For the years 1861-1868, this is continued in an article by Hermann Gottlieb Mannhardt, *Christlicher Gemeindekalender,* (1919). For the last period see Emil Händiges "Historisches Memorandum zur Wehrlosigkeit der Mennoniten," *Der Bote,* (January 17, 1941) p. 5.

[3]Wilhelm Mannhardt, *op. cit.*, p. 191 ff.

[4]Letter of Elder Johann Wall, Hansau, (a friend of Johann Cornies), *Mennonitische Blätter,* (March, 1858).

[5]Jacob Mannhardt wrote in *Mennonitische Blätter*, (Sept., 1870) p. 41: "Seit dem Jahre 1866 ist unsere Stellung zu dem Kriegswesen eine veränderte geworden."

[6]Hermann Mannhardt, *Die Danziger Mennonitengemeinde,* (Danzig, 1919) p. 168.

[7]*Op. cit.*, p. 178.

[8]*Mennonitische Blätter,* (January, 1868).

[9]Peter Bartel, "Deputationsreise nach Berlin," *Mennonitische Rundschau,* (October 12, 1898).

[10]*Mennonitische Blätter,* (May, 1870) p. 34.

[11]Peter Dyck, *Reisebeschreibung II,* p. 6. Microfilm, BCHL.

[12]As he said himself, he read first of the Mennonites in America in the book of Wilhelm Mannhardt, *Die Wehrfreiheit der Altpreussischen Mennoniten,* (Marienburg, 1863). See preface to: *Sammlung von Notizen über Amerika* (Danzig, 1872) in Appendix.

[13]Cornelius Jansen, "The Mennonites," *The Free Press,* Mt. Pleasant, Iowa, (Jan. 18, 1876). Helena Jansen relates (*Der Herold*, June 11, 1931) p. 61, that one of the Quakers had been in the United States the year before they came to South Russia. The full passage reads: "In dieser Zeit kam in Angelegenheit das Weizengeschäfts ein junger Herr Joseph Sturge nach Südrussland und traf mit meinem Vater zusammen. Er gehörte zu den Quäkern. Dieser teilte mit, dass zwei ihrer Prediger nach Südrussland kommen würden. Einer wäre unlängst in den Vereinigten Staaten gewesen und würde über manches Aufschluss geben können. Der junge Sturge machte in unserem Hause sein Hauptquartier und auf diese Weise erfuhren wir über die amerikanischen Verhältnisse im Allgemeinen und über die Wehrfreiheit in Amerika noch besonders. Mein Vater bekam durch ihn auch Adressen von Mennoniten, die hier schon lange wohnten, bei denen er dann brieflich anfragte." See also Cornelius Jansen, *Sammlung von Notizen ....*, p. 21.

[14]Cornelius Jansen, *Sammlung von Notizen über Amerika* (1872), pp. 15-44; *Mennonitische Blätter,* (September, 1870) pp. 53-55.

[15]*Eine Deputationsreise von Russland nach America vor vierundzwanzig Jahren* (Elkhart, 1892) p. 7.

[16]*Mennonitische Blätter,* (Sept., 1869) p. 58, and (Feb., 1870) p. 16.

[17]*Ibid.*, (Feb., 1870) p. 16.

[18]*Ibid.*, (May, 1870) p. 31 f.

[19]"The Mennonites," *The Free Press,* (Jan. 13, 1876). The version given by C. B. Schmidt, *op. cit.*, p. 8. That the Mennonites of Russia read "no newspapers" is, however not correct. Cornelius Jansen and many other read papers. What struck him "like a bolt of lightning" must have been the unexpected developments along these lines.

[20]Dietrich Gaeddert, "Aufzeichnungen über die Auswanderung der Mennoniten von Süd-Russland nach Nord-Amerika," 1892 (Dietrich Gaeddert Collection, BCHL). According to Dietrich Gaeddert's version in this letter, he was the first one to discover that the Mennonite privileges were in danger, as early as 1861. In Dietrich Gaeddert's diaries which are preserved and in part for the period from March 25, 1857, to Feb. 7, 1871, in possession of the Bethel College Historical Library, nothing can be found referring to the citation just quoted. Another event asserting that the preparation of a universal conscription law was known before 1870, is told by Peter Bartel, a Mennonite elder in West Prussia and once delegate to Berlin. In February, 1868, the Prussian crown prince in an audience given to the Mennonite elders, commented on their plans of going to South Russia, if nonresistance would be denied to them, saying that they should be assured of the possibility of returning for what had happened in Prussia would soon also happen in Russia. See Peter Bartel, "Deputationsreise nach Berlin," *Mennonitische Rundschau,* (Oct. 12, 1898).

[21]*Op. cit.*, p. 3.

[22]"Christian Krehbiel and the Coming of the Mennonites to Kansas," Cornelius Krahn, (ed.), *From the Steppes to the Prairies,* (Newton, Kansas, 1949), p. 27.

[23]*Sammlung* . . . , pp. 8-12; A passage in the diary of Margaretha Jansen of January 25 (o.s.), reads: "Wir haben wieder kein Mädchen doch, jetzt ist wenigstens Akolienka gesund. Wie wir nach Hause kamen war das Mädchen schon fort, und dann heisst es: 'selbst arbeiten.' Nun das schadet uns nichts. Wir bereiten uns für Amerika vor, wo man ja sehr schwer Leute begommen kann und selbst arbeiten muss."

[24]Kempes Schnell, "John F. Funk and the Mennonite Migrations of 1873-85," *From the Steppes to the Prairies,* (Newton, Kansas, 1949).

[25]Cornelius Jansen, *Sammlung von Notizen über Amerika* (Danzig, 1872), pp. 5-8.

[26]*Ibid.*, pp. 12-14. According to Jansen's *Correspondenz* his letter was written Feb. 11, 1871, (o.s.). Unfortunately, the letters of Cornelius Jansen are not preserved in the John F. Funk archives so we have only the notes of Cornelius Jansen. This first time on February 11, Jansen ordered three copies of the *Herold der Wahrheit* and also books such as a Mennonite church history.

[27]July and October, 1950, pp. 201 and 352 respectively.

[28]*Sammlung von Notizen über Amerika,* pp. 15-27.

[29]*Ibid.*, pp. 28-44.

[30]*Correspondenz* 1871-1873.

[31]Leonhard Sudermann, "Bericht über unsere Reise nach St. Petersburg, in den ersten Monaten des Jahres 1871," *Herold der Wahrheit,* (1898) pp. 307, 322f, 357f, and 373. See also, D. H. Epp, *Die Chortitzer Mennoniten,* (Rosenthal 1888) pp. 100 ff; Gerhard Wiebe, *Ursachen und Geschichte der Auswanderung der Mennoniten aus Russland nach Amerika* (Winnipeg), p. 19 ff.

[32]P. M. Friesen, *op. cit.*, p. 495; Franz Isaac, *op. cit.*, p. 161.

[33]"Meine Aussprache über der Englischen Königin ihre Äusserung," CJC.

[34]"Bitte um Verwendung in Pr: für eine Deputation nach Amerika und Druck des Sendschribens."—The missive here spoken of is probably the same as the above-mentioned last missive of the Quakers. Whether it was printed then, is unknown.

[35]Diary of Margaretha Jansen, June 24, 1872.

[36]On May 28 he sent Ewert, among other papers "eine Copia von Brief an Fr: Sturge wegen unsere Reise." See also letter by J. Watt and J. M. Holmes in *Sammlung* . . . (pp. 44-47).—On May 15, 1871, (o.s.) Cornelius Jansen had sent R. S. 1500 by William Wagner, on July 1 (o.s.) R.S. 1300 by E. Mahs and Company, both times to the banking house of Bordier Brothers at Hamburg for the account of Heinrich Schütt. —At the end of the year, on December 11, 1871 (o.s.), R.S. 1500 were sent to Hamburg by Mahs for Abraham Matthies. —During these years Cornelius Jansen also frequently asked his business friends at Odessa for information on the rates of exchange.

[37]Letter to Consul Smith and *Correspondenz,* (CJC).

[38]Cornelius Jansen, *Sammlung* . . . . p. 44.

[39]Ernst Correll Collection, Goshen College.

[40]Timothy C. Smith to U. S. Department of State, July 22, 1871, Ernst Correll Collection, Goshen College.

[41]*Correspondenz,* Jan. 8, 1872 (o.s.)

[42]*Sammlung von Notizen über Amerika.*

[43]*Op. cit.*, pp. 6-8.

[44]Gaeddert writes literally: "Fast wollte es scheinen, als ob Bruder Cornelius Jansen . . . hier zu weit gehen wollte; denn er hatte den Muth, es der ganzen Predigerschaft, respt. Conferenz, zu sagen, dass es höchst nothwending sei, der hohen Regierung Russlands zu bekennen, dass wir Mennoniten schon zu weit abgewichen seien von unserem Glaubensbekenntnisse und hätten auch namentlich im Krimmkriege die Grenzen unsers so theuren Glaubensbekenntnisses überschritten, indem man den Schiessbedarf und Anderes dem Kriegsplatze zugeführt habe; man habe grosse Ursache Sr. Majestät und die hohen im Reiche nächst Gott Abbitte zu thun, und nachdem erst um Glaubens und Gewissensfreiheit zu bitten. Mann solle sich gerne bereit erklären, die von den Alten erwirkte Freiheit von Brantweinbrennen und Bierbrauen einbüssen zu wollen und zu vertauschen mit völliger Religionsfreiheit die die Alten zu sichern vergessen hatten. Natürlich fand der grösste Theil dieser Conferenz die Rede des C. Jansen absurd . . . ."

When evaluating this report we have to realize that it was especially written for Cornelius Jansen. —Jansen had expressed similar ideas in a letter to Leonhard Sudermann, on Feb. 25, 1871: "So wie die Auswanderung hierher (to Russia) mit irdischem Ziele begann, wovon dass auf unchristliche Weise verehrte Privilegium zeugt, indem durch Brennerei und Brauerei etc.: Freiheiten der Säuferei Rechnung getragen wurde; aber von keiner Buch-Druckerei oder anderem geistigen Bedürfniss auch nur Andeutung zu finden ist, so wird auch das Ende sein," (CJC).

[45]Dispatch of Consul Smith to Department of State, Jan. 6, 1872. Ernst Correll Collection. *Op. cit.*, p. 8.

[46]In his report Gaeddert writes that here for the first time he noticed that he was not isolated in his opinion. Speaking of himself in the third person, he writes: "Hier erfuhr D. Gaeddert es klar und nachhaltig, dass er mit seiner Anschauung der Verhältnisse nicht so ganz isoliert in der Welt dastand, sondern an Br. Jansen nicht nur einen Gleichgesinnten gefunden, sondern einen Vorläufer and hellen Kopf."

[47]Original draft in German in CJC. An English translation is published by G. Leibbrandt, *op. cit.*

[48]The English translation is reproduced by Ernst Correll: "Mennonite Immigration into Manitoba," *MQR,* (July, 1937) p. 211.— P. Lohrenz is not known as a leader of that time, he probably happened to be first to sign the letter. The other names are not given by Correll.

[49]Not to Yalta, as noted by C. H. Smith, *op. cit.*, p. 46f., and repeated by G. Leibbrandt, *op. cit. MQR,* (Oct., 1932) p. 208 f; Fr. Isaac, *op. cit.*, p. 308 f. It is of interest to note that of the later leaders of the emigration Isaak Peters was a member of this delegation while Jacob Buller and Dietrich Gaeddert signed the authorization. Jacob Wiebe, Karassan, Crimea, also elected to the delegation, did not participate.

[50]Dietrich Gaeddert writes (*op. cit.*, p. 9) that Leonhard Sudermann, who had been a member of the first delegation to St. Petersburg, was not elected to this second one because he was held to be influenced too much by Cornelius Jansen: "Ältester L. Sudermann, Berdyansk, wurde dieses Mal schon nicht gewählt, weil man glaubte, er sei schon zu sehr bearbeitet für das Sündenbekenntnis von C. Janzen und er könnte dann in Petersburg noch die ganze Geschichte verderben." Sudermann, however, writes in "My First Journey as Deputy in South Russia" (*Family Almanac,* Elkhart, 1896): "The confidence of the church toward me was in no way weakened by the course I had taken, as was subsequently proven when they sent me on three different occasions to represent the church in matters of the highest importance, and was even called upon the fourth time but resolutely declined to go after I had fully decided to emigrate to America." Only Franz Isaac was a member of both delegations.

[51]Franz Isaac (*op. cit.*, p. 310) reports: "Was uns aber in dieser Audienz fast in Erstaunen setzte, war die bis ins Einzelne genaue Kenntnis die Se. Exzellenz vor dem am 11. Januar d. J. in Alexanderwohl abgehaltenen Konferenze hatte. Nicht

nur hielten Se. Exzellenz uns vor, dass in derselben von einem Ausländer Propaganda für Auswanderung gemacht, sondern auch eine Deputation abgefertigt sei, bei der Regierung das Recht auszuwirken, in Zukunft nicht einmal mehr das tun zu dürfen, was wir bisher getan haben (wie z.B. die Podwodleistungen im Krimkriege) und ausserdem auch das Recht zu erlangen, im ganzen Reich Proselyten zu machen." The allegations were not "ridiculous changes," as Jacob Sudermann says in his article, "The Origin of Mennonite State Service in Russia, 1870-1800," *MQR,* (January, 1943) p. 31, but, of course, exaggerated. Since the deputies, according to Franz Isaac, had not heard about these "changes" Jansen perhaps had made his statements to a smaller circle only.

[52]Fr. Isaac, *op cit.*, p. 310f.

[53]Ernst Correll, *op. cit.*, p. 212f.

[54]*Ibid.*, p. 210.

[55]*Ibid.*, p. 216.—Named as receivers are "Sudermann, Hiebert, Penner, Jansen and other Mennonites."

[56]*Ibid.*, p. 214 f.

[57]Ernst Correll Collection, Goshen College.

[58]Ernst Correll, "Mennonite Immigration into Manitoba," *MQR,* (July, 1937) p. 217 f.

[59]The draft of this letter by hand of Jansen, and designated "Copia," is preserved in Cornelius Jansen Collection. It differs from the apparently final copy, found in the Public Archives of Canada, and published by Ernst Correll, *op. cit.,* p. 220 f. Also, the date is not the same. The following is the draft.

"Sir Exellenz
den Herrn Gen: Gouvernour von Canada.
B: 10/22 July 72.
Exellenz!
Dankbar is der durch Se. (?) Consul Zohrab erbetener Bescheid betreff einer Aufnahme unserer Mennoniten-Gemeinschaft in Canada, entgegen genommen worden.
Die trüben Erfahrungen betreff unserer Verweigerung der Theilnahme an jederlei und sei es der geringste Armeedienst im Militärgesetz, veranlassen uns jedoch zu der ehrerbietigen B. (Bitte) an Ew Exellenz uns, wenn möglich umgehend darüber Bescheid geben zu wollen, wie der Ausdruck zu verstehen ist, wenn es in Ihrer ges: Antw: heisst: Die Mennoniten haben gleich den Quäkern keinerlei Verpflichtung zum Armeedienst, ausgenommen derjenigen welche der Gen: Gouvernour sich aufzuerlegen gedrungen fühlen könnte.—Hierdruch erwächst hier die allgemeine Besorgniss dass wir dann auch mit vermeintem vollen Recht bei vermeinter 'Notwendigkeit" zum Armeedienst gezogen werden können, worin sich nur das wiederholen würde was hier in Russland und Deutschland zur Zeit auch für "Notwendig" angesehen wird. Im Auftrage der hierigen Gemeinde bitte ich Exellenz ganz ergebenst doch keinerlei unzurechtfertigende Zweifel sondern einfach das Bedürfniss eines klaaren Bescheides für uns sehen zu wollen, den, wenn möglich, wir uns in deutscher Sprache erbitten.
Ehrerbietigst
C. Jansen"

[60]Report of the Committee of the Privy Council approved by the Governor-General, September 25, 1872. Ernst Correll, *op. cit.*, p. 269 f.

[61]Ernst Correll Collection. See also G. Leibbrandt, *op. cit., MQR,* (Oct., 1932) p. 224 f.

[62]*Ibid.*, Instruction of Hamilton Fish to Eugene Schuyler, April 22, 1872.

[63]Jansen's last letter contained "Bescheid über den Bericht und Bitte um Meldung über unsere Angelegenheit nach Washington." *Immigration Letter-File*, April 8, 1872 (o.s.), CJC.

[64]Letter of Secretary John Lowe, June 1, 1872. E. Correll, *op. cit.*, *MQR*, (July, 1937) p. 220.

William Hespeler (1830-1921) was born at Baden-Baden, Germany, came to America in 1850, engaged in different occupations, most of the time living in Ontario. Following his activity for the Mennonite immigration he became Commissioner of Immigration and Agriculture at Winnipeg, and later was German Consul in that city. See E. Correll, *op. cit.*, p. 203.

[65]E. Correll, *op. cit.*, p. 226.

[66]E. Correll, *op. cit., MQR,* (Oct., 1937) p. 268.

[67]E. Correll, *op. cit., MQR,* (July, 1937) p. 227.

[68]E. Correll, *op. cit., MQR,* (Oct., 1937) p. 267.

[69]The English copy and two copies in German by the hand of Cornelius Jansen are in the *Immigration Letter-File* of CJC.

[70]Consul Zohrab to Earl Granville, Aug. 5, 1872. E. Correll, *op. cit., MQR,* (July, 1937) p. 223.

[71]E. Correll, *op. cit.*, p. 224 f., the letter closes: "I am of opinion therefore that Mr. Zohrab having informed the German Mennonites of the willingness of the Canadian Government to receive them and the terms on which they will be received as emigrants he should abstain from making any further advance to them. They appear to have a keen eye for their own interests, and should they finally decide on emigration (which I very much doubt) will be governed in the selection of their future home by the advantages which may be offered to them.

[72]John Low to Wm. Hespeler, Sept. 17, 1872. E. Correll, *op. cit., MQR,* (Oct., 1937) p. 268 f. The presumptive deputation were the young Russian Mennonites on their private trip.

[73]*Ibid.*, p. 271.

[74]*Ibid.*, p. 269.

[75]Letter to Isaac Robson and Thomas Harvey, *Immigration Letter-File,* Oct. 29, 1872 (o.s.), CJC.

[76]Consul Zohrab reported on a conversation held with Cornelius Jansen on August 5, 1872: "Mr. Jansen also stated that letters had been received from the Mennonites in the Crimea reporting that they and the Lutherans were very dissatisfied with the new laws and wished to quit the country and that they were closely watching the course pursued by the Mennonites here; it resulted in their quitting Russia they would leave also." E. Correll, *op. cit., MQR,* (July, 1937) p. 224.

[77]See Melvin Gingerich, "The Alexanderwohl 'Schnurbuch'" in *Mennonite Life,* (January, 1946) pp. 45-47. The BCHL has numerous other contracts and lists of mutual aid similar to this one.

[78]We do not know the names of these delegates. One of the latter was one of the visitors to America just returned, probably Peter Dyck, *Immigration Letter-File,* CJC.

[79]E. Correll, *op. cit., MQR,* (Oct., 1937) p. 278 f.

[80]Dietrich Gaeddert, *op. cit.*

[81]A short time before, Pastor Hans had tried to influence the Mennonites by a general (probably printed) letter addressed to all elders of the Mennonite congregations, which letter was inspired by Government officials, according to Abr. Görz, *op. cit.*, p. 7. "Vom 6. Mai 1872 liegt von Pastor Hans folgender Brief vor, den er, nach seinem Inhalt zu schliessen, wahrscheinlich im Auftrage hoher Regierungsbeamten geschrieben hat."

[82]Fr. Isaac, *op. cit.*, p. 313 f.

[83]Dietrich Gaeddert, *op. cit.*, p. 13ff.

[84]Gerhard Wiebe, *op. cit.*, p. 21 ff; D. H. Epp, *op. cit.*, p. 107.

[85]Dietrich Gaeddert, *op. cit.*, p. 13f; Franz Isaac, *op. cit.*, p. 316 ff.

[86]Gerhard Wiebe, *op. cit.*, p. 23 ff; Klaas Peters, *Die Bergthaler Mennoniten* p. 7 ff; Cornelius Krahn, "The Bergthal Settlement," *Mennonite Weekly Review,* (Feb. 22, 1951) p. 6.

[87]*Immigration Letter-File.* The payment for this and the following printings was advanced by Louis Eduard Zimmermann, Jansen's friend at whose home Heinrich von Riesen stayed during this time. Twenty-four and a half talers for printing and paper (3½ sheets of paper) and 1½ talers for binding.

[88]The only copy of *Sammlung of Notizen von Amerika* available at this time is located in the BCHL. The preface appears as Appendix IV in this publication.

[89]Oct. 29, 1872. Draft in CJC.

[90]1871 (?). We know that Cornelius Jansen went to see the Governor-General at Odessa at the end of the year 1870. It is possible that one year later he repeated this visit.

[91]The bill was dated and paid on August 5. The price paid for the printing of pamphlets indicates something about their length: for the first, 6½ talers were paid; for the second, and third, 4½ and for the fourth and fifth, 3 talers.

[92]This obviously cannot be the right title, since these pamphlets were in the German language. It probably was a translation of American documents against war. In a letter to C. H. Zimmerman written during this time, Jansen enclosed "American papers witnessing against war" ("Ausschluss der American Paper als gegen Kriege zeugend"). *Immigration Letter-File*, June 23, 1872 (o.s.).

[93]Cornelius Jansen, "The Mennonites," *The Free Press,* (Jan. 20 and Jan. 13, 1876).

[94]*Immigration Letter-File*, August 20, 1872 (o.s.).

[95]Draft of letter of October 29, 1872, CJC.

[96]Speaking about his pamphlet, *Thoughts on Our Duties Towards Magistrates,* Jansen said in his talk (*op. cit.*, Jan. 20, 1876): This and a few others about religious liberty of the Peace Society, were not very long afterwards shown to a friend of mine at Petersburg, with the question whether he knew the publisher of them by the name of C. F."—The last letter, thus printed in *The Free Press,* certainly is mispelled, the "J" in the German handwriting being easily mistaken for a "F."

[97]For printing, paper (half a sheet each) and binding 6 talers were billed on January 27, 1873, to Louis Eduard Zimmerman. To judge from the presumptuous title, it was not a product of Cornelius Jansen himself, but rather a translation of some Quaker tract. In Jansen's correspondence of that time a "Tracktatchen von Robson" is mentioned repeatedly. See *Immigration Letter-File.*

[98]"Unser armes laues Volk soll trotz aller bisherigen Trägheit, doch noch die Ehre und Freude einigen Antheils an der Bekämpfung des ebenso abscheulichen als sündlichen Krieges haben und wir wollens nicht verstehen." Letter to Leonhard Sudermann, Berdyansk, Feb. 25, 1871 (o.s.). Draft, CJC.

[99]*Family Almanac,* (Elkhart, 1896). In a letter from Canada Cornelius Jansen wrote to his relatives (Oct. 9, 1873): "Ueberhaupt hat es für jeden Christen so etwas tröstendes und aufmunterndes in sich der Welt gegenüber die dort in Europa so gerne über uns frohlocken und uns zu ihrer Beruhigung überwunden sehen möchte, ein offenes Zeugniss abzulegen, dass das Friedensevengelium unseres Herrn und Heilandes wie einst so auch heute Menschen willig findet, seine irdische Behaglichkeiten aufzugeben um Ihm zu dienen viel mehr für uns opferte."

[100]Cornelius Jansen Collection.

[101]*Op. cit.*, p. 501.

[102]Manuscript in CJC. See Appendix II.

[103]*Thoughts on Indirect Military Service*, etc. See Appendix III.

[104]Letter to Leonhard Sudermann, Feb. 25, 1871. "Dass einzige Zeugniss was wir geben können ist wie unsere Väter, zu gehen, und dass will ich tun so mir mein Herr und Heiland hilft und sollte ich mich täuschen in der Wahl und meine Kinder in dieselbe Noth kommen, so wird mein Zeugniss ihnen das Weiterwandern erleichtern. Ich habe sie nicht nach Reichthum trachten gelehrt, aber sie wissen auch gut dass mich nichts, nichts treibt, meine für mich viel zu gute behagliche Stellung zu verlassen, als für mich und sie die Freiheit der Kinder Gottes, Gewissenfreiheit, zu bewahren." P. M. Friesen, *op. cit.*, p. 508.

[105]This he expressed in his letter to Robson and Harvey, Nov. 1, 1872 (o.s.), in which he wrote that he had tried to reject an opposing argument 'in a large congregation of ministers and elders," (CJC).

[106]A brother of Philip Wiebe, Elder Jacob Wiebe from the Crimea, not to be confused with the founder of the Krimmer Mennonite Brethren Church, opposed emigration sharply in a letter written in 1876, reproduced by P. M. Friesen, *op. cit.,* p. 511 ff. A copy has been preserved in BCHL.

[107]Kozelitzke, March 19, 1875.

[108]Heinrich Dirks wrote regarding the emigration question, written at Pakanten, Sumatra, July 18, 1872:

> "Wo will unser armes Mennoniten-Volk in dieser gegenwärtigen bösen Zeit in der argen Welt ein Plätzchen finden wo es ihm in etwa wieder heimisch würde, und wo es auch nur das zurück fände, was ihm in Russland noch immerhin bleiben wird," (CJC).

[109]Letter to Robson and Harvey, Sept. 29, 1872 (o.s.).

[110]For instance, *Thoughts on Indirect Military Service*, etc. See Appendix III.

[111]To his business friend Carl Heinrich Zimmermann, "Vorsteher" of the Danzig Mennonite Church, Cornelius Jansen wrote an "Entschuldigung betreff der Kränkung," *Immigration Letter-File,* June 23, 1872.

[112]Letter to Robson and Harvey, Sept. 29, 1872.

[113]Letter to Robson and Harvey, September 29, 1872 (o.s.). On August 8 (o.s.) the house was sold to a certain Büttner, "Olga Suckau's Mann." Diary of Margaretha Jansen, August 8, 1872.

[114]Cornelius Jansen, "The Mennonites" etc., *The Free Press,* (Jan. 20, 1876).

[115]The "Ukase" appears in translation in Appendix. The Russian and several English copies have been preserved, CJC. Wilhelm Loewens, a Mennonite architect, apparently from Danzig, who had spent a few years in America, was asked for information.

[116]Helena Jansen, *op. cit.*

[117]*Op. cit.*, p. 20; "As he was still a Prussian citizen, he sent a long telegram to Count Bismarck, who was then in the zenith of power at Berlin. The Count really took an interest in the matter, as Father had frequently communicated with him during the time he was Consul and Bismarck was Ambassador at St. Petersburg."

[118]Quoted from official translation, copy in Ernst Correll Collection, Goshen College.

[119]"The Mennonites."

[120]*Ibid.*, p. 30.

[121]*Ibid.*

III. THE PROMISED LAND

[1]*Tagebuch,* Cornelius Jansen, April 22, May 4, 1873. His words, "Viele Gäste." In this short diary Jansen covers the period from April 15, 1873 to March 13, 1874. His entries are very brief but rather to the point. They cover the family's overland journey from Berdyansk to Danzig and other places they visited in Germany; their stop at Leeds, England, where they visited the Quakers, the voyage to Quebec, Canada, their overland journey to Berlin, Ontario, and the first travels in the United States with the Russian Mennonite delegation.

[2]Helena Jansen, "Value of Liberty. . . ."

[3]A bill of the firm Kylius and Co., printers at Berdyansk, of May 11, 1873, contains "24 Sheet-Poems for Silver Wedding."

[4]*Ibid.*, also Cornelius Jansen, *Tagebuch,* May 15, 1873.

[5]"Am 25ten Mai 1873 sagte Papa mir die Blätter bezüglich Tautes Cto. aus den verschiedenen Büchern herauszunehmen, ich verbrannte das Uebrige, und, darunter leider auch die Cto's von Stadtabgaben und Hausreparatur welche Papa mir nicht speciell bezeichnet hat. P. Janzen." Handwritten note, CJC.

[6]Leonhard Sudermann, Jacob Buller and Rudolf Riesen left for Prussia on the 15th of April. They expected to meet Wilhelm Ewert in Prussia and then leave together with others for America. Apparently David Goerz had some difficulty with his passport.

[7]*Immigration Letter-File*, April 4 and 5, 1873.—("2050 for M/Th. (?), 2950 for American obligations").

[8]C. Jansen, *Tagebuch,* May 26, 1873 or June 7 (n.s.).

[9]*Ibid.*

[10]*Ibid.*, May 26 - June 2, 1873: Peter Jansen, *op. cit.*, p. 31.

[11]Peter Jansen, *op. cit.*, p. 31.

[12]C. Jansen, *Tagebuch*, June 1 and 2.

[13]*Ibid.*

[14]*Ibid.*, June 16 and 17.
[15]See Simplified Chart of the Penner Family in Appendix I.
[16]Peter Jansen, *op. cit.*, p. 31.
[17]C. Jansen, *Tagebuch*, June 18, July 6, 1873.
[18]*Ibid.*, July 12.
[19]Peter Jansen, *op. cit.*, p. 32.
[20]CJC; C. Jansen, *Tagebuch*, July 14 and 19, 1873.
[21]*Ibid.*, July 15.
[22]*Ibid.*
[23]*Ibid.*, July 19 to 22, 1873.
[24]*Ibid.*, July 24 to 29, 1873.
[25]Peter Jansen, *op. cit.*, p. 32.
[26]C. Jansen, *Tagebuch*, November 10, 1873.
[27]This is an indication that Cornelius Jansen was beginning to turn over some of his responsibility to his son Peter. This was to become increasingly more true from now on.
[28]Letter, Allen Bros. & Co., Liverpool to Falk and Co., Hamburg, May 21, 1873. Also, Falk & Co. to C. J., May 24, 1873.
[29]Peter Jansen, *op. cit.*, p. 30.
[30]C. Jansen, *Tagebuch*, July 28 to 31, 1873.
[31]*Ibid.*, August 1 to 10, 1873
[32]Peter Jansen, *op. cit.*, p. 32.
[33]C. Jansen, *Tagebuch*, August 10 to 14, 1873; Peter Jansen, *op. cit.*, p. 33.
[34]C. Jansen, *Tagebuch*, August 14 to 19, 1873.
[35]*Ibid.*, August 20, 1873.
[36]Leonhard Sudermann, *Eine Deputationsreise von Russland nach Amerika.* (Elkhart, 1897) p. 78.
[37]Leonhard Sudermann, Diary (typed copy) p. 25, BCHL.
[38]C. Henry Smith, *The Coming of the Russian Mennonites*, (Berne, Indiana, 1927) pp. 51-52.
[39]*Ibid.*, p. 52.
[40]*Ibid.*, pp. 57-69.
[41]*Ibid.*, pp. 69-70. L. Sudermann, *Eine Deputationsreise*, p. 78., writes that the agreement was made in Philadelphia on the 19th. If so, then Jansen did not attend this meeting.
[42]C. Jansen, *Tagebuch*, August 20, 1873. The presentation and discussion of the Mennonite request in Congress have been presented in detail by Leland Harder in "The Russian Mennonites and the American Democracy under Grant" in *From the Steppes to the Prairies* (Newton, Kansas, 1949) edited by Cornelius Krahn.
[43]*Ibid.*, August 21 to 27, 1873.
[44]*Ibid.*, August 28 to Sept. 12, 1873.
[45]*Ibid.*, Sept. 8-12, 1873.
[46]Dietrich Gaeddert, *op. cit.*
[47]Letter, C. Jansen to Holden or Hollen n. d. but found on p. 28 of *Conto-Corn. Jansen-Correspondence* with Amos Herr et. al. 1873-1875, CJC. These letters found in this book appear to be rough notes he took, probably to dictate them to his stenographer. That he had a stenographer during the first years in America is referred to in his daughters' diaries.
[48]C. Jansen, *Tagebuch*, Sept. 12 to Oct. 1, 1873.
[49]Letter, C. Jansen to "Geehrter Herr," Feb. 21, 1874, found in *Conto-Cornelius Jansen-Correspondence* to Amos Herr et. al. 1873-1875.
[50]C. Jansen, *Tagebuch*, Oct. 29, 1873.
[51]Letter, Peter Jansen to his friend Dec. 2, 1873, in No. I. *Manuskript-Heft* by Peter Jansen, CJC, BCHL.
[52]*Ibid.*, also C. J., *Tagebuch*, of Nov. 10.
[53]Letter, Cornelius Jansen to Mr. Forney, Editor of the *Press*, Nov. 28, 1873, in *Conto, op. cit.*

[54]Letter, Peter Jansen to his friend Dec. 2, 1873, *op. cit.*, also C. Jansen, *Tagebuch*, Nov. 16, 1873; See also *The Friend, A Religious, Literary and Miscellaneous Journal*, (Vol. XIII, No. 158) p. 3. See letter of Thomas Harvey in *The Friend*.

[55]*Memoirs of Peter Jansen*, p. 35.

[56]*Ibid.*; C. Jansen, *Tagebuch*, Nov. 14 to 20, 1873; See also Leland Harder, *op. cit.*

[57]Letter, P. Jansen to his friend Dec. 2, 1873, *Manuskript-Heft;* C. Jansen, *Tagebuch*, Nov. 21 to 26, 1873.

[58]Letter, P. Jansen, to Forney, Nov. 23, 1873, in *Conto, op. cit.*

[59]Letter of P. Jansen of Dec. 2, *op. cit.*; C. Jansen, *Tagebuch*, Nov. 24 to 29, 1873.

[60]Ernst Correll, "President Grant and the Mennonite Immigration from Russia," *MQR* (July, 1953) pp. 149-150).

[61]James A. Richardson, *A Compilation of the Messages and Papers of the Presidents*, 1789-1897, (Washington, 1898) Vol. VII, p. 253.

[62]Letter, C. Jansen to Forney, Nov. 23, 1873, *Conto, op. cit.*

[63]Letter, C. Jansen to Amos Herr, Nov. 10, 1873, *Conto, op. cit.*

[64]"Christian Krehbiel and the Coming of the Mennonites to Kansas," an Autobiography, (Tr. and ed. by Edward Krehbiel) in *From the Steppes to the Prairies* (1874-1949) ed. by Cornelius Krahn, (Newton, Kansas, 1949) p. 39.

[65]C. Henry Smith, *op. cit.*, p. 77.

[66]C. Henry Smith, *op. cit.*, pp. 77-79.

[67]Margarete Jansen, *Tagebuch*, December 1, 1873, to January 10, 1874. BCHL has a microfilm copy of this diary which starts on October 21, 1873, and ends with Margarete's death, January 6, 1875. The last entries are made by her father.

[68]Letter, Secretary of Interior C. Delano to Cornelius Jansen, Feb. 9, 1874, Ernst Correll Collection, Goshen College.

[69]Letter, C. Jansen to Secretary of Interior, C. Delano, Feb. 16 or 18, 1874, *Conto, op. cit.* This letter, like all those in this book appears to be the first copy of a letter which was rewritten.

[70]Margarete Jansen, *Tagebuch*, March 26 to April 8, 1874.

[71]Letter, C. Jansen to "Meine Geliebten!" April 13, 1874. See also Peter's letter to his mother and "Geschwister" of March 28, 1874, CJC. The family received this letter on the 16th (See M. Jansen, *Tagebuch*, April 16, 1874).

[72]Margarete Jansen, *Tagebuch*. See first page of diary which gives the places and dates for this trip. See also entry of April 23, 1874 and C. H. Smith, *op. cit.*, pp. 88-91.

[73]Margarete Jansen, *Tagebuch*, April 16, 1874.

[74]C. Henry Smith, *op. cit.*, pp. 80-81.

[75]C. Henry Smith *op. cit.*, p. 81, especially Herr's letter to Jansen regarding the Dakota lands and Herr's interest in lands of other states.

[76]*Ibid.*, pp. 77-91, also Leland Harder, "The Russian Mennonites and American Democracy under Grant," in, *From the Steppes to the Prairies*, pp. 51-65.

[77]"The Diary of Paul Tschetter, 1873," (trnsl. & edited by J. M. Hofer), *MQR* (July, 1931) p. 217.

[78]Leland Harder, *op. cit.*, p. 61f.

[80]C. Jansen, *Tagebuch*, March 25, 1873.

[81]Berdyansk, April 7, 1873 (o.s.), Ernst Correll Collection, Goshen College.

[82]Cornelius Jansen, "The Mennonites," *The Free Press*, (Jan. 27, 1876).

[83]*Memoirs of Peter Jansen*, pp. 46-47, Theodore Schmidt, "The Mennonites of Nebraska," (M.A. thesis, BCHL) p. 51.

[84]Theodore Schmidt, *op. cit.*, p. 51.

[85]Letter, C. Jansen to Amos Herr, 10/12/73, *Conto, op. cit.* In his letter to Hollen or Holden *op. cit.*, he writes that he wants to do what he can to assist the emigration whether they settle in "the North, West or South just so they leave Russia and Germany." See also C. Jansen's letter in the Chicago *Daily Tribune*, Jan. 5, 1875, p. 2. c7f.

[86]Georg Leibbrandt, "The Emigration of the German Mennonites from Russia to the United States and Canada in 1873-1880": I, *MQR* (Oct., 1932) p. 211.

[87]Thomas Harvey, editor of *The Friend*, (Samuel Harris & Co., London. First Month, 1st 1874) p. 3.; *Ibid.* (Tenth Month 1st, 1873) pp. 247-248.

[88]Berdyansk, April 7, 1873 (o.s.), Ernst Correll Collection, Goshen College.

[89]Marshall Jewell, U. S. Minister to Russia, to Hamilton Fish, No. 77, May 20, (1874) and Hamilton Fish, Secretary of State to Marshall Jewell. No. 16, June 12, 1874, Ernst Correll Collection, Goshen College.

[90]Letter, C. Jansen to Anthony Kimber, undated but it must have been written shortly after Jansen's interview with the Kimber brothers in November, 1873. *Conto., op. cit.*

[91]Marshall Jewell letter, *op. cit.*; also, Gerig Leibbrandt, *op. cit.*, MQR, Oct., 1932, pp. 221-226.

[92]C. Jansen, *Tagebuch*, August 16, 1873.

[93]Letter, Peter Jansen to Whiting, August 26, 1873. The year is omitted, but since the letter is dated Berlin, Ontario, it must be 1873, CJC.

[94]C. Jansen, *Tabeguch*, December 22-24, 1873.

[96]*Herald of Truth* (Elkhart, Indiana, Jan., 1874) pp. 9-10.

[97]*Ibid.*

[98]*The Friend* . . . The articles start in October, 1873 and continue through 1876. See New Series Vol. XIII No. 154, p. 247, BCHL.

[99]*Ibid.*, (Third Month 1st, 1875) pp. 73-74.

[100]*Ibid.*

[101]*Ibid.*, (Fourth Month 1, 1875) pp. 93-94.

[102]*Ibid.*

[103]*Ibid.*, (10th Month 1st, 1875).

[104]*The British Friend, A Monthly Journal Chiefly Devoted to the Interests of the Society of Friends*, (London, Vol. XXXIV, No. VII. 7th Month 1, 1876) pp. 203-204.

[105]*Ibid.*

IV. SETTLEMENT IN RETROSPECT

[1]*Memoirs of Peter Jansen*, p. 33.

[2]Cornelius Jansen, *Tagebuch*, August 14, 1873.

[3]Margarete Jansen, *Tagebuch*, October 6, 1873. Margarete Jansen kept a diary beginning October 21, 1873, but she went back as far as her memory allowed her, to the latter part of September, 1873. She carries it to the end of her life in January, 1875.

[4]*Ibid.*, October 13, 1873.

[5]*The Friend* (Tenth Month 1st. 1874) pp. 299-300.

[6]*Ibid.* (Third Month 1st, 1875) pp. 73-74.

[7]*Memoirs of Peter Jansen*, p. 33.

[8]*Ibid.*, p. 33.

[9]*Ibid.*, p. 35.

[10]*Ibid.*

[11]Letter, C. Jansen to *Mein Herr Onkel*, 11/10/73, *Conto, op. cit.*

[12]M. Jansen, *Tagebuch*, Nov. 16, 1873.

[13]*Ibid.*, April 12 and 19, 1874.

[14]Letter, Peter Jansen to his friend at Goldschar, Dec. 2, 1873. No. 1 *Manuskript-Heft*, CJC.

[15]*Memoirs of Peter Jansen*, p. 40.

[16]M. Jansen, *Tagebuch*, May 16, 1874.

[17]*Ibid.*, December 31, 1873; May 30, 1874.

[18]*Ibid.*, December 13, 1873.

[19]*Ibid.*, January 22, 1874; M. Gingerich; Jacob Y. Shantz . . ." *MQR* (July, 1950) p. 244.

[20]*Ibid.*, April 19, 1874.

[21]*Ibid.*, April 5 and 6, 1874.

[22]*Ibid.*, December 31, 1873.

[23]Letter, C. Jansen to T. Robson and T. Harvey, T. Whiting, W. Sturge and their families. n.d., *Conto, op. cit.*

[24]Letter, P. Jansen to T. Whitney, Aug. 26, 1873.
[25]Letter, Gertrude Penner to Peter Jansen, Jan. 6, 1874.
[26]M. Jansen, *Tagebuch*, March 4, 1874.
[27]*Ibid.*, March 10 and 21, 1874.
[28]C. Jansen, *Tagebuch*, March 1-13, 1874. (His last entries).
[29]M. Jansen, *Tagebuch*, Oct. 10, 1873 and May 20, 1874.
[30]*Ibid.*, March 22, 1874.
[31]*Ibid.*, March 26; April 8, 21, 23; May 6, 14, 20, 1874.
[32]*Ibid.*, Jan. 7, 1874.
[33]C. Jansen, Letter, to John Lowe, June 27, 1874. *Letter File, Various Documents and Letters copies and originals*, 1868-1875. The Jansen Collection contains the list of all Mennonites that came to Manitoba, 1874-81, which was kept by Schantz. His help given to Schantz must have been considerable.
[34]Letter, Peter Jansen to his friend at Goldschar, "*Reisebericht,*" Dec. 2, 1873, No. 1. *Manuskript-Heft.*
[35]Letter, P. Jansen to Jno. Abbott, Esq. Nov., 1873, *op. cit.*
[36]M. Jansen, *Tagebuch*, June 1, to June 4, 1874.
[37]*Ibid.*, July 13 to 26, 1874.
[38]*Ibid.*, July 13, 26; August 14, 1874.
[39]*Ibid.*, Sept. 3 and Oct. 1, 1874.
[40]*Memoirs of Peter Jansen*, pp. 40-42.
[41]*Ibid.*, p. 43.
[42]*Ibid.*, p. 42.
[43]M. Jansen, *Tagebuch*, Sept. 3, 1874. She had failed to make a daily entry, so she reviewed what had happened on the 3rd.
[44]Dietrich Gaeddert, *op. cit.*
[45]C. Henry Smith, *The Coming of the Mennonites*, pp. 115-119. According to Voth the only offer Schmidt did not meet was when Touzalin said, "You tell Mr. Richert that the C. B. & Q. will give them the necessary land for nothing."
[46]M. Jansen, *Tagebuch*, Oct. 9, 1874.
[47]*Ibid.*, July 26; Sept. 6, 13, 20, 27; Nov. 27, 1874.
[48]*Ibid.*, July 26, 1874.
[49]*Ibid.*, Sept. 24 and Oct. 27, 1874.
[51]*Ibid.*, December 7, 1874 to January 6, 1875.
[52]Anna Jansen, *Tagebuch*, January 10, 1875. Anna Jansen, the second oldest daughter in the family, started her diary on this date. Her first entry is as of November 29, 1878. BCHL has a microfilm copy of this diary. It has many omissions, but it is the most valuable source for the next three years.
[53]*Memoirs of Peter Jansen*, p. 42.
[54]A. Jansen, *Tagebuch*, January 19 and 22, 1876.
[55]Letter, C. Jansen to Aron Claassen, April 18, 1876.
[56]*Ibid.*, April 1, 1876.
[57]*Ibid.*, May 23, 1876.
[58]A. Jansen, *Tagebuch*, March 13, 16, Sept. 25 and Oct. 2, 1875.
[59]Chicago *Tribune*, January 5, 1875, p. 2.
[60]*Ibid.*
[61]"The Mennonites and their Colonies in Nebraska," in *Various Documents and Letters. Copies and Originals*, etc. CJC. It is possible that this was the original of the article published in the Chicago *Tribune*, Jan. 5, 1875.
[62]Letter, Mrs. C. Jansen to Aron Claassen, Feb. 29, 1876.
[63]*Ibid.*, March 10, 1876.
[64]*Ibid.*, Feb. 29, 1876.
[65]Anna Jansen, *Tagebuch*, May 18 and 26, 1875.
[66]*Ibid.*, Sept. 1, 1875.
[67]*Ibid.*, Oct. 11, 1875.
[68]*Ibid.*, Feb. 11, May and June, 1876.
[69]*Ibid.*, March 24 and April 25, 1876; also Letters, C. Jansen to A. Claassen Feb. 18, 1876 and Mrs. Jansen to A. Claassen March 10, 1876.

[70]*Tagebuch*, April 26, 1876.
[71]*Memoirs of Peter Jansen*, p. 47.
[72]*Ibid.*
[73]*Ibid.*, p. 48. Cornelius Jansen, Jr., *Tagebuch*, Nov. 17, 1879.
[74]Anna Jansen, *Tagebuch*, January 2, 1877.
[75]*Memoirs of Peter Jansen*, p. 43.
[76]A. Jansen, *Tagebuch*, entry of Dec. 30, 1875.
[77]*Memoirs of Peter Jansen*, p. 43.
[78]*Memoirs of Peter Jansen*, pp. 44, 49.
[79]*Ibid.*, pp. 44, 45.
[80]A. Jansen, *Tagebuch*, February 28, 1876.
[81]A. Jansen, *Tagebuch*, entry of June 28, 1876, *Memoirs of Peter Jansen*, p. 44.
[82]Peter Jansen, *op. cit.*, p. 44.
[83]*Beatrice Weekly Express*, January 20, 1876.
[84]A. Jansen, *Tagebuch*, April 10-27, 1875.
[85]Cor. Jansen, Jr., *Tagebuch*, April 17, 1882. This diary starts Jan. 1, 1879 and ends Jan. 1, 1884, CJC, BCHL.
[86]*Memoirs of Peter Jansen*, pp. 44 and 51.
[87]*Ibid.*, p. 52.
[88]*Memoirs of Peter Jansen, op. cit.*, p. 48; Anna Jansen, *Tagebuch*, March 13, to May 4, 1877.
[89]Peter Jansen, *op. cit.*, p. 48; A. Jansen, *Tagebuch*, July 18, 1877.
[90]A. Jansen, *Tagebuch*, July 18, 1877.
[91]Peter Jansen, *op. cit.*, p. 48.
[92]*Memoirs of Peter Jansen*, p. 46.
[93]A. Jansen, *Tagebuch*, December 11, 1877.
[94]*Memoirs of Peter Jansen*, p. 45.
[95]*Ibid.*, pp. 53-54.
[96]Mrs. G. A. Penner, daughter of Peter Jansen, indicated in an interview that she remembers vividly the fact that there were four windmills on the home place and that this was often a point of considerable comment by visitors.
[97]L. A. Penner, Route No. 1, Beatrice, Nebraska, a nephew of Peter Jansen who as a boy used to spend his vacations "on the Ranch with Uncle Pete."
[98]*Fairbury Gazette*, June 30, 1883.
[99]*Ibid.*, May 7, 1892.
[100]*Fairbury Gazette*, (August 4, 1888) states that "Peter Jansen went to Colorado and bought 8,000 sheep for his ranch," and in February 22, 1890, refers to "Peter Jansen and Company" having "shipped three carloads of sheep."
[101]The exact issue in which this appeared was not found. The letter is dated February 5, 1909, and is addressed to Bill Cramb who was at that time the editor of the *Fairbury Journal*, clipping in CJC.
[108]Peter Jansen, *Tagebuch*, Vol. 1, pp. 114-119. Peter started his diary January 1, 1884 and continued it to March 13, 1895. It contains many omissions, CJC.
[109]*Numerical Index*, Township 3, Range 4, Sec. 30. Register of Deeds Office, Jefferson County, Fairbury, Nebraska.
[110]D. Paul Miller, "An Analysis of Community Adjustment—A Case Study of Jansen, Nebraska," (Ph.D. dissertation U. of N., 1953) map p. 93. Notice especially, Sec. 26. BCHL.
[111]*Numerical Index, Section* 34, Register of Deeds Office, Fairbury, Nebraska.
[112]Circular preserved in CJC, BCHL.
[113]D. Paul Miller, *op. cit.*, p. 49.
[114]March 26, 1887, issue.
[115]The information on the businesses in Jansen in the first two decades was taken from the "Jansen News Items," *Fairbury Gazette*.
[116]D. Paul Miller, *op. cit.*, pp. 109-128.
[117]*Ibid.*, Appendix III-e.
[118]*Fairbury Gazette*, (August 18, 1888).
[119]*Ibid.*, (May 28, 1892).

[120]*Ibid.*, (August 6, 1892).
[121]D. Paul Miller, *op. cit.*, pp. 129 ff.
[122]Peter Jansen, *Tagebuch*, July 23-31, 1891.
[123]*Ibid.*, Nov. 14-20, 1891.
[124]*Ibid.*, June 29 and August 1-17, 1892.
[125]Peter Jansen Real Estate Deeds, CJC, BCHL.
[126]Peter Jansen, *Tagebuch*, Oct. 29, 1894 Peter wrote that he had made no entry in his diary for a long time, because the times were so trying he had not felt like writing.
[127]Mrs. C. Jansen, *Tagebuch*, June 14, 1892.
[128]*Ibid.*, June 22, 1892.
[129]*Memoirs of Peter Jansen*, p. 61.
[130]*Op. cit.; Lincoln Sunday Journal and Star*, (August 2, 1936) Section C and D, p. 3; *Mennonite Life*, (October, 1947) p. 41 ff.
[131]*Beatrice Daily Sun*, (February 9, 1911).
[132]*Beatrice Daily Sun*. Clipping in CJC, BCHL.
[133]*Memoirs of Peter Jansen, op. cit.*, p. 60.
[134]*Ibid.*, p. 62.
[135]Clipping in CJC, BCHL.
[136]E. S. Bayard in "Down the Pike," *Pennsylvania Farmer*, (Harrisburg, Pennsylvania, February 12, 1944).
[137]*Memoirs of Peter Jansen*, p. 85f.; p. 91f.
[138]A. A. Friesen Collection, BCHL; *The Mennonite* (June 21, 1923) p. 4.
[139]*Mennonite Life*, (Oct., 1947) p. 41.
[140]Anna Jansen, *Tagebuch*, June (no date) 1877. Also *Memoirs of Peter Jansen*, p. 48. But Cornelius Jansen, Jr., wrote Nov. 17, 1879: "Yesterday, two years ago we came to Nebraska." In Jansen's obituary it states that he and his family left Mt. Pleasant on November 16, 1876, and moved to Beatrice, Nebraska, CJC.
[141]A. Jansen, *Tagebuch*, June, 1877.
[142]Cornelius Jansen, Jr., June 9, July 30-Aug. 2, 1879; May 21, 1880, and Mar., 1882.
[143]*Ibid.*, April 22, 1880, Nov. 2, 1881.
[144]*Ibid.*, (June 26, 1883).
[145]A. Jansen, *Tagebuch*, Jan. 2, 1877.
[146]Mrs. Cor. Jansen, Sr., *Tagebuch*, June 11-14, 1892.
[147]*Ibid.*, Feb. 18, 1890; Aug. 14, 1892.
[148]Cornelius Jansen, "Aufsatz," dated "3 mo. 81." It is to be found at the close of Anna Jansen's *Tagebuch*. Mrs. C. Jansen, *Tagebuch*, Feb. 18, 1890.
[149]C. Jansen, Jr., *Tagebuch*, December 21, 1879. Theodore Schmidt, "The Mennonites of Nebraska," on page 59 writes that the first building which burned was built in 1880. Cor. Jansen, Jr., however records it in his diary on December 21, 1879. Both agree that it happened the Sunday before Christmas, but disagree on the year.
[150]C. Jansen, Sr., "Aufsatz," *op. cit.*
[151]T. Schmidt (*op. cit.*, p. 59) gives the date as 1902.
[152]Mrs. C. Jansen, *Tagebuch*, April 8, May 5, Aug. 15, 1892.
[153]*Ibid.*, June 20 and 21, 1892.
[154]"Obituary of Cornelius Jansen, Sr.," *Family Almanac*, (1896).
[155]Beatrice *Daily Express*, Dec. 14, 1894, P.M., *Cornelius Jansen Memorial*.
[156]*Der Christliche Apologete, op. cit.*
[157]*The Christliche Bundesbote, op. cit.*
[158]Letter of Mr. J. F. Funk to Helene Jansen, Dec. 28, 1894, *op. cit.*
[159]These were the five children of Peter Jansen before the death of Father Jansen.
[160]Mrs. C. Jansen, *Tagebuch*, March 31, April 1 and 6, 1890.
[161]*Ibid.*, Nov. 24, 1877.
[162]*Ibid.*
[163]*Ibid.*, Dec. 9, 1877.
[164]*Ibid.*, Dec. 31, 1877.
[165]*Ibid.*, Dec. 19, 1877.

[166]*Ibid.*, Nov. 29, 1878.
[167]Cornelius Jansen, Jr., *Tagebuch*, Jan. 4, 1879.
[168]*Ibid.*, Jan. 9, 1879.
[169]*Ibid.*, Nov. 20, 1879.
[170]*Ibid.*, Oct. 11, 1881.
[171]*Ibid.*, Aug. 10 and 11, 1882.
[172]*Ibid.*, May 6, 1883.
[173]C. Jansen, Jr., *Tagebuch*, July 5, 1879.
[174]*Ibid.*, May 15, 1882.
[175]*Ibid.*, May 23, 1882.
[176]*Ibid.*, June 14, 1882.
[177]*Ibid.*, August 24, 1882.
[178]*Memoirs of Peter Jansen*, *op. cit.*, p. 48.
[179]Peter Jansen, *Tagebuch*, Jan. 29-March 4, 1884.
[180]C. Jansen, Jr., *Tagebuch*, June 21, 1883.
[181]Peter Jansen, *Tagebuch*, Dec. 24, 1894.
[182]*Ibid.*, January to March 15, 1884.
[183]Mrs. C. Jansen, *Tagebuch*, May 16, 1893.
[184]*Ibid.*, May 16 and 17, 1893.
[185]*Ibid.*, May 26, 1893.
[186]A. Jansen, *Tagebuch*, January 2 and 8, 1877; C. Jansen, Jr., *Tagebuch*, Nov. 14, 1879, mentions Helena's birthday.
[187]A. Jansen, *Tagebuch*, January 8, 1877.
[188]*Ibid.*, July 14 and 18, 1877.
[189]C. Jansen, Jr., *Tagebuch*, August 18 and 199, 1881.
[190]*Ibid.*, August 9 and 10, 1882.
[191]*Ibid.*, March 21, 1883.
[192]*Ibid.*, April 10, 1879.
[193]*Ibid.*, January 6, and March 3, 1882.
[194]*Ibid.*, July 17, 1882.
[195]*Ibid.*, August 31, 1882.
[196]*Ibid.*, October 2, 1882.
[197]*Ibid.*, Nov. 10, 1882.
[198]*Ibid.*, Dec. 22, 1882.
[199]*Ibid.*, Jan. 27, 1883.
[200]*Ibid.*, March 5, 1883.
[201]*Ibid.*, May 21, 1883.
[202]*Ibid.*, Nov. 1, 1883.
[203]*Ibid.*, Jan. 1, 1884.
[204]Letter, J. E. Rhoads to Cornelius Jansen, Jr., Dec. 29, 1894, *Cornelius Jansen Memorial.*
[205]Mrs. C. Jansen, *Tagebuch*, July 5, Aug. 16, 18, 19, 21, 29, 31 and Sept. 1, 1892.
[206]*Ibid.*, Sept. 18, 1893.
[207]C. Jansen, Jr., *Tagebuch*, Oct. 2, 1882.
[208]*Ibid.*, July 1, 1882.
[209]*Ibid.*, August 27, 1883.
[210]*Ibid.*, April 8, 1882.
[211]Mrs. C. Jansen, *Tagebuch*, March 22, 1892.
[212]Margarete Jansen, *Tagebuch*, April 16 and 23, July 4, 6, 12 and 13, 1874.
[213]Cornelius Jansen, Sr., Letter, to John Lowe, June 27, 1874, *op. cit.*, chap. 29, p. 68.
[214]M. Jansen, *Tagebuch*, April 16, 23, July 4, 6, 12, 13, 1874.
[215]Anna Jansen, *Tagebuch*, April 6, 1874.
[216]*Ibid.*, March 13, Sept. 25, Nov. 8, 1875.
[217]*Ibid.*, Dec. 21, 30, 1875.
[218]*Ibid.*, March 7, 1876.
[219]*Ibid.*, Jan. 2, 1877.
[220]C. Jansen, Jr., *Tagebuch*, July 30, 1883.

[221]Mrs. Cor. Jansen, *Tagebuch*, August 20-22, 1892.
[222]*Ibid.*, June 9, 1893.
[223]*Ibid.*, November 27-29, 1893.
[224]Peter Jansen, *Tagebuch*, March 20 and 23, 1894.
[225]*Ibid.*, December 13, 1894.
[226]*Ibid.*, December 1, 1894. Apparently Peter entered this after his father's death.
[227]*Ibid.*
[228]Beatrice *Daily Express*, Dec. 14, 1894, *Cornelius Jansen Memorial.*
[229]*Cornelius Jansen Memorial* (Clipping and *Christl. Bundesbote* clipping).
[230]*Cornelius Jansen Memorial.*
[231]*Ibid.*, letter of C. B. Schmidt.
[232]*Cornelius Jansen Memorial.*
[233]Letter, Wm. I. and Annie Graham to Mrs. C. Jansen, Dec. 16, 1894, *Cornelius Jansen Memorial.*
[234]Letter, Anna M. Harvey to the Jansen Family, Jan. 2, 1895, *Ibid.*
[235]Letter, George Hume to Jansen Family, Jan. 2, 1895, *Ibid.*
[236]Letter, Wm. G. Hubbard to Jansen Family, Dec. 26, 1894, *Ibid.*
[237]Ludwig Keller to Peter Jansen Dec. 30, 1894, *Ibid.* Peter gave him the requested information which enabled him to write the obituary.
[238]Letter, C. B. Schmidt to Peter Jansen, Dec. 20, 1894, *Ibid.*
[239]*Kansas City Journal*, Friday, January 29, 1915, p. 3, col. 1-5 and p. 4, c. 3.
[240-243]From letters in *Cornelius Jansen Memorial.*
[244]The Beatrice *Daily Express*, Dec. 14, 1894, P.M.
[245]Obituary in *Cornelius Jansen Memorial.*

APPENDIX I

GENEALOGICAL BACKGROUND OF CORNELIUS JANSEN

According to a *Certificat* dated January 24, 1866, Cornelius Jansen states that he has no inheritance claims on the Peter Penner estate, it can thus be assumed that his sister, Johanna, must have died prior to that date. Cornelius Jansen died in December, 1894 and Peter Penner on February 7, 1895 (or 1896). After this, Mrs. Cornelius Jansen of Beatrice, Nebraska, wrote to the widow of Peter Penner (second wife) at Elbing, West Prussia, inquiring about the property of her brother-in-law to which the elder of the Mennonite Church at Elbing-Ellerwald, W. Dückmann, replied that Cornelius Jansen and Peter Penner had made a settlement regarding the estate in 1866 confirmed by the copy of this Certificat sent her.[1] Peter and Johanna Penner must have had no children. When Mrs. Cornelius Jansen received this letter from Elder W. Dückmann, she wrote on the envelope that she recalled vividly this settlement, but since her husband's sister Johanne, had had, prior to her marriage, a property of $2,000-$3,000, they had expected that the Cornelius Jansen children would have been remembered in the will of Peter Penner.

The father of Anna Buhler Jansen, Wilhelm Buhler[2] was born in 1749 and died on March 7, 1830 at Petershagen. He was a farmer and in 1789 he owned about thirty-seven acres of land (one *Hufe*) in this village. Two marriages are recorded. In 1795 he married Margaretha Schultz of Petershagen (born 1769), who died the following year. His last wife was Anna Warkentin, born September 15, 1765 in Neustädterwald (Tiegenhof area). He married Anna Warkentin as a widow having been previously married to Cornelius Lepp (1725-1749). From this first marriage, she had a son Cornelius, whose son, Wilhelm Lepp, a merchant, migrated to the United States.

Besides their oldest daughter, Anna, (Mrs. Daniel Janzen) Wilhelm and Anna (*nee* Warkentin) Buhler had three more children who left no descendants: Wilhelm, born 1802, drowned 1835; Peter, born 1804, was not married, died 1875; and Margaretha, born 1806, died 1844, as wife of Peter Dyck of Kalteherberge, West Prussia. When Peter Buhler died, October 23, 1875, at Wedhornskampe, West Prussia, his nephew, Cornelius Jansen, at that time living at Mount Pleasant, Iowa, was mentioned as the only heir.

The parents of Anna Warkentin were Peter Warkentin of Neustädterwald (1725-1794) and Margaretha Froese (died 1782). Their only son died in infancy. One daughter was married to Peter Goosen, a distiller from Elbing, with whom she migrated to South Russia.

Cornelius Jansen's grandfather, on his father's side, was Cornelius or Cornels Jantzen, who in 1789 owned a small house (*Kate*) at Tiegenhof. It is not known to whom he was married. The Grosswerder Mennonite Church records name four children who were baptized at Tiegenhagen: Cornels (1806); Sara (1807); Daniel (1815); and Maria (1817). Cornelius Jantzen and Daniel, his brother, both lived at Tiegenhof at the same time. Daniel's children, Wilhelm, Maria, and Cornels, were baptized between 1799 and 1801.

These two brothers, Cornelius and Daniel, are recorded in the Danzig Flemish Mennonite Church as sons of Cornelius Jantzen (I) who lived at Alt-Schottland and St. Albrecht, suburbs of Danzig. Daniel was born in 1757 and Cornelius (II), October, 1761. The latter was baptized in Danzig, 1780. Daniel had a twin sister, Maria.

Cornelius Jantzen (I) was baptized in 1755 and died March 20, 1763. His wife, Catharina de Veer, born January 12, 1734 was a daughter of Jacob and Maria (*nee* Berentz) de Veer. The de Veers were a leading Mennonite family of Danzig whose ancestor, Ghysbert de Veer, had come from Amsterdam in the latter part of the 16th century. After the death of her first husband, Catharina married Heinrich Sudermann (1739-1771). From this marriage, she had three children, a daughter, a son who died in infancy, and a son, Heinrich, who must have stayed with one of his half-brothers, because he was baptized at Tiegenhagen 1780. After the death of Heinrich Sudermann, Catharina was admitted to the "Home" (*Hospital*) of the Mennonite Church of Danzig. It is probable that her children were taken care of by relatives and that because of their relationship to the Buhlers, Daniel and Cornelius (II) Jantzen came to Tiegenhof.

The parents of Cornelius Jantzen (I) were Dirck Jantzen and his second wife, Anna Buhler, a sister of Elder Hans Buhler of the Grosswerder Mennonite Church. Dirck Jantzen was a younger brother of Elder Anthony Jantzen of the Flemish Mennonite Church of Danzig; he had been elected deacon in 1712 and into the ministry in 1719. When, in 1725, the so-called Danzig Mennonite churches of Amsterdam and Rotterdam were in need of an elder, they wrote to their brethren in West Prussia asking for help. Thus, Dirck Jantzen was elected elder and went to Amsterdam, where he stayed for eight years. After his return he served as elder of the Flemish Mennonite Church at Danzig until his death, November 25, 1750.

CORNELIUS JANSEN GENEALOGY

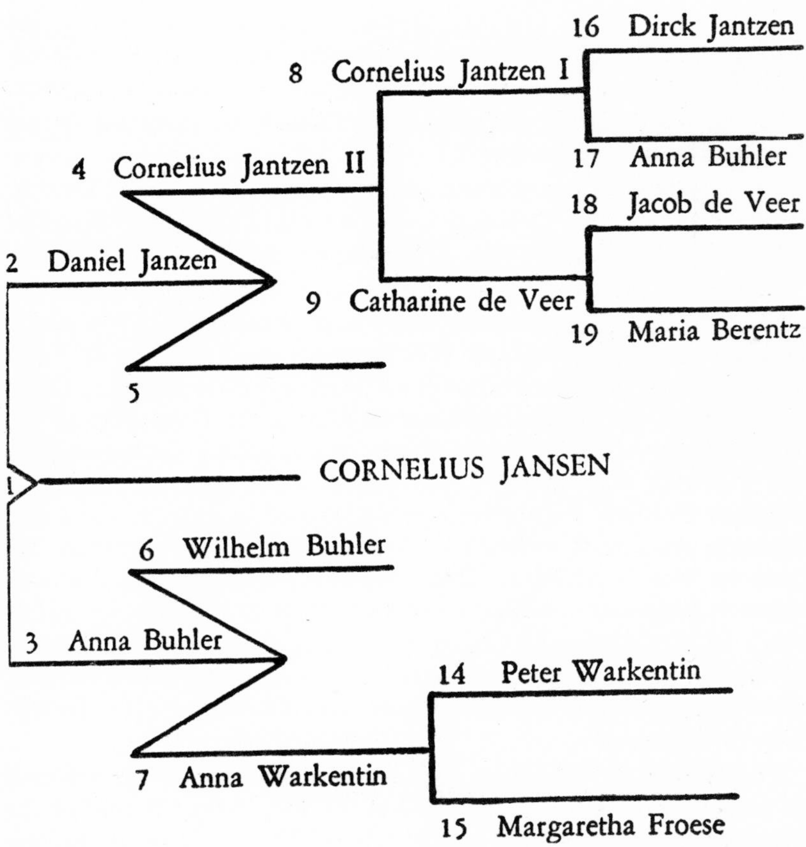

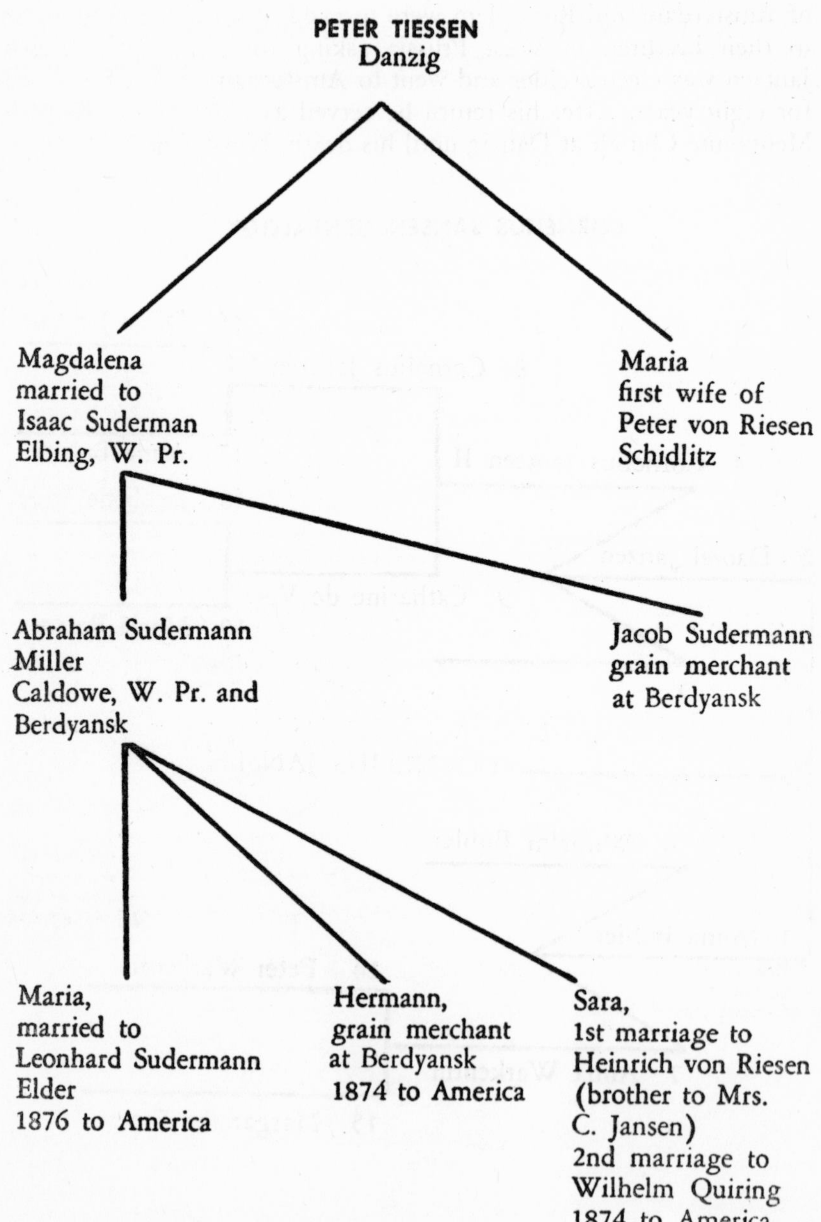
PETER TIESSEN
Danzig
Magdalena
married to
Isaac Suderman
Elbing, W. Pr.
Maria
first wife of
Peter von Riesen
Schidlitz
Abraham Sudermann
Miller
Caldowe, W. Pr. and
Berdyansk
Jacob Sudermann
grain merchant
at Berdyansk
Maria,
married to
Leonhard Sudermann
Elder
1876 to America
Hermann,
grain merchant
at Berdyansk
1874 to America
Sara,
1st marriage to
Heinrich von Riesen
(brother to Mrs.
C. Jansen)
2nd marriage to
Wilhelm Quiring
1874 to America

BERDYANSK AND KLEINE GEMEINDE

RELATIONSHIP TO BERDYANSK NEIGHBORS

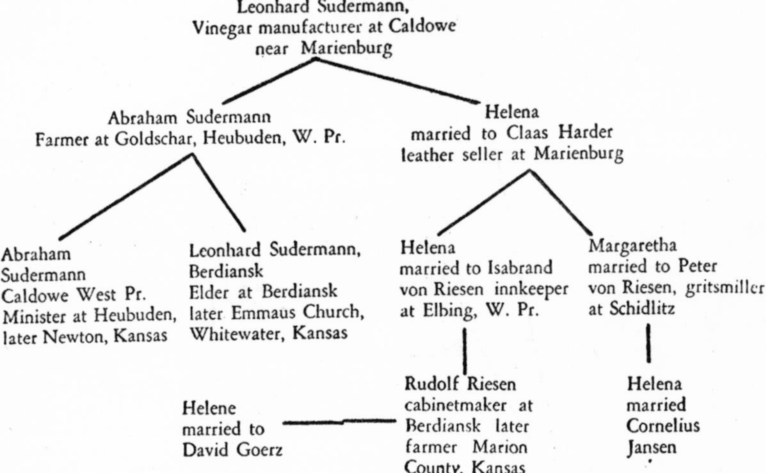

RELATIONSHIP TO LEADERS OF THE KLEINE GEMEINDE

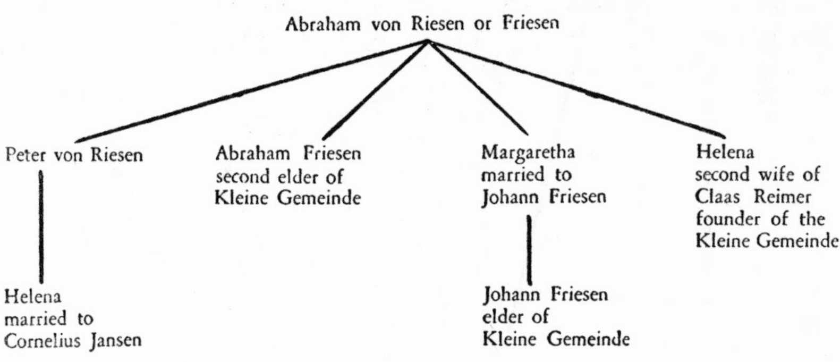

CHART OF THE PENNER FAMILY

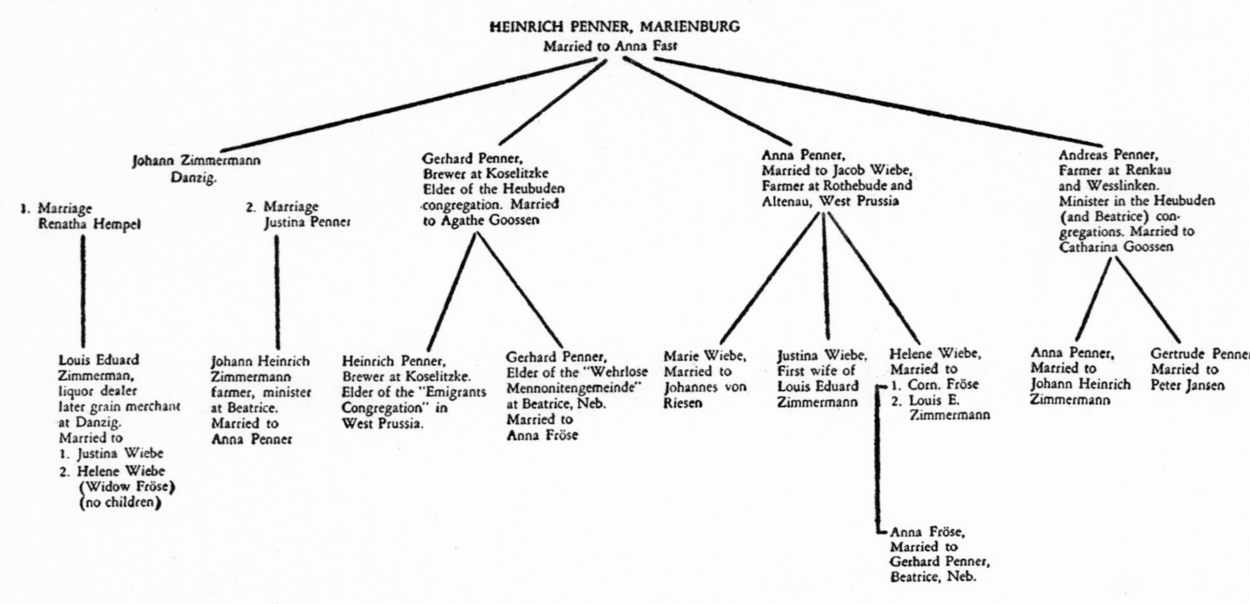
HEINRICH PENNER, MARIENBURG
Married to Anna Fast
Johann Zimmermann
Danzig.
1. Marriage
Renatha Hempel
2. Marriage
Justina Penner
Gerhard Penner,
Brewer at Koselitzke
Elder of the Heubuden
congregation. Married
to Agathe Goossen
Anna Penner,
Married to Jacob Wiebe,
Farmer at Rothebude and
Altenau, West Prussia
Andreas Penner,
Farmer at Renkau
and Wesslinken.
Minister in the Heubuden
(and Beatrice) con-
gregations. Married to
Catharina Goossen
Louis Eduard
Zimmerman,
liquor dealer
later grain merchant
at Danzig.
Married to
1. Justina Wiebe
2. Helene Wiebe
(Widow Fröse)
(no children)
Johann Heinrich
Zimmermann
farmer, minister
at Beatrice.
Married to
Anna Penner
Heinrich Penner,
Brewer at Koselitzke.
Elder of the "Emigrants
Congregation" in
West Prussia.
Gerhard Penner,
Elder of the "Wehrlose
Mennonitengemeinde"
at Beatrice, Neb.
Married to
Anna Fröse
Marie Wiebe,
Married to
Johannes von
Riesen
Justina Wiebe,
First wife of
Louis Eduard
Zimmermann
Helene Wiebe,
Married to
1. Corn. Fröse
2. Louis E.
Zimmermann
Anna Fröse,
Married to
Gerhard Penner,
Beatrice, Neb.
Anna Penner,
Married to
Johann Heinrich
Zimmermann
Gertrude Penner
Married to
Peter Jansen

APPENDIX II

REGARDING NONRESISTANCE IN RUSSIA

Etwas ueber unsere gegenwaertigen Zustaende betreff dem Wehrdienst

Von Cornelius Jansen

Wenn wir die Strömung zur Russifizirung, in der unser Volk in diesem Lande mit dem neuen Gesetz vom 4/16 June 1871, für die Colonisten bereits sich befindet, und in die wir noch mehr durch zu erwartende Anordungen hinein kommen, einen ihrer Stärke angemessenen Damm entgegensetzen wollen, so brauchen wir für die Zukunft unbeschränkte Religionsfreiheit.

Wen wir nun doch erneuerte Bittgesuche für unserer Existenz in diesem Lande machen, so lasset uns offen sein, um so eine entscheidende Antwort von Seiten der Regierung zu erhalten, wenn wir uns in Zukunft nicht selbst täuschen, auch nicht getäuscht sein wollen.

Wir berechnen die Tragweite der Gefahr und der Willkühr nicht, der wir uns für die Zukunft mit unsern Kindern und Gemeinden aussetzen, und wenn wir unsere Lage nüchtern besehen und würdigen lernen, können wir leicht dazu kommen, dass, wenn man gegenwärtig sich beruhigend sagt: "Noch wollen oder dürfen wir uns nicht nach etwas anderem umsehen," man nach Ablauf der zehn Jahre leider zu spät sagen wird: "Wir wollen aber hier nicht bleiben."

Nicht eine vorherschende Neigung zum Proseliten machen bestimmt uns, eine wahre Religionsfreiheit zu beanspruchen, sondern die fernere Existenz unsere Gemeinden dringt zu der vorher gesagten unumgänglich nothwendigen Bedingung.— Den Vertrag den unsere Regierung mit unseren Vorfahren hier einst gemacht, hat Erstere, ohne uns zu fragen, gebrochen, sie sieht ihn als entledigt an, und gibt uns, wenn wir uns den neuen Verhältnissen nicht fügen wollen, zehn Jahre lang den Weg der Auswanderung frei. (*Marginal addition*: Mit dem Einwilligen in eine Pflicht zur Regierung, haben wir nicht Wahl sondern Gehorsam gegen diese zur Pflicht.)

Leicht ersichtlich ist es, dass wir unter den anbrechenden Verhältnissen nicht bleiben können, wenn wir unserem Bekenntniss treu bleiben wollen, oder wir müssen für die Zukunft einen neuen Vertrag mit der Regierung schliessen, und werden gut thun damit recht gründlich zu sein und zu Werke zu gehen, wozu Alles bisher hier erfahrene aufs ernstlichste mahnt.—Wir werden doch nicht so Herz-und Gedankenlose Väter sein wollen, die ihren Kindern so etwas von Freiheiten hinterlassen worunter sie, wenn sie am innern Menschen noch nicht ganz gestorben sind, doch später nur seufzen und uns anschuldigen.—

Ein Blick in die Zukunft lehrt, dass ihnen nur Leiden und Verfolgungen bevorstehen, wenn sie anders ein Gewissen haben und halten wollen. Oder sollten wir uns denen anschliessen wollen, die in Oberflächlichkeit nur für ihre eigene Person an ein gutes Fortkommen denken, und ihre Kinder unter allerhand gehaltlosen Vorwänden, in Wahrheit dem Schicksal Preis geben? Ich wiederhole aus tiefster Überzeugung und im Geiste unseres Herrn und Heilandes, um in diesem Staate uns behaupten zu können, brauchen wir volle vollkommene Religionsfreiheit, eine Duldung allein kann nicht genügen.—

Voraussichtlich kommt es bald dazu, dass der Land-Wirth seinen Landbesitz zum Eigenthum erhält, dem sich das Recht zum Verkauf nach Belieben anschliesst; wird es zu verhüten sein, dass es in den Colonien russische Eigenthümer von Wirthschaften gibt? Täuschen wir uns in diesem doch nicht!— Sei es dass sich die Gemeinden eine Zeitlang ernstlich sträuben, wird man sich aber erhalten können? Man bedenke doch, dass die Beamten gerade in Interesse und dem Plan dieser Regierung angewiesen sind, wo nur möglich, deren Zweck zu verfolgen, und die Landeskinder sei es heimlich oder offen zu unterstützen.— In einem Molokaner Dorfe in unserer Nähe war es genug, wenn drei streitige Subjekte zur russischen Kirche übergingen, um ihnen eine solche hinzubauen und zu unterhalten; ebenso ist es bekannt, wie dieses schon Veranlassung zur Ausweisung von 9 Familien aus der Molokaner Gemeinde nach dem Amur war, von wo wieder ein Theil nach Nord-Sibirien verbannt wurde. Solches steht in Zukunft auch unseren Colonien bevor. In Halbstadt ist an der Bezirksschule der erste Lehrer bereits ein Russe während vielen andern Schulen russische Lehrer beigegeben sind, und man erzählt aus Halbstadt, das gegenwärtig schon der russische Geistliche bis zweimal die Woche auf ein Tag dort Besuch macht. Ist das von ungefähr? Auch wird der Lehrer seinen Einfluss auf die Kinder selbstverständlich nicht versäumen geltend zu machen. Wenn auch den Religionsunterricht einer unserer Brüder gibt, wird es diesen freistehen ähnlich und offen für unsere Wahrheiten einzutreten, wie Jenem Verdächtigungen dieser gestattet sind?

Wenn aber als natürliche Folge erst Geistliche in unseren Colonien wohnen, mit der unbeschränkten Freiheit für die Landeskirche zu werben, und unsere Prediger haben keine Gleichberechtigung, müssen vielmehr sich immer fürchten, dass sie gegen das Landesgesetz verstossen laut, Paragraph 58: "Ein Andersgläubiger der irgend einen Russen zu seinem Glauben verführt, in welchem Falle und unter welchem Vorwande dieses auch immer geschehen, und welchem Glauben der Verführer auch angehören möge, ist sofort unter Wache zu nehmen und mit dem Verführten zugleich dem Gericht zu überliefern." (*Crossed out*: Werden unsere Prediger dann nicht bald Hirten ohne Heerden sein? Wollte Gott ich täuschte mich mit dem Gedanken, dass laut den, in gegenwärtigem Landstreit dargelegten Gesinnungen, es nicht wenige giebt, die, wenn sie ihr vermeintliches Recht nicht bekommen, dazu fähig sing, selbst ihren Volk diesen unausbleiblichen Ruin in Bälde anzubahnen.) Mit erleuchteten Augen für geistige Zustände in, wenn auch nur schwache Klarheit und Treue, können wir leicht die Wahrheit des vorher Gesagten erkennen. Berechnet man aber lieber die Opfer die uns eine Entscheidung in so wichtiger Sache kosten könnte, dann hofft man gerne auf einen vielleicht "einigermassen günstigen Ausgang," lässt sich trösten und dahin halten mit dem allgemeinen Lieblingsgedanken: "es wird so schlimm nicht werden," dieser oder jener vernünftige und dabei reiche Mann, ist ja auch noch ruhig, sollten wir ärmeren eher gehen?

Die sprechensten Beispiele in den Ostseeprovinzen stehen eben so gut zur ernsten Mahnung da, und weisen uns darauf hin, was unserem Volke wartet, wenn nach zehn Jahren der Thoresschluss geschehen.— Und wir wollen diesem allen gegenüber blind für die Gefahr sein, und nicht entschieden versuchen uns entweder durch eine neue gründliche Abmachung zu behaupten, und wenn hierin nicht gewilligt wird, eben so entschieden wie Tausende unsere Vorfahren oft unter Drangsal und Noth, mit Hintenansetzung alles irdischen Gutes nach dem Beispiel des Königs Davids im Anblick der Gefahr sagen: "Auf! Lasst uns fliehen denn hier wird kein Entrinnen mehr sein vor Absalom, eilet, dass wir gehen, dass er uns nicht ereile und greife uns, und treibe ein Unglück auf uns."

2 Sam. 15, 14, und den Vers 16 heisst es: "und der König ging hinaus zu Fuss, mit seinem ganzen Hause."

Das Wort Gottes ist die Wurzel von jedem Thun eines Christen, von den uns darin gegebenen Verpflichtungen und Verheissungen, wird, wenn auch Himmel und Erde vergehen, doch nicht der kleinste Buchstabe vergehen, und der Christ bewegt sich aus Dankbarkeit und Liebe gerne in den Schranken dieses göttlichen Gesetzes; die Liebe aber ist des Gesetzes Erfüllung, die Liebe zu Gott, und die Liebe zum Nebenmenschen; aber auch die indireckte Militär-Leistungen (*Marginal addition*: und das Dortbleiben ist allemal eine Anerkennung und nur die Möglichkeit durch Fortgehen zu zeugen.) verletzen durch Förderung einer schlechten Sache, dieses Gebot, wofür nicht nur die so Handelnden, sondern auch wir verantwortlich werden, wenn wir unsere unerfahrenen Kinder nicht entschieden dafür zu bewahren suchen; wir sind in Gefahr des Himmelreichs verlustig zu werden, wenn wir ein, wenn auch nur klein scheinendes Gebot auflösen helfen, wie viel mehr wird aber der Strafe leiden, der (*Marginal addition*: wie in diesem Falle) das Höchste, das Gebot der Liebe verletzt?—

Keineswegs möchten wir aber in der entschiedenen Zurückweisung der auch indirekten Wehrpflicht so verstanden sein, als wenn wir ein Thaten-und Theilnahmloses Wesen während einer Kriegsnoth, wenn der Herr solche noch etwas um der Herzenshertigkeit willen, zu lässt, befürworten wollten, dass sei ferne! Wir würden uns im Gegentheil verpflichtet fühlen bei solcher traurigen Gelegenheit alles Ernstes uns und unsere Brüder dahin zu ermahnen, was in unsern Kräften ist zu thun der leidenden Menschheit beizustehen, und den unsäglichen Jammer und herzzerreissende Drangsal des Krieges lindern zu helfen.

(Manuscript in Cornelius Jansen Collection)

APPENDIX III

THOUGHTS ON INDIRECT MILITARY SERVICE, AS THAT OR ARTISANS, TRAINDRIVERS, THE SANITARY SERVICE, ETC.

By Cornelius Jansen

From the circumstance that the law pronounced the obligation to military service over all estates, every one must personally satisfy the law. Though the required fulfillment of duty may not consist in direct bloodshed, yet the rendering of such service in military law is simply a satisfaction of military obligation, and one ceases, as a matter of course, to belong to the opposite, i.e., to those NOT under military obligation.

In an army, the individual corps have always the most varied tasks to perform. One part march against the presumed enemy, with the task of annihilating, of killing, mutilating, or taking prisoners; another part subserve this work of annihilation and bloodshed with earthworks, fortifications, bridge-building, etc., without themselves doing the first. But those who are wrestling in sanguinary combat need, moreover, thousands of other hands for indirect cooperation in the work of annihilation, as, the healing as rapidly as possible of the wounded, to make them available for new combats, getting together the dead, burying these, and, in general, clearing the battlefields. All this is no less an indispensable requisite than the transport service in bringing up new troops, munitions, forage, etc., etc. Each has his distinct, and for the whole Very Important function; one is subservient to the other, and taken together they form a whole, from which the individual members must on no account be wanting, whatever may be their special task. The united object is the annihilation of the opponent, by murder, robbery, burning, destruction of provisions, hence hunger, thirst, etc., and to this purpose All are subservient, from the office clerk, ambulance bearer, and waiter on the sick, train-driver, etc., up to the slaughterer of men. No one who cooperates herein remains faithful to the chief principle of the gospel of peace, the foundation of the truth—compassionate love. When his service becomes an army-service, he is, as those belonging to those under military obligation, liable to military duty, a member in this whole, and is connected with it as the helper of the thief. What is here said must be intelligible to mere love of the truth and to reason itself, without any special Christian knowledge.

But in a Christian community there are, moreover, many other duties in most manifest contradiction with the recognition of any service in the army, however slight in appearance; and our forefathers in recognition hereof, decidedly refused demands similar to those now made on the so-called Mennonites. Our subsisting church order, regulated according to Christ's demand, and the first

Christians' example, is subverted by the accepance of any military duty, by whatever name it may be called. All mutual duties in the community, as well those of elder, preacher, deacon, as those of members of the community in mutual brotherly service, are annulled by the duty of the army, whereby there is an end of mutual supervision, and exhortation and assistance, and whatever is therein connected. A glance at so-called Christendom shows how the want of Christian economy in the church renders any true sanctification of the same impossible. Now, if the mercy of God has hitherto kept us in such truth, ought we now, perchance, to give it up for a wretched mess of lentils, and help to change it into a lie, and serve the creature rather than the Creator? Shall we, instead of God's help to build satan's kingdom, through a wretched misappreciation of the mission which the Lord has entrusted to us?

When, perchance, do our dear young people need more assistance in soul and body, exhortation, supervision? And when, perchance, is evil more seductive than when it is designed to take our youths for army service? Where is every virtue more trodden under foot, and the poisonous effluvium of vice of every kind—which although invisible, is yet not the less body and soul alike destroying—more inhaled than in the army services? No matter, though it consist of office, lazaretto, train, or such like service?

Pray let us no longer regard the rendering of such services so superficially as even, by advocating sanitary services UNDER MARTIAL LAW, to be willing to avail ourselves of that absurd conception of "Samaritan service" and so deceive ourselves and others.

Lazaretto service, without the deepest inner conviction and free sense of duty, such as, to our deepest shame, was exhibited to us in the last war by MANY even from other distant parts of the world, and even with the sacrifice of their own lives, without this Christian freedom, lazaretto service, in its mere performance, is, moreover, one of the Most Dangerous and Burthensome of all army services, for epidemics and contagious diseases carry off even more than are murdered in the field of battle, and death is absolutely equally near and nearer . . . .

Now, fathers, who, on account of advanced age, are themselves free from the obligation as regards themselves, yet undertake the same for their posterity, how heavy will be, in this case, the responsibility! They bequeath something to their children, under which the latter will groan, and accuse their fathers with, unhappily only too much reason. Will our youths undertake such lazaretto services voluntarily? By no means. The fathers would be building for their children a bridge which surely leads to direct service in the army.

Sad, if this should become clear, for the first time, on our deathbed! But still more sad, if any here continue to resist the truth against better light! And shame upon him, who, for the sake of thirty pieces of silver, should be contributing to render obscure the gospel of peace, and to lead the weak astray. Nor will his reward for such a Judas-deed be wanting. Warm or cold applies, moreover, herein, for to the Lord the lukewarm is a thing to be spewed out.

(From Cornelius Jansen Collection)

APPENDIX IV

PREFACE TO "SAMMLUNG" by Cornelius Jansen

Sammlung von Notizen über Amerika, Danzig, 1872. Druck von Paul Thieme, 1. Damm 2.

Vorwort

Durch Dr. W. Mannhardts Denkschrift: "Die Wehrfreiheit der Mennoniten" aufmerksam geworden auf die grosse Anzahl unserer Bekenntnisgenossen in Amerika, fühlte ich mich gedrungen, mir Gewissheit über die religiöse Stellung unserer Gemeinde in jenem, mir bis dahin höchst gleichgültigem Lande zu verschaffen, und schrieb damals den, in den mennonitischen Blättern von J. Mannhardt in Danzig (1870, No. 7) von Herrn P. Wiebe in Rolla, Missouri theilweise erwähnten und somit bekannt gewordenen Brief vom 15. Februar 1870. Ausser der brüderlichen Theilnahme des Herrn P. Wiebe, wurde mir solche auch von Andern, und übergebe ich einige dieser Liebesbeweise, wie auch andere auf Amerika bezügliche Notizen hiemit der Oeffentlichkeit, um damit dem, unter uns so allgemeinen Vorurtheile gegen Amerika entgegen zu treten, und häufigen, an mich gerichteten Anfragen zu begegnen.

Wenngleich Amerika ein Land der Freiheit ist, so gilt diese dort wahrlich nicht als eine Freiheit vom Gesetz, sondern im Gesetz; und in religiöser Beziehung nicht "Irreligiösität" sondern im vollsten Sinne des Wortes "Schutz für Religion"; und diesen Schutz hat

Amerika auch über 180 Jahre unseren Mennonitenbrüdern geboten.— Die amerikanische Constitution empfing seiner Zeit zur Grundlage die Gesetze, welche der friedliebende William Penn Pennsylvanien gegeben.— Und wenn Amerika von Verbrechern als Zufluchtsstätte aufgesucht und benutzt wird und wir uns wohl sagen müssen, dass auch dort wie hier überall: "die Sünde als der Leute Verderben" unter dem Volke herrscht, so bietet Amerika doch auch den, in ihren Glaubensverhältnissen Bedrängten, eine sichere Zufluchtsstätte.

Die Einführung der allgemeinen Wehrpflicht in Preussen und hier giebt mir Veranlassung, auch andre meiner Glaubensbrüder, denen ihre Gewissensfreiheit lieb ist, aufzumuntern, sich mit unseren Bekenntnisgenossen in Amerika bekannt zu machen, um so die Verhältnisse dort näher kennen zu lernen. Es ist wohl Grund anzunehmen, dass wir dort eine Heimat finden werden, wo wir unter dem Schutze der Regierung unserem Glauben in Frieden und Einigkeit nachleben dürfen.

Möge Gott der Herr diese Sammlung, die ich aus Liebe zu ihm und den Brüdern veröffentlicht, mit seinem Segen begleiten.

Berdiansk im März 1872.

C. Janzen.

(A copy of *Sammlung von Notizen über Amerika* is a part of the Cornelius Jansen Collection of the Bethel College Historical Library.)

APPENDIX V

TRANSLATION OF CORNELIUS JANSEN EXPULSION UKASE FROM RUSSIA

No. 1509

(Ukase of His Imperial Majesty, Emperor of all Russia.) From the Tauride Provincial Department to the Berdyansk Police District Court.

According to Imperial Ukase, at the Provincial Department was heard the proposal of the Director of the Taurida Court of Exchequer, in the absence of the Governor, on the 6th of March of the present year under No. 406 in which it is set forth:—That according to the representations made to the Governor of the Province in regard to the sending abroad of the Prussian subjects Cornelius Jansen and Loewens, residing in the district of Berdyansk, for spreading amongst the Mennonite inhabitants false ideas of their condition, and persuading the Mennonites to cease being Russian subjects and to emigrate to America, the Acting Governor General was informed by telegram of 3rd March that the Minister of the Interior had decided to send abroad the Prussian subjects Jansen and Loewens with the prohibition, for the future, of returning to Russia. In giving this information, the Government Regency directs for the carrying out of the same that the Governor be informed of the time of the sending away of the said foreigners and to forward the marks and descriptions of the persons sent away:—

DECREED, According to the proposal made by The Director, in the absence of the Governor of the Province, to order the Berdyansk District Police Court, to send abroad immediately, through the Prussian Consul at Berdyansk, the Prussian subjects Jansen and Loewens, residing in the Berdyansk District and at the same time to authorize the Police office, before the sending away of Jansen and Loewens, to make arrangements for their being photographed and twelve copies of each with the precise marks and descriptions of Jansen and Loewens be sent to the Tribunal at the time it is informed of the date of their being sent abroad. The necessary expenses for photographing to be claimed from Jansen and Loewens and if they are insolvent to use the office money and send the original account signed by the photographer, so that measures may be taken for refunding the same.
March 10th 1873.

The original signed by the Counsellors present and Chief of Office.

(Signed)
Bielousoff, Secty.

This is to certify that the foregoing is a true and correct copy of the original and given to the Prussian subject C. Jansen, according to his petition. In faith of which the Berdyansk Police Court hereto affixes its seal and signature 29th March 1873.

(Signed) Prince Maksutoff
Chief of the Port
(Seal) Bielousoff, Secty.

Telegram No. 915 (Translation)

Simferopol 24th March, 7.4 p.m.
received Berdyansk 24th March, 8.25 p.m.

To the Chief of the Berdyansk District.

Execute immediately the ukase of the Provincial Tribunal No. 1509 as to the sending away of Jansen and Loewens, and telegraph what has been done.

Reuthern.

Certifying true copy of telegram.

(Signer) Prince Maksutoff
Chief of the Port
Bielousoff, Secretary

APPENDIX VI

THE WILL OF CORNELIUS JANSEN, DATED JAN. 30, 1880

(Translation)

IN THE NAME OF GOD, AMEN! I, Cornelius Jansen, Sr., mindful of my mortality do hereby make and publish my last Testament, as follows:

I bequeath to my beloved wife Helena *nee* von Riesen all of my real and personal property which after my death appear to be mine, for her unrestricted use during her lifetime, excepted from these are: the house together with all other building, appurtenances and conveniences on and with lots 1, 2, 3, and 4 (all in Block 72, City of Beatrice, Nebr.) to purchase of which my beloved sister-in-law Anna von Riesen gave and presented to us a certain sum of money, and with regard to the property my beloved wife and sister-in-law shall have mutual discretion.

Because we all are under many grateful obligations toward our sister-in-law, aunt and sister Anna von Riesen, all personal property such as horse, cow, carriage, furniture, bedding etc., shall remain in her undisputed joint use with my above named wife and in case of my wife's death, she shall have the unrestricted use of the above during her natural lifetime.

My children and heirs are herewith most emphatically admonished to render all possible assistance and show all deference to their aunt until her death.

Further, if after the death of my wife and sister-in-law there shall remain unmarried children or a child of mine, then these or this one shall remain in undisputed possession of the above described property in the same manner as their mother and aunt had it.

They shall also have the privilege and right to derive a revenue by renting or leasing this city property, however they shall have no right to sell the same.

After the death or marriage of my unmarried children, this property may be sold and the proceeds divided equally among my children or grandchildren.

Furthermore I order and desire that as my son Peter is now living on our land in Jefferson County, and some of my other children may also do so, and as the manner of farming these lands may change with the times, that unless I make a special disposition later, he or they shall for five years after my death not be disturbed, or the conditions under which they hold the property be changed, unless by the voluntary consent of these children living there.

The revenue from this property shall (as heretofore to myself) go to my beloved wife Helena Jansen and in case of her death to my heirs in equal parts.

After the expiration of these five years all shall be equal heirs, but shall divide the property only in a manner approved by my Executors hereafter named.

To these my Executors I again express my special desire that all possible considerations shall be shown to those of my children living in Jefferson County, as far as this can be done without injustice to my other children.

It is my express will and order that in case there should arise any difference of opinion over any point in this my Testament, no recourse shall be had to law, but the question shall be definitely and conclusively decided by my executors or by arbitrators selected by them and their decision shall be accepted as final.

I herewith appoint as my executors, my beloved wife Helena Jansen and my beloved sister-in-law Anna von Riesen, and in the event of the death of one of them, the other shall select one of my children to act with her under the same conditions. After both die, my two eldest children shall be the executors.

In Witness Whereof, I, the aforenamed Cornelius Jansen, have signed and sealed this my last will with my own hand in the presence of the witnesses named below, this 30th day of January, in the year of our Lord, Eighteen hundred and Eighty at Beatrice, Gage County, Nebraska.

(SEAL) CORNELIUS JANSEN

Signed, sealed, published and declared by the said Cornelius Jansen as and for his last Will and Testament, in the presence of us, who at his request and in his presence and in the presence of each other, have subscribed our names as witnesses thereto.
Beatrice, Nebraska, January 30th, 1880.

Witnesses:

COCHRAN S. BLACK

EDWARD BOEHMLER

JOHN NICHOLS

(A "Codicil" of 1894 is found in the copy of the "Will" in the Cornelius Jansen Collection which adds some details.)

APPENDIX VII
EARLY JANSEN COMMUNITY

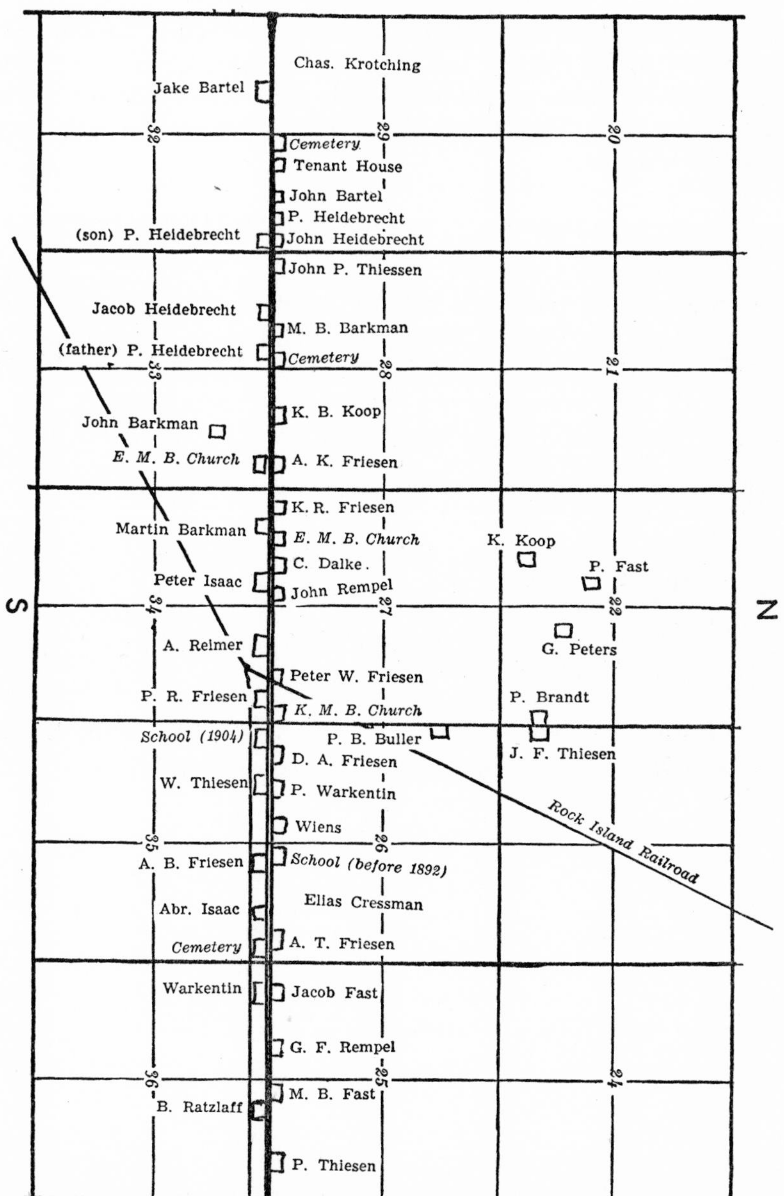